The recent work of Jürgen Habermas

D1216658

The recent work of Jürgen Habermas

Reason, justice and modernity

Stephen K. White

Department of Political Science
Virginia Polytechnic Institute and State University

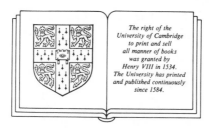

The right of the
University of Cambridge
to print and sell
all manner of books
was granted by
Henry VIII in 1534.
The University has printed
and published continuously
since 1584.

Cambridge University Press

Cambridge

New York   Port Chester   Melbourne   Sydney

Published by the Press Syndicate of the University of Cambridge
The Pitt Building, Trumpington Street, Cambridge CB2 1RP
40 West 20th Street, New York, NY 10011, USA
10 Stamford Road, Oakleigh, Melbourne 3166, Australia

First published 1988
Reprinted 1988
First paperback edition 1989
Reprinted 1990

Printed in Great Britain at the University Press, Cambridge

British Library cataloguing in publication data

White, Stephen K.
The recent work of Jürgen Habermas: reason, justice and modernity.
1. Habermas, Jürgen–Political science
I. Title
320'.5'092'4   B3258.H324

Library of Congress cataloguing in publication data

White, Stephen K.
The recent work of Jürgen Habermas.
Bibliography.
Includes index.
1. Habermas, Jürgen.
2. Sociology–Germany.
3. Frankfurt school of sociology.
I. Title.
HM22.G3H348 – 1987   301'.0943   87–3005

ISBN 0 521 34360 7   hard covers
ISBN 0 521 38959 3   paperback

TO PAT

Contents

Acknowledgements

Some of part III, chapter 2, as well as section IV of chapter 4, appeared in modified form in "Toward a Critical Political Science," in Terence Ball, ed., *Idioms of Inquiry: Critique and Renewal in Political Science* (Albany: State University of New York Press, 1987), reprinted with permission. Some of section II, chapter 2 was included in a slightly different form in "Post-Structuralism and Political Reflection" *Political Theory* (forthcoming). Earlier versions of section IV, chapter 3, and sections I and II, chapter 4 were included in "Habermas' Communicative Ethics and the Development of Moral Consciousness," *Philosophy and Social Criticism* vol. 10 no. 2 (1984), pp. 25–47, reprinted with permission. A revised version of section III, chapter 6 appeared in "Foucault's Challenge to Critical Theory," *The American Political Science Review* vol. 80 (June 1986), pp. 419–432, reprinted with permission. The author is grateful for permission to reprint portions of the following: Jürgen Habermas, "A Reply to My Critics," in John B. Thompson and David Held, eds., *Habermas: Critical Debates* (MIT Press and Macmillan Press, 1982); Jürgen Habermas, *Reason and the Rationalization of Society*, vol. 1 of *The Theory of Communicative Action*, Introduction and English translation, copyright © 1984 by Beacon Press and Basil Blackwell; Jürgen Habermas, *Theorie des kommunikativen Handelns* (Suhrkamp, 1981); Lawrence Kohlberg, "From Is to Ought," in Theodore Mischel, ed., *Cognitive Development and Epistemology* (Academic Press, 1971).

This book had a long gestation period. During that time several people, through their ideas, opinions, and encouragement, helped me along, especially Peter Bachrach, Marshall Cohen, Fred Dallmayr and Dante Germino. In the early stages of the project, I received grants from the American Council of Learned Societies, the National Endowment for the Humanities, the Virginia Tech Foundation and the Deutsche Akademische Austauschdienst. The last of these supported me during the fall of 1982, at the University of Konstanz, West Germany. Albrecht Wellmer, my host, was a source of numerous subtle insights about Habermas and communicative ethics. The National Endowment for the Humanities' renewed generosity in

1984 allowed me to attend William Connolly's N.E.H. summer seminar on "Genealogy and Interpretation" at the University of Massachusetts in Amherst. Many of the ideas in chapter 6 percolated out of the lively discussions that took place there.

Deeply perceptive criticism came from those who read the entire manuscript. My sincerest thanks go to my colleague Timothy W. Luke, and to Thomas McCarthy and J. Donald Moon. The book would have been far poorer had it not been for their insights. Thanks is due also to Jürgen Habermas for his encouragement at the early stage, and his continued willingness to answer my inquiries. For both he and Wellmer, communicative ethics is something more than a matter of academic interest. Unfortunately Wellmer's book, *Ethik und Dialog: Elemente des moralischen Urteils bei Kant und in der Diskursethik*, did not reach me soon enough to take its arguments about communicative ethics into account.

Susan Allen-Mills and Margaret Deith of Cambridge University Press handled the review and editing of the manuscript with commendable professional skill. I could not have produced the manuscript without the word processing skills of the secretaries in the Department of Political Science at the Virginia Polytechnic Institute and State University. I am grateful in particular to Sandra Howell, Debra Harmon, Terry Kingrea, Ann Rader, Maxine Riley, and Pat White (no relation). I also want to express my thanks to some able graduate research asistants: Gerd Hagmayer-Gaverus, Pedro Assuncao, Gunther Dettweiler, Ian Walden, and Hiltrud Moor.

My greatest debt is to my wife, Pat, who gave unselfishly of her editorial skills and, more generally, put up with me while I was engaged in the project. I dedicate the book to her.

Abbreviations of Habermas's works

CES *Communication and the Evolution of Society,* translated by T. McCarthy. Boston: Beacon Press 1979

KHI *Knowledge and Human Interests,* translated by J. Shapiro. Boston: Beacon Press 1971

KK *Kultur und Kritik.* Frankfurt: Suhrkamp 1973

LC *Legitimation Crisis,* translated by T. McCarthy. Boston: Beacon Press 1975

LSW *Zur Logik der Sozialwissenschaften.* Frankfurt: Suhrkamp 1970

MKH *Moralbewusstsein und kommunikatives Handeln.* Frankfurt: Suhrkamp 1983 [English translation forthcoming, MIT Press.]

PDM *Der Philosophische Diskurs der Moderne: Zwölf Vorlesungen.* Frankfurt: Suhrkamp 1985 [English translation forthcoming, MIT Press.]

QCQ Questions and Counterquestions. *Praxis International* 4 (1984), 229–49

REPLY Reply to My Critics, in J. Thompson and D. Held (eds.), *Habermas: Critical Debates,* pp. 219–83. Cambridge, Massachusetts: MIT Press 1982

RHM *Zur Rekonstruktion des Historischen Materialismus.* Frankfurt: Suhrkamp 1976

TCA *The Theory of Communicative Action,* vol. 1, *Reason and the Rationalization of Society,* translated by T. McCarthy. Boston: Beacon Press 1981

TG *Theorie der Gesellschaft oder Sozialtechnologie: Was leistet die Systemforschung?,* with Niklas Luhmann. Frankfurt: Suhrkamp 1971

TKH *Theorie des kommunikativen Handelns,* vol. 2, *Zur Kritik der funktionalistischen Vernunft.* Frankfurt: Suhrkamp 1981 [English translation forthcoming, Beacon Press.]

TP *Theory and Practice,* translated by J. Viertel. Boston: Beacon Press 1973

TRS *Toward a Rational Society,* translated by J. Shapiro. Boston: Beacon Press 1970

VET   *Vorstudien und Ergänzungen zur Theorie des kommunikativen Handeln.*
            Frankfurt: Suhrkamp 1984

WAHR   Wahrheitstheorien, in H. Fahrenbach, ed., *Wirklichkeit und*
            Reflexion: Walter Schulz zum 60 Gebürtstag, pp. 211–63. Pfullingen:
            Neske 1973

Introduction

The aim of this book is to introduce the recent work of Jürgen Habermas and show its significance for ethics, social theory and the philosophy of the social sciences. By "recent" I mean what he has written since *Knowledge and Human Interests* appeared in English in 1971. Without a doubt there is a unity of perspective which runs through all of Habermas's thought. Nevertheless, around 1970 some distinctive new themes and directions began to emerge. These include the ideas of communicative rationality, universal pragmatics, communicative ethics, the ideal speech situation, a reconstruction of historical materialism and a legitimation crisis in advanced capitalism. Through the 1970s Habermas refined and modified these ideas. In 1981, he published the German edition of *The Theory of Communicative Action*. This massive and complex work combines the various strands of his recent thought into one synthetic vision of modernity and critical theory. Naturally, then, my analysis will focus closely on this text, but also on subsequent essays and books which further elucidate the topics presented there. In this introduction, I want to give some general sense of the direction Habermas's work has taken over the period I will be considering.

One of the most distinctive (and contested) aspects of this work has been its commitment to a universalistic perspective on rationality and ethics. This appears in Habermas's notion of universal pragmatics, which asserts that competent speakers raise certain invariable, universal validity claims, and in his belief that in argumentation over specific claims we also impute an ideal speech situation, which provides us with a rational basis for testing the truth or legitimacy of these claims. The contestability of these assertions, made in the early 1970s, became even more apparent by the end of that decade when the general philosophical climate began to change markedly. The universalist, rationalist tradition of the Enlightenment came under increasing fire from various quarters. Contextualist and relativist positions were articulated by analytic philosophers, moral and political theorists, social anthropologists, feminists and post-structuralists.

Habermas has tried to meet this shift in philosophical consciousness in a way which admits some of their insights, but which nevertheless retains a clear emphasis on universalism. From the perspective of this book, I am interested in two aspects of this endeavor: the notion of communicative reason and ethics, on the one hand, and the theory of modernity and modernization, on the other.

The challenge facing communicative reason and ethics can perhaps be brought into focus most simply by drawing attention to the fact that a number of contextualist philosophers have shown a tendency to assign, however reluctantly, some sort of favored status to moral appeals which stress equality as well as mutual recognition and appreciation of different forms of life.[1] I will discuss this further in chapter 1 but, for the moment, the question which is raised is: Can such appeals be more systematically elaborated and possibly accorded some sort of universally valid defense? Or do such appeals have an ineradicably vague or abstract quality, which can only be removed at the cost of culturally concretizing them and thus making their validity contextual? Habermas's communicative ethics attempts to answer the first question in the affirmative and show that the ideas of equality and mutual recognition can be articulated in a way which is not totally vague or indeterminate. Chapters 3 and 4 will examine this effort.

The second challenge with which the changing philosophical climate has confronted Habermas is the necessity of developing a sophisticated defense of modernity. In terms of his analysis of universal validity claims, the result of this pressure can be seen in his moving from assertions about what is implicit in the speech actions of all actors to assertions about "the intuition of competent members of *modern* societies."[2] With this shift, Habermas takes on the burden of defending a vision of modernity which corresponds to his interpretations of subjectivity and reason.

Habermas's critical defense of modernity will be misconstrued, however, if it is understood simply as his response to a change in the philosophical climate. His underlying concern is with the historical situation he sees reflected in this changed climate. He sees a "new obscurity" facing Western industrialized countries, based on a growing sense on the political center and left that their traditional economic and political programs no longer have the same power to illuminate situations and motivate action.[3] These programs – orthodox socialism and welfare-state liberalism – have always drawn their motivating power from values deeply embedded in the Enlightenment and the revolutionary traditions of the nineteenth century. Thus, to say that these programs are exhibiting signs of exhaustion is also to raise deep questions about some of the central values of modern culture.

In this situation only the neo-conservatives seem untroubled by an obscured vision. They point self-confidently to the cause of the currrent ills of industrialized, capitalist society: precisely those values in modern culture upon which welfare liberalism and socialism are constructed. The ascendence of these values, the neo-conservatives argue, has made modern culture deteriorate into a soup of permissive secular hedonism.[4] And it is this cultural degeneracy that is responsible for our present problems, not the economic and political structures of capitalism.

The task for Habermas is one of presenting an interpretation of modernity that defends key aspects of modern culture and shifts the critical focus back to the economic and political systems. Yet he must, at the same time, develop this focus in such a way that he can show why the traditional economic and political programs of welfare liberalism and socialism are themselves too closely entangled in the logic of modernization underlying these systems; in short, he must explain why these programs no longer appear to offer convincing responses to our current malaise. The interpretation which Habermas thinks will accomplish these ends is one which turns on developing the distinction between the achievement of a *modern culture*, on the one hand, and the processes of *societal modernization*, on the other.[5] The particular thesis he offers emerges from his rethinking of Horkheimer and Adorno's critique of modernity in *Dialectic of Enlightenment*, his ingenious appropriation of Weber and finally his own notion of how communicative reason is distinguished from both instrumental and functional reason. As I will show in chapter 5, his argument is that Western modernization has constituted a "one-sided" – and thus distorted – development of the rational potential of modern culture. He refers to these distortions with the concepts "colonization of the lifeworld" and "cultural impoverishment." It is only from such a perspective, Habermas argues, that we can adequately expose the causes of the new obscurity as well as gain some new normative "self-assurance" drawn from our own cultural resources.[6]

Of all the current philosophical positions that have challenged the values of modernity, the one which Habermas finds most intellectually provocative is post-structuralism.[7] The critique of reason and modernity which emerges from the work of post-structuralists, such as Jacques Derrida and Michel Foucault, engages him in an especially acute way. For one thing, the post-structuralist critique of the entwinement of instrumental reason and domination has some strong affinities with the work of Habermas's theoretical ancestors in the Frankfurt School. Hence in one sense the post-structuralists are following out critical theory's own lead in exposing the operation of power in places previously unseen by other radical critics of bourgeois society. And yet this new departure seems to include an aesthetic drift, in relation to which all ideas of collective political action and the potential of a more just society become deeply problematic. It is this general implication of post-structuralism which is most disturbing to Habermas. The basis of his dispute with post-structuralism is perhaps best summed up in his remark that critical theory must try "to formulate an idea of progress that is subtle and resilient enough not to let itself be blinded by the mere appearance [*Schein*] of emancipation. One thing, of course, it must oppose: the thesis that emancipation itself mystifies."[8]

I will bring Habermas's work into a dialogue with post-structuralism in parts of chapters 2 and 5, but most fully in chapter 6. The primary emphasis will be on Foucault's work, partly because of its more explicit social and political character and partly because of the instructive way he treats the problem of modern subjectivity.

This problem emerges most explicitly for Habermas in *Der philosophische Diskurs der Moderne*, where he traces the philosophical discourse on modernity from Hegel to Foucault. Already in Hegel, the modern subject appears as both distinctive achievement and source of anxiety. He/she is the free, rational subject of both knowledge and action; but the activity of such a subject seems inevitably corrosive of the possibility of a free ethical life with others.[9] Habermas argues that neither Hegel nor later critics of modernity have adequately laid the problem of subjectivity to rest. Chapter 6 will discuss this problem as it relates to Foucault.

Ultimately Habermas wants to claim that adequately handling the problem of subjectivity requires a radical paradigm change in philosophy and social theory. Along with the radical critics of modernity, from Nietzsche to Adorno to the post-structuralists, Habermas argues that the paradigm of a "subject-centered" "philosophy of consciousness" is "exhausted." But these critics, he maintains, all remain entangled in the *aporias* of this paradigm, however much they struggle against it. An adequate critique – as well as an adequate defense – of modernity can be mounted only by shifting to the "paradigm of understanding."[10] This paradigm is focused on the structures of intersubjectivity which are implicit in the understanding achieved in ongoing linguistic interaction, or "communicative action" as Habermas calls it. Making this communicative model plausible has been the underlying goal of all of Habermas's work since around 1970, and these efforts come to fruition in *The Theory of Communicative Action*.

Although Habermas presents numerous arguments as to why his approach is superior to its competitors, he believes that ultimately its persuasiveness will depend in large degree on the success of the research program for the social sciences which can be built upon it. His inspiration here is the early interdisciplinary work of the Frankfurt School in the 1930s, rather than Horkheimer and Adorno's later writings.[11] I will be using this notion of a critical research program as a central orienting idea throughout the present work.

In chapter 1, I try to provide a way of locating the different levels of such a program, building upon the work of those who have applied Imre Lakatos's notion of a research program to the social sciences. The key insight here is that the "core" of any social science research program must be constituted at least partially by some account of subjectivity or human agency.[12] Now it might seem rather strange to speak of Habermas's account of subjectivity, given the distance he tries to put between himself and traditional subject-centered philosophy of consciousness. However, an account of subjectivity can be derived in more than one way. For example, rational choice theory develops an account of the subject which does indeed build upon the tradition in which each agent inhabits a monological world of cognition and volution. Habermas, on the other hand, constructs an account of subjectivity which is derived from his analysis of the structures of intersubjectivity implicitly pre-supposed by ongoing interaction. In both cases, a minimal model of the sub-ject is presented – that is, one sketched out in terms of reason and action – but the underlying theoretical positions yield quite different views of these two concepts.

In chapter 1, I will point out some of the problems with other contem-porary ways of handling the concepts of action and rationality. This sets the stage for chapter 2, where Habermas's communicative account is presented. This conceptual core structures all of the other aspects of his work. Succeed-ing chapters elucidate this connection in relation to communicative ethics (chapters 3 and 4), and the interpretation of modernity and contemporary capitalism (chapters 5 and 6).

Recasting his thought as a research program is not something Habermas did simply because he wished to return to the founding spirit of the Frankfurt School. Rather, it constitutes a fundamental acceptance of the ten-tativeness and fallibility of his basic concepts. Once they are interpreted as part of the core of a research program, they can no longer be advanced with the self-confidence of orthodox Marxism or the tradition of German idealism. And in this sense Habermas is explicitly distancing himself from the lingering foundationalism that characterized a work such as *Knowledge and Human Interests*. Ultimately, the basic conceptual framework must be judged by how "progressive" his research program is over a period of time.[13] And yet what it means for a research program in the social sciences to be progressive is anything but clear.[14] Certainly it must generate cogent interpretations and explanations, as do research programs in the natural sciences. But "success" for a social science research program may also depend partially on the practical, normative insight it generates. In this sense, I think Habermas would stake his claim on the ability of his communicative model simultaneously to give modernity grounds for a "self-assurance" to be found in its own cultural resources, and yet also to locate the sources of the new obscurity in the increasing "colonization of the lifeworld" and "cultural impoverishment" in advanced industrial societies.

The reader will no doubt quickly sense that my treatment of Habermas is fairly sympathetic. This is partially a result of the fact that I do agree with a number of Habermas's positions; but it is also partially the result of the nature of the task in hand: introducing a body of work whose density, scope and complexity continue to make it relatively inaccessible and easily misunderstood. If nothing else, I hope this book clears away some of the underbrush of misunderstanding and thus establishes a fairer basis from which criticism of Habermas's project can proceed.

1

Rationality, social theory and political philosophy

Some years ago Imre Lakatos suggested that the theoretical landscape of the natural sciences can best be conceptualized as a terrain of competing research programs or general strategies for interpretation. Lakatos distinguishes between the "core" concepts of a program, which are themselves not susceptible to direct empirical testing, and the interpretations and explanations constructed from those concepts which are. The core concepts thus constitute a "negative heuristic" for a research program and the specific interpretations and explanations the "positive heuristic."[1]

More recently, it has been suggested that Lakatos's model can be appropriated for the social sciences as well, although not without some significant changes. One thing that is distinctive about the idea of a social science research program is that its core must include some model of the subject; that is, some minimal conceptualization of what it is to be human. Moreover, not only is such a model conceptually necessary, it is also necessarily normative.[2] These features introduce some distinctive problems for social science.

Now it may be the case that, in the future, some research program will be devastatingly successful in its range of convincing explanations and interpretations. Were this to be so, and were the normative implications entailed by the corresponding model of the subject to diverge radically from our most reflective moral judgements, we would probably do well to question the cogency of those judgements.[3] However, I suspect that no research program will have such unqualified success. If this is true, then the choice of one or a combination of programs as the "best" will be strongly underdetermined. But that means that the relationship of our considered moral judgements to the normative implications of a given model is not going to be one where wholesale questioning is advisable in the former, but rather one where the latter are assessed in terms of the former. That is, it seems reasonable to think that *one* plausible criterion for assessing the overall adequacy of a research program is to ask how well the normative implications of its model of the subject stand up under the scrutiny of our most reflective moral judgements. Other criteria of assessment will of course be related to the cogency of the interpretations and explanations which can be developed on the basis of the core conceptual components of a given program. How one weighs the normative criterion against the interpretive and explanatory ones will no doubt be a complex matter.

Another, related source of complexity is bound up in the phrase "our considered moral judgements." A research program will implicitly or explicitly specify the referent of "our." Theoretically, a program could be oriented toward any collectivity, from a particular group to all of humankind. Which collectivity is thematized will be deeply intertwined with how social theorists perceive the historical problems confronting society.[4]

The history of modern social theory is full of what appear to be radically different answers to these problems, for example, Marxism, on the one hand, and rational choice theory, on the other. But, for all their differences, most of these approaches have oriented themselves, through their core concepts, toward a conception of modern mankind which functions as a normative standard (even though this standard – the referent of "our" – is seen as being realized in different actors on the stage of modern history). Now this common orientation to modern mankind has just as commonly, if sometimes only implicitly, been equated with an orientation to all of humankind.

One of the distinctive qualities of the current philosophical climate, alluded to in the Introduction, is a strong suspicion of this equation (a suspicion which goes hand in hand with a new sense that modernity is facing something like a crisis in self-assurance). Given this change, it must now be more clearly recognized that the model of the subject with which a social theorist operates highlights qualities and experiences of distinct collectivities. This means that the normative discourse associated with the core of a research program must always be linked with broader questions about the exemplary value of the qualities and experiences of the relevant collectivity.

I will be arguing in this book that Habermas's work since *Knowledge and Human Interests* is best understood in terms of the perspective just outlined for social science research programs. Although Habermas did not explicitly begin around 1970 with such a perspective, he seems to have developed this sort of theoretical self-understanding as his work progressed.[5] This assertion might appear more easily acceptable if it were phrased in a way that makes clearer reference to traditions in philosophy and social theory which are usually associated with critical theory. Thus, Habermas's minimal model of the subject, constructed from his "communicative" understanding of rationality and action, can be thought of as comprising what might be called the quasi-Kantian dimension of critical theory. The need for systematic analysis in this dimension has often been misunderstood by critical theorists, and Habermas has accordingly often been criticized for taking a long philosophical journey, the fruits of which appear to have little to do with critical theory.[6] On the contrary the quasi-Kantian dimension constitutes an outline for a distinctive model of the subject which, although it is clearly different from Marx's, nevertheless allows social and political theory to preserve some of Marx's intentions, at least in relation to illuminating complexes of power and ideology, by "recovering a potential for reason encapsulated in the very forms of social reproduction."[7]

Such a core or model of the subject is a condition of the possibility of generating interrelated explanations and interpretations of contemporary social phenomena. These latter are one part of what might be called the Hegelian–Marxian dimension of critical theory. The other part of this dimension is constituted by reflection on the qualities and experiences of the collectivity which are reflected in the model of the subject. Habermas's task in this dimension thus includes not only the analysis of advanced capitalism in all its facets, but also a normative defense of *modern* consciousness as still possessing the resources necessary to provide us with some minimal ethical–political orientation toward our "new obscurity."

My plan is to lay out and show the interconnections between the different components of Habermas's project. I will first assess the significance of the communicative model of action and rationality as compared to other models. Then I will turn to an examination of his attempt to develop the specific normative implications of that model into a "communicative ethics." Next I will demonstrate how this model structures Habermas's interpretations of key concepts such as power and ideology, as well as how it both reflects and informs a general interpretation of modernity. Finally, I will show how these interpretations in turn lend themselves both to the construction of explanations of social, cultural and political phenomena of advanced capitalism and to the development of an ethical–political orientation to these phenomena.

My initial line of inquiry in this chapter will be somewhat indirect. I will focus first on ways of thinking about rationality which are more familiar than Habermas's communicative approach. My specific concern will be how different conceptions of rationality can serve as part of the core of a research program for social theory. Given this focus I will be more specifically concerned with practical rationality; that is, what constitutes good reason for actions. The choice of a particular conception of practical rationality will have, as I suggested above, both normative implications and implications for interpretation and explanation. And the overall adequacy of a conception will thus ultimately be related to both normative and empirical-theoretical criteria.

I will briefly consider two conceptions of practical rationality which are alternatives to Habermas's communicative conception. Strategic rationality is the familiar means–ends conception. Contextual rationality, on the other hand, is a notion associated with recent philosophical discussions in social anthropology. Here rationality is taken to mean "conformity . . . to norms."[8] Action is understood as norm-guided behavior and can be evaluated as rational or irrational depending upon whether or not it conforms to the beliefs and social norms in the context of which it occurs. Thus, on the contextual account, what counts as rational action will vary with the social context.

An examination of the implications and limitations of strategic and contextual rationality is crucial for understanding the significance of Habermas's communicative conception of reason and action.

I. Strategic rationality

The dominant conception of practical reason in social science today is the strategic one. This conception is most explicitly embraced by those who consider themselves rational choice theorists.[9] This school attempts to provide a clear delineation of a minimal model of the subject and to be theoretically rigorous in tying its assumptions about the subject's characteristics to its hypotheses about political phenomena. Its characterization of the subject is clear in relation to what are two essential aspects of any minimal model: a conception of action and rationality. Action is conceptualized as the intentional, self-interested behavior of individuals in an objectivated world, that is, one in which objects and other individuals are related to in terms of their possible manipulation. The rationality of action is correspondingly conceptualized as the efficient linking of actions-seen-as-means to the attainment of individual goals.

It is important to point out that the inclusion of the assumption of self-interested motivation in the foregoing description is not conceptually necessary to the strategic model. Intentional action and means–ends rationalization can in principle be combined with any type of motivation. For most forms of collective action, however, rational choice theorists usually add the assumption that rational agents are motivated by self-interest; that is, they are egoistic, utility maximizers. This assumption is made because self-interest seems to be the most easily universalizable motivation; that is, it can explain a larger fraction of collective behavior than any other single motivational assumption.[10] Most rational choice theorists are careful to point out, however, that there is no necessary reason why other motivational assumptions, such as moral ones, cannot also be employed to yield explanatory models.[11] The only thing which is not permitted is the use of the concept of rationality to make normative judgements about the types of ends pursued or the motivation which stimulates action.

Rational choice theorists see themselves as engaged primarily in the task of building a naturalistic social science by beginning with simple assumptions about rationality and then predicting how individuals will behave in a given set of conditions.[12] In a strict sense, such a theory neither endorses nor recommends any moral position or course of action. In particular, it does not directly recommend to individuals a course of prudential action as does Hobbes. Rational choice theory simply aims at predicting how individuals *will* act in a given situation, *if* they do in fact act rationally in the strategic sense.[13] In other words, they elucidate a logic of rational action, but do not necessarily recommend that an agent value rationality and thus tailor his actions to its logic. Nevertheless, the conclusions of rational choice theory are important for ethics and political philosophy, since the logic they elucidate demonstrates what sort of cooperative collective action can be expected among individuals who share an attachment to strategic rationality, however divergent their other basic values might be. Thus rational choice theory throws light on the kind of question Hobbes tried to answer: Can individuals who share nothing more than strategic rationality come to agree upon a set of collective arrangements, the result of which will be in the public interest or a good for all? Or, put more generally, to what degree can we account for the cooperative as well as the conflictual dimension in political life without any appeal to motivations which are not exclusively self-interested and to some moral sense of rationality?

Thus when one explores the implications of making strategic rationality the sole criterion of rationality in political life, one is probing questions which have both normative and explanatory significance. Rational choice theorists, however, tend to focus only on explanatory questions. The difficulty they struggle with when attempting to construct political theory on an exclusively strategic–rational basis is that cooperation often in fact takes place when their model would lead us not to expect it. The point at which this difficulty becomes evident is, I will show, also the point at which a contextualist account comes into its own. The contextualist perspective, however, will also be shown to have some theoretical shortcomings, as well as some disturbing normative implications (disturbing at least to anyone who wishes to hold open the possibility of some minimal moral universalism).

The problem I want to examine in relation to the strategic conception has been widely discussed. It involves the problem of cooperative action among strategically rational individuals for the purpose of providing themselves with "public" or "collective goods," that is, goods which, if they are provided at all, must (for all practical purposes) be provided to all members of a community. [14] This problem's connection with that of Hobbes results from the fact that a just set of political arrangements falls into the category of collective goods.

The difficulty involved with cooperative action to provide collective goods revolves around the results of a rational actor's calculations as to whether the costs of participating in such action outweigh the benefits. For example, in regard to voting, it appears that a rational individual would decide not to vote, for the simple reason that the cost in time and effort of that act is far too high when measured against the benefit of having his favored party win, once he considers the likelihood that his one vote will make the difference between his party winning or losing. By not voting, the individual does not measurably change the probability of the collective good (his party in office) being supplied: if his party loses, it would have done so even if he had not voted; if it wins, he gets the benefit of the collective good without any cost, that is, as a free rider. [15]

The conclusion that it is not rational to vote – *even in the most just of democratic systems* – has disturbing implications both for political philosophers and rational choice theorists. The latter must, of course, explain the fact that large numbers of people often do vote. Unless these theorists are ready to place voting generally into the category of non-rational or irrational action, they need some way of understanding it as rational.

The problem which arises with voting is actually a general one which applies to many other types of participation whose aim is to provide some collective good. [16] And, given the fact that not only voting but also these other forms of collective action do in fact occur, rational choice theorists have been continually perplexed by the "logic of collective action," for it seems to indicate a crucial explanatory shortcoming in their approach. Over the last two decades immense effort has gone into investigating ways of overcoming this problem. Some have tried to show that non-cooperativeness is not always as rational a strategy as was first thought. [17] Others have investigated how, in collective action situations, contributing to the provision of a collective good may become rational because of the fact that simultaneously some private good may be obtained or some private harm may be avoided. This is called the provision of "selective incentives."[18] Such lines of research have clearly extended the terrain over which strategic rational explanations can successfully be deployed. However, I think it is fair to say that substantial areas of cooperative behavior remain unexplained and would thus require recourse to some "extra-rational motivations" on the part of actors.[19]

An attempt to avoid this conclusion has been made by some rational choice theorists. They have taken the basic concept of selective incentive and inflated it to include not just tangible incentives but also ones which are intangible or social–psychological. For example, it has been suggested that a voter might get some private benefit or satisfaction from *conforming to the norms* of good citizenship or fairness in a democracy.[20] However, it has been persuasively argued that this kind of conceptual move is not very productive. Such a "portmanteau concept of 'satisfaction'" simply lumps together purely self-interested motivations with other kinds which are not purely self-interested, and it does this without any clear increase in the *kind* of predictive power that rational choice theory promises – universally applicable predictions derived from very simple premises. One would have to say that the proposed inflation strategy really constitutes a departure from the basic research program of rational choice theory.[21]

Clearly such a strategy might allow for a weak sort of predictive power, once the theorist gains a substantial amount of *particular* knowledge about such things as the kinds of moral and political norms which exist in a given society. The important thing to realize, however, is that the adoption of this strategy would mean that the theorist is no longer using only a *lawlike model* of social science, with its assumption of *strategic* rationality, but also an *interpretative model* of social science, with its assumption of *contextual rationality*.[22] The premises of an explanation would no longer contain only simple behavioral postulates, but also "thick descriptions" of background beliefs, norms, traditions and institutions.[23] Thus predictions about action would no longer be derived in a strictly logical way, but rather would express how a certain action would or would not tend to cohere in a given situation with what the applicable beliefs and norms would lead one to expect.

II. Contextual rationality

It was pointed out earlier that the question of the motivation of action is one which in a strict sense is normally taken by rational choice theorists to be outside the domain of rationality. In other words, no judgement of rationality can be made in regard to particular motivations being present or absent in an agent's action. However useful this way of entirely separating questions of motivations from questions of rationality may be for the operational purposes of rational choice theory, it does seem to conflict with the way we ordinarily use the concept of reason in our judgements of actions. What I want to suggest is that it makes perfectly good sense to think of the concept of practical rationality as incorporating at least some minimal motivational assumptions. By saying there are minimal motivational assumptions incorporated in the idea of rational action, I mean to suggest that we would judge an individual to be acting irrationally, not only if he, say, chose inefficient means to particular ends, but also if he showed no evidence whatsoever of having two general types of motivation which are *constitutive* of what we understand as *human* action.

Such a conceptual argument about general orientations of action will help to demonstrate why it makes sense generally to think of both a strategic and a contextual sense of rationality. It will also help one understand the sort of conceptual arguments Habermas makes from the perspective of his communicative model. I say this because in his recent work (as I will show in chapter 2) he has moved away from the epistemological approach to reason which characterized *Knowledge and Human Interests*. He has relinquished the strong transcendental claims about knowledge – constitutive interests. But Habermas still apparently wants to capture in his communicative model some features of what he earlier referred to as "technical interest" and "practical interest."[24] Only now these features must be drawn out in a theory of action and language.[25] The best initial access to this question can be obtained, I think, by a conceptual argument about action in which a strategic orientation replaces technical interest and intersubjective–contextual orientation replaces "practical interest."[26] Although Habermas does not explicitly make the argument I will put forward, something like it does seem to be an implicit basis for the more explicit conceptual arguments he makes about communicative action, which I will take up in chapters 2 and 3.

I suggested that the presence of two basic orientations of action is a constitutive part of what constitutes rational action. The absence of either one in the ongoing behavior of a subject is grounds for throwing his claim to reason radically into doubt.

The first is simply the motive of self-interest or orientation to self which, although rooted in the motive of simple physical self-preservation, is by no means limited to this. Rather it can take on a multitude of forms mediated by the particular social world in which the individual lives. It is the persistence of this motivation which makes strategic–rational accounts plausible for large classes of human action. Without such motivation, we might be able to find some instances of rational calculations on a given individual's part, but these would pale in comparison with our judgement that his actions as a whole were irrational. In other words, if we observe an individual who perhaps pursues certain particular ends quite efficiently, but who is totally oblivious to the need to feed and clothe himself, are we not likely to question his claim to rationality?

The limitation of thinking in terms of a single basic orientation, however, is illustrated by the familiar fact that we are sometimes quite willing to attribute rationality to an action in which self-interest and even self-preservation are overridden by other motivations. Such situations are ones in which the overriding motivation has an intrinsically *intersubjective* or *social* character in that it expresses a *recognizable* orientation to the values of some community as they are manifested in some basic moral, religious or social norms.[27] It is in relation to this sort of orientation that we are often willing to consider even an action endangering self-preservation as possibly rational.

It is important to be clear at this point that what I am talking about is not captured adequately, or at least not very clearly, by Weber's notion of "value-rational" (*wertrational*) action. An action is value-rational, according to Weber, if it expresses "ultimate values" and is undertaken by an individual "regardless of cost" to himself.[28] Weber's way of speaking about individuals and ultimate values tends to obscure an important difference between situations in which the overriding of self-preservation may be rational and those in which it is not. Consider the following situations. In the 1980 war between Iran and Iraq, it was reported that soldiers of the former country showed what seemed to be an extraordinary readiness to sacrifice themselves. For example, when Iranian armor was stopped by the presence of land mines on the approaches to Iraqi-held towns, individual soldiers would volunteer to ride bicycles down the road to set off any mines that might be there, thus paving the way for an advance. Contrast this with the hypothetical behavior of an Iranian soldier who, upon hearing that an assassination attempt had been made on the Ayatollah Khomeini, reflected for a few minutes and then shot himself in the foot as a way of expressing his solidarity with the regime and his willingness to sacrifice his personal well-being in its service. Within Weber's framework, both actions would be deemed equally value-rational, since both concern an individual's absolute commitment to a cause and willingness to express that commitment in deliberate acts, regardless of the personal cost. This categorization, however, glosses over an important difference between the two situations.

15

In the first, there is a much stronger case for ascribing rationality, because the overriding of self-preservation is explicable in terms of the traditional normative expectations of a soldier of Islam, expectations which the current regime in Iran has been able to rekindle. On the other hand, in the second example, one is likely to question the individual's rationality. This is so because he has not chosen a mode of expressing his commitment which coheres with any pattern of norms existing in the religious and political community to which he wishes to express his allegiance. In other words, not just any act of self-inflicted injury *counts* as an *expression* of commitment.[29] For it to count, it must be consistent with the expectations generated by the beliefs and norms of an existing or potential community. Weber's way of speaking tends to obscure the significance of just such expectations for judgements of rationality.[30]

The recognition as rational of those actions in which an orientation toward social norms takes precedence over self-interest derives its plausibility from our implicit recognition of a second basic motivation which is constitutive of human action. This might be called simply an intersubjective–contextual orientation. To be motivated in this way means to orient one's actions not only toward self but also toward creating or maintaining institutions and traditions in which is expressed some conception of right behavior and a good life with others.

This motivational dimension expresses our character as creatures who seek meaningfulness for our individual lives by creating and maintaining intersubjectively binding normative structures. Clearly the particular forms this motivation takes vary widely across cultures and through history. There is within this variation, however, a common denominator which allows us a perspective from which we can begin to sort the rational from the irrational.

What I am suggesting here can be grasped if one imagines situations in which social motivation is totally lacking. Isaiah Berlin, in trying to make a similar point about rationality, offers an apt example. He asks us to imagine an individual who possesses the capacity to reason only in a strictly strategic manner and who obtains his most intense satisfaction from sticking pins into surfaces with a particular resiliency.[31] It makes no difference to him whether these surfaces are tennis balls or human skin. And he goes about satisfying his desire in a perfectly systematic (means–ends rational) way. If questioned about his activity, he readily asserts that he would not like others to stick pins in his own skin, but simply cannot understand why he should refrain from sticking them in others as often as circumstances permit. Berlin's concern here is to suggest, on the one hand, that such an individual falls within the bounds of strategic reason, but to question, on the other hand, whether we would feel entirely comfortable calling this man rational. The source of our questioning here is the total absence of any interest in or even understanding of what it means to participate in interaction governed by intersubjectively valid norms.

A further illustration of this point, this time on a collective level, can be seen in the radical disintegration of any intersubjective orientation among the Ik, a tribe in northern Uganda, studied by the anthropologist, Colin Turnbull.[32] Because of some changes in the conditions of their collective life over which they had no control, the Ik have begun to disintegrate as a society; that is, intersubjective orientation has increasingly been displaced by exclusive concern for individual survival. The pursuit of this end by whatever means necessary has systematically penetrated every relationship of Ik society. For example, the elderly are allowed to starve and children of three years of age are driven away by their parents. Both children and elderly are seen simply as competitors for scarce food.

One way to interpret life among the Ik is to see it as confirmation of ethical relativism, that is, as an instance of a society with radically different values from those with which we are familiar. (For example, the Ik word corresponding to our "good" seems to have evolved to the point of meaning something like "having a full stomach.")[33] Such an interpretation, however, misses the truly radical character of Ik life: it is ceasing to possess part of what is constitutive of human action, that is, the presence of some intersubjective–contextual orientation in individuals.[34] Turnbull also seems to arrive at something like this conclusion, at least implicitly, for he makes a recommendation as to how to deal with the Ik problem, which is astonishing to find coming from a veteran anthropologist, for whom a confrontation with a radically different society is a familiar experience. Essentially he recommends social surgery reminiscent of Plato's proposal in *The Republic.* Children and adults alike should be forcibly rounded up into small, random groups and taken away to be resettled into other tribes. The groups must be small and random so that the Ik patterns of behavior will die out without infecting the host societies.[35] Hence, although the Ik are not themselves ultimately responsible for creating the conditions of their decline, their behavior, like that of the pin-pusher, falls into a category which seems in some way to be beyond the bounds of reason as that concept applies to human action.

If the foregoing arguments are correct, it makes sense to think of two basic motivations which are constitutive of human action. Thus, when an individual's behavior manifests no evidence of either one or the other, we

17

bring its rationality into doubt, in the sense of questioning its coherence with our most basic conceptions of what constitutes a human being. Of course, the rationality of particular actions which fall into either of these motivational categories can also be brought into question. Here is where the usefulness of the distinction between strategic and contextual rationality comes into play. In relation to the motivation of self-interest, the appropriate criterion is strategic or means–ends rationality. In relation to social motivation, however, both strategic and contextual criteria may be appropriate. Strategic criteria can, of course, be applied to assess how effective a given action is as a means for achieving some end which is not purely self-interested. However, this means–end consistency by itself is an insufficient criterion for adequately separating out the rational from the irrational in cases where social motivation is involved. This inadequacy can be seen, for example, in the fact that a strategic-rational altruist, like his counterpart, the strategic–rational egoist, will often find it rational not to participate in a cooperative effort when collective goods are involved.[36] If this is the case, one is then still left with the necessity of categorizing much cooperative action as nonrational or irrational. It is only by resorting to the contextual criterion that this sort of intuitively inappropriate categorization can be avoided. Within a contextual–rational framework, participatory actions such as voting can now be understood as manifestations of social motivation in relation to an intersubjectively valid set of democratic norms. In other words, voting is a socially appropriate way of *conforming* to the expectations associated with the role of a citizen of a democratic polity, and thereby *expressing* one's commitment to the shared values on which such a polity is based.

Thinking in terms of social motivation and contextual rationalization involves a fundamental shift in the way action is conceptualized. The model or conceptual framework is no longer monologically intentional and consequentialist, but rather *conventional* or *norm-guided*. On this model, action has an intentional structure, but only in the sense that the actor intends to *express* something *in making his action conform* to a structure of norms.

The idea of contextual rationality is often closely associated, at least among Anglo-American philosophers, with Peter Winch's work. For present purposes, his basic argument can be summed up in the claim that the meaning and rationality of an action are derived from understanding its role in relation to the prevailing norms and beliefs of the form of life of which it is a part.[37] Winch's work has been the subject of much discussion and criticism.[38] I want to leave aside his strong claims about the *exclusively* interpretive nature of social theory and keep the focus on the idea of contextual rationality as one tool for understanding and evaluating social and political phenomena. Taken in this spirit, contextual rationality is a necessary complement to strategic rationality, because the latter cannot adequately account for the role of action which is not motivated purely by self-interest, but which at the same time seems to be in some sense rational. From the context-rational perspective, an act such as voting can be judged as rational or irrational once we understand the norms defining democratic citizenship.[39]

One of the underlying goals of Winch's analysis has been to sensitize us to the danger of making quick judgements about the irrationality or non-rationality of unfamiliar actions or beliefs.[40] This problem has often manifested itself in Western judgements about both primitive societies and contemporary non-Western societies. Winch argues that our assessments of the rationality or irrationality of actions and beliefs in such societies will be inappropriate if we do not understand that an essential part of the criteria for such assessments is constituted by the context within which those actions and beliefs have their place, in particular, the prevailing social norms and world view. Winch has sometimes been interpreted as saying that different societies or forms of life have their own *completely* independent criteria of rationality. If this were Winch's view – and some of his initial remarks on the subject do lend themselves to such an interpretation – then it would indeed warrant the harsh criticism it received.[41] Winch has, however, clarified his initial remarks in such a way that the argument now has the following form. There are indeed some universal criteria of rationality, and for actions these would include such things as transitivity. Such criteria are not in themselves sufficient, however, to pick out what in a given society *counts* as consistent or rational action in particular circumstances. For that, he says, we require more "particular knowledge about the norms [individuals] appeal to in living their lives."[42] In this form, the contextualist argument offers a useful framework for avoiding inappropriate ethnocentric judgements about the irrationality of actions and institutions in non-Western societies, as well as for making sense of our intuitive feeling that it is not irrational for a citizen in a democratic political system (which he holds to be at least partially just) to act in ways which help preserve it.

Although the adoption of a contextualist framework as a supplement to a strategic one can provide insight into the foregoing problems, it nevertheless carries with it some limitations and disturbing implicaitons for social theorists and political philosophers, at least insofar as they wish to give some account of the concepts of power, ideology and social change, and maintain, at the same time, some universalistic moral orientation to political life.

As compared to the strategic framework, the contextualist framework provides us with a more satisfactory way of understanding the consensual and integrative dimension of society. In particular, it provides at least a rough way of understanding how action reproduces the symbolic structures of a social world and how, in turn, that world both endows individual life with meaning and is taken to be valid by the individual in a way which is not reducible to strategic considerations. However, the contextualist perspective's advantages in this regard are gained at a substantial price, for, within this perspective, the phenomena of conflict and power are rendered relatively opaque. Basically, it provides no way of asking whose interests a given normative structure favors. This problem is related to the one of adequately comprehending the phenomenon of ideology. The contextualist perspective provides a more adequate way of conceptualizing the dimension in which ideology manifests itself (collective beliefs and norms), in the sense of understanding the function of that dimension in endowing individual life with social meaning. This initial advantage which the contextualist has over the strategic perspective, however, cannot be capitalized upon, because the former cannot comprehend collective beliefs and norms in terms of power and systematic misperception.[43]

Another drawback of contextualism which has often been noted is its inability to provide an adequate conceptual framework within which processes of social change can be comprehended. While the contextual model may be able, as Winch has suggested, to comprehend some sorts of change along the lines of Wittgenstein's notion of "going on in the same way" in new circumstances, it hardly seems adequate for an understanding of the various ways in which norms, for example, break down under the impact of conflicting interests or systemic changes in social structures.[44]

The strategic–rational perspective can of course provide some account of social change in terms of shifting constellations of power and interests (although, as I will show in chapter 4, its conceptualization of power is inadequate).[45] If we shift the focus, however, from particular changes to broader questions of the direction of change and its meaning, then it is no longer so clear what orientation the strategic–rational perspective offers. More precisely, what significance does it attach to that specifically *modern* phenomenon, the systematic expansion of strategic rationality into more and more areas of social life, which increasingly replaces norm-guided action with action oriented to individual self-interest? Rational choice theorists tend not to raise this question directly and they could, if pressed, probably argue that they are not necessarily constrained by their assumptions to take any one position. Nevertheless, the position most rational choice theorists seem, at least tacitly, to adhere to is one which takes the systematic expansion of strategic rationality to be a beneficial process which clears the necessary cognitive and social ground for an ever greater degree of individual freedom and welfare, coming to fruition in the modern democratic state.[46] This interpretation of social rationalization has a systematic one-sidedness, however, insofar as it seems to be conceptually blind to the possibility of perceiving a negative side to modernization. That is, if one wishes to entertain the Weberian question of a "loss of meaning" entailed by Western modernization, the strategic perspective alone is inadequate for that purpose, since it cannot conceptualize the meaning–endowing function of traditional normative structures.

Turning to the normative implications of contextual rationality, the most important problem it raises is its apparent preclusion of a universalist moral perspective, in particular, one which somehow links reason and justice. This results from the fact that, within the contextualist account, the giving of reasons to justify an action or institution is an activity which is exhausted by drawing connections between that action or institution and the social context of beliefs and norms. An appeal to universal principles instead of traditional norms thus has no special, higher power of moral rationalization. Such an appeal does not therefore differentiate a specific universalistic, moral sense of practical rationality. In other words, requirements that our actions conform, for example, to the principle of universalization and accordance of respect to all others as free and equal beings have a justificatory power no different from any other normative framework for judging actions.

The fact that Western societies tend to accord a privileged status to the rationalization of action in terms of abstract universalizable principles is to be explained as simply one possible way of creating a hierarchy of types of normative justification. In other words, an appeal to the kind of moral principles just cited must be thought of as a culturally specific activity whose force ultimately depends upon the fact that others share what one might call the deep normative structure of Western moral and political consciousness. The upshot of this line of argument is that what counts as rational in the moral realm will be thoroughly dependent on whatever moral norms happen to be in force in a given culture. To sum up, the contextualist perspective, which offers a necessary explanatory supplement to the strategic one, is also a perspective which appears to exclude the possibility of making a certain sort of claim about justice, i.e., a universalist one.[47]

III.   Universalism, justice and rationality

Whether because of the foregoing contextualist argument or related ones, it is becoming increasingly clear that universalism in moral and political philosophy is currently experiencing serious difficulties finding a satisfactory form in which to defend itself.[48] In many areas of morality, the abandonment of universalism is entirely appropriate and a healthy sign of waning Western ethnocentrism. However, in that one area of morality which is centrally related to politics – justice – such an adjustment is more unsettling, at least to some. This is because "Claims of justice have always been the preferred examples of moral claims that are to be recognized by reason, as founded in the nature of things, as not essentially diverse, and as not contingent upon any sort of social order."[49] Certainly such a conviction stood behind Rawls's *A Theory of Justice*.[50] And yet even Rawls had to back away from the strong universalist claims of his book, now arguing that the theory of justice is only directly valid within a "democratic society under modern circumstances." In other words, the persuasiveness of his arguments extends only as far as that deep normative structure of modern Western consciousness.[51]

If universalism is having difficulty finding an adequate framework within which to defend the link between reason and justice, where exactly does contextualism leave us on this question? At this point it is rather interesting to note what one leading contextualist, Richard Rorty, is forced to admit when he is faced with the question of how to defend his own preference for one of two different moral–political positions which appear equally compatible with a contextualist perspective. Rorty prefers the moral–political language game of William James or John Dewey over that of Nietzsche or Foucault, for the former seems to involve some appeal to the human community and a hope for solidarity, whereas the latter seems to rest on a basic "inhumanism." (I am not concerned with the validity of this description of the Foucault–Nietzsche position.) Justifying this preference would involve, Rorty admits, a "full scale discussion" of "public morality, a concern for justice."[52] Rorty is certainly right about this, but the question is: what would a fully contextualist account of justice look like? Fortunately just such an account has been offered recently by Michael Walzer.[53] Much of what Walzer says is compelling, but in his preface and conclusion, there is a curious admission which indicates that his position as a whole relies on retaining a minimal aspect of universalism. "For the purposes of this book," he assumes "our *recognition* of one another as human beings." We recognize, or ought to, that we are "one another's *equals*" by virtue of our

22

characteristics as "culture-producing creatures [who] make and inhabit meaningful worlds."[54]

Now how is one to understand this universalistic appeal to *equality* and intersubjective *recognition*? Walzer gives us no systematic answer. It is in this context of seeking a systematic answer to the problem of a *minimal* universalism that I want to turn to Habermas's work.

He offers a universalist position which makes strong claims and yet attempts to accommodate the insights of contextualist critics. His position is quite distinct from that of a Dworkin, a Kohlberg or a Rawls: although Habermas thinks that we can legitimately speak of universalistic procedural criteria for assessing the justness of normative claims, he does not think it is possible to claim that these criteria unequivocally pick out one determinate principle or set of principles for acting justly or creating just institutions.

Habermas argues that minimal criteria of justice are derivable from his conceptions of communicative action and communicative rationality. The universalist claim raised by this interpretation of the moral sense of rationality is developed in a complex set of arguments about "performative contradictions," moral development and modernity; and these arguments are integrated into the framework of a general theory of society which, in turn, offers an account of power and ideology.

It will be the task of chapter 2 to explain the communicative model of rationality and action, and contrast it with the strategic and contextual models. It will also be shown how Habermas's turn to the communicative model both continues certain themes present in the work of earlier critical theorists and yet also constitutes a substantial departure from that work.

I will then focus in chapter 3 on an evaluation of Habermas's argument that a "communicative ethics" can be derived from the notions of communicative action and rationality. Specifically, he maintains that universalistic "norms of rational speech" are implicit in ongoing linguistic interaction and that this fact can be demonstrated by reconstructing what is intuitively known by every competent speaker.[55] This argument is found to be partially successful but not successful enough to carry all the weight Habermas, at least initially, attributed to it. The ultimate justification for the claims of a communicative ethics must rely on a defense of certain *modern* structures of consciousness.

Before turning to Habermas's theory of modernity in chapter 5, I further develop in chapter 4 the idea of a communicative ethics. The focus here is on distinguishing it from other conceptions of post-conventional ethics, such as Rawls's or J. L. Mackie's. Then I propose a way in which the normative implications of this "minimal" communicative ethics connect up with a central problem in political theory: the analysis of power. The communicative model provides a persuasive way of rethinking this "essentially contestable" concept.

Chapter 5 takes on the task of elucidating the complex interpretation of modernity which Habermas puts forward in *The Theory of Communicative Action*. It is shown how the communicative model helps Habermas structure an interpretation of modernity which allows him to be critical of it, as other critical theorists and post-structuralists have been, but also to locate a potential for rationality within it. I argue that this distinctive interpretation permits Habermas to develop a critical perspective on the societal processes of modernization, which is in some ways similar to Foucault's, but which does not suffer from Foucault's difficulties with the notions of normativity and subjectivity. Finally I draw out and assess some specific hypotheses about the structures and processes of contemporary capitalism, which Habermas derives from his reading of modernity. These constitute the "positive heuristic" of Habermas's research program.

Chapter 6 reflects on the overall project Habermas has set for himself. It considers the criticisms which have been made of his particular brand of conceptual and moral universalism. The charge of foundationalism is first shown to be inaccurate. Then I take up the most penetrating critiques, in particular the claims that an interpretation of modernity and subjectivity such as Habermas's cannot adequately comprehend the true dimensions of the subjugation of both outer and inner nature in the modern world. The perspectives of, respectively, radical ecologists and Foucault, present particularly important problems for Habermas, because critical theory has always claimed to be sensitive to subjugation and domination in whatever guise they appear. I consider how one can respond to these challenges from a Habermasian perspective and ultimately argue that the later is more defensible than the critiques.

2

Communicative action and rationality

In this chapter I will begin to examine Habermas's conceptions of communicative action and communicative rationality, and to show why he thinks they constitute both a universalistic perspective on normative legitimacy and the core of an alternative research program. Although the formal elaboration of the theory of comunicative action and rationality comes only with the "linguistic turn" in Habermas's thinking which occurred around 1970, his interest in rationality has been evident since his earliest writings. It will thus be useful to begin my analysis with a brief overview of why he took up the problem of rationality in the first place, and why his initial treatment of it was unsatisfactory. I will then turn in Section II to a consideration of the claims he makes about how a rational reconstruction of communicative competence gives one the necessary bearings for an adequate conception of rationality. This will lead in Section III to an extended discussion of communicative action, followed in Section IV by a consideration of some of the problems to which that model gives rise.

I. The critique of positivism and the linguistic turn

What constitutes the idea of socialism, for me, is the possibility of overcoming the capitalistic simplification of the process of rationalization (to use Weber's terminology). Simplification, that is, in the sense of the rise to dominance of cognitive–instrumental aspects, through which everything else is driven into the realm of apparent irrationality.[1]

The central problem of Habermas's thought has been how to demonstrate that an exclusively instrumental or strategic understanding of rationality is somehow inadequate and that therefore the historical process of increasing Weberian rationalization of the world represents a threat to the full potential of human beings to bring reason to bear on the problems of their social and political existence. The significance of this threat was brought home to Habermas in the 1950s by Max Horkheimer and Theodor Adorno's *The Dialectic of Enlightenment.* They argued that the unparalleled success of modern

Western civilization in freeing itself from the constraints of the natural world through the increasing development of science and technology did not bring with it the freedom envisaged by Marx, or Enlightenment thinkers, but rather ever more effective and subtle forms of domination.[2] Horkheimer and Adorno, however, in spite of all their emphasis on reason and the possibility of a "rational society" in which reason, freedom and justice would be harmoniously linked, were never very successful in developing a coherent notion of reason, within which an instrumental or strategic–rational orientation to the social and political world could be illuminated in a way which would demonstrate clearly exactly how limited or one-sided it is.[3]

Habermas's efforts to develop a "more comprehensive" [*weitergehende*] conception of reason initially took the form of a critique of the "positivistic self-understanding" of science.[4] For Habermas's purposes, the claims of positivism about knowledge, reason, and moral and political values can be summarized in three propositions: first, that knowledge on the hypothetical-deductive model is the only genuine form of knowledge in both the natural and the social sciences; secondly, that this form of knowledge is value-free, in the sense that its validity is not dependent on the prior acceptance of any normative commitments, or at least none with any moral or political content; thirdly, that the domain of values and norms is taken to fall outside "the scope of rational discussion." As a result of this third element, positivism also sanctions an understanding of politics in which rationality refers only to the efficiency of the means for carrying out individual and collective ends, not to the ends themselves.[5]

Habermas's attack on positivism is directed primarily against the claim that the validity of science is independent of any normative commitment on the part of the scientist. In particular, Habermas wants to question whether scientific knowledge is in fact really "released from every normative bond."[6] It is with this problem in mind that he begins to work toward his theory of "knowledge-guiding" or "knowledge-constitutive interests" which emerges full blown in *Knowledge and Human Interests*.[7] Now both Horkheimer and Adorno had considered one of critical theory's primary tasks to be the elucidation of the embeddedness of scientific research in the larger context of the reproduction of capitalism and thus in the world of conflicting social interests.[8] Habermas's theory of knowledge-guiding interests attempts to perform this kind of task but in a more radical way, by locating science in relation to certain "anthropologically deep-seated" interests of the human species as a whole.[9] The validity of scientific theories cannot, according to this view, be separated from the underlying "interest" of man in the "domination" of nature which allows the material reproduction of the species.[10] It is in response to this "technical interest" that science constitutes the world as one of potentially manipulable bodies. However, the human species also has another universal interest: its "practical interest" in maintaining that level of intersubjectivity which is achieved in ordinary language communication and is necessary for the reproduction of man as a social–cultural being.[11] It is in relation to this "interest" that one can speak of knowledge as the understanding subjects achieve on questions of how to order their social and cultural life.

Positivism, then, fails both to reflect on the technical interest which informs science and to differentiate this normative orientation from the practical interest of mankind. These failures allow positivism to play an ideological role in relation to the problem of adequately understanding the relationship between scientific and technological progress, on the one hand, and questions about the proper shape and direction of social and cultural life, on the other. The latter questions are declared to be beyond the scope of rational discussion, except in a technical, instrumental sense. This reduction of the practical dimension in the name of the exclusive claim of the technical actually constitutes a tacit answer to a basic normative question: what is the proper relationship between the different knowledge-guiding interests? Positivism, in the final analysis, not only fails to allow one some conceptual framework for a broader understanding of the technical rationalization of the world, but it also implicitly endorses that process.[12]

Habermas's theory of knowledge-constitutive interests has been subjected to extensive criticism on a variety of grounds.[13] The most incisive criticism is that his scheme constitutes a mode of philosophical foundationalism. Habermas has tried to meet this problem by shifting his center of theoretical attention away from epistemology to the theory of language and action.[14] This shift has not, however, changed the underlying aim of his work, by which I mean the rehabilitation of the idea that there is a universalistic sense of rationality which applies to the moral–practical dimension, a sense which, when properly explicated, will both help reveal the "one-sidedness" of technical rationalization as well as allow for a better understanding of "a potential for reason encapsulated in the very forms of social reproduction."[15]

Habermas now pursues this aim by means of a "rational reconstruction" of linguistic interaction. The pursuit of this strategy has fostered the development of his distinctive conceptions of communicative action and rationality.[16] In the remainder of this chapter, I will lay out these conceptions, show why Habermas thinks them superior to others and why he thinks they form the basis of a universalistic perspective in ethics and political philosophy. Problems related to the epistemological status of rational reconstructions will be taken up in chapter 6.

II.   Communicative competence and communicative rationality

In shifting his focus to language and action, Habermas's aim has been to illuminate how ongoing linguistic interaction has built into it a sense of rationality which is not reducible to strategic or contextual dimensions. His claim is that the speech acts of communicatively competent actors conform to a set of rules, some of which establish the criteria of communicative rationality. What Habermas calls " rational reconstruction" is the task of rendering what is a universal competence or implicit know-how into a set of explicit rules; in this case he is reconstructing "formal–pragmatic" rules. [17]

Such rules describe the competence an actor has for *using sentences* in *utterances* aimed at "reaching an understanding." As the analysis of speech acts since J. L. Austin has shown, speakers, in *saying* something, also *do* something. [18] This doing of something is what Austin called the "illocutionary force" of an utterance. Habermas wants to argue that the *universal* core of the many and varied things speakers do in uttering sentences is to situate those strings of symbols in a system of validity claims. When a speaker orients himself toward understanding – that is, engages in communicative action – his speech acts must raise, and he must be accountable for, three rationality or "validity claims" [*Geltungsanspruche*]: truth, normative legitimacy and truthfulness/authenticity. [19] Only if a speaker is able to convince his hearers that his claims are rational and thus worthy of recognition can there develop a "rationally motivated agreement" [*Einverständnis*] or consensus on how to coordinate future actions. [20]

From the perspective of communicative action, utterances can be assessed as rational or irrational because they raise criticizable validity claims, that is, ones which are fallible and open to objective judgement.

In contexts of communicative action, we call someone rational not only if he is able to put forward an assertion and, when criticized, to provide grounds for it by pointing to appropriate evidence, but also if he is following an established norm and is able when criticized, to justify his action by explicating the given situation in the light of legitimate expectations. We even call someone rational if he makes known a desire or an intention, expresses a feeling or a mood, shares a secret, confesses a deed, etc., and is then able to reassure critics in regard to the revealed experience by drawing practical consequences from it and behaving consistently thereafter. [21]

In developing the ability to speak and act, each individual acquires the know-how required both to differentiate the three dimensions of validity and to employ the standards appropriate to each dimension for the purpose of assessing particular claims. For a given agent this know-how may be more or less conscious, but it is always intuitively accessible.[22]

The development of this communicative competence depends upon the development of particular but interrelated competences in the dimensions of cognition, speech and action. Each of these can be reconstructed theoretically as a system of rules over which an agent has mastery. The schema Habermas has in mind links up with the work of others, such as Chomsky and Piaget, and has the following form. Communicative competence, as the mastery of the rules for raising and redeeming the different types of validity claims, encompasses:

1 "Cognitive competence": mastery of the rules of formal, logical operations (Piaget).
2 "Speech Competence" [*Sprachkompetenz*]: mastery of the linguistic rules for producing situations of possible understanding.
   a) mastery of the rules for producing grammatically well-formed sentences (Chomsky's "linguistic competence").
   b) mastery of the rules for producing well-formed utterances (universal or formal pragmatic rules).
3 "Interactive Competence" or "Role Competence": mastery of the rules for taking part in increasingly complex forms of interaction.[23]

Habermas's specific contributions to this schema fall under categories 2b and 3. The latter will be discussed in chapter 3. The former are the rules which enable a sentence to take up one of the three formal or "universal pragmatic functions of language" which correspond to the three validity claims: "to represent something in the world, to express the speaker's intentions, and to establish legitimate interpersonal relations." It is only on the basis of having taken up these cognitive, expressive and interactive functions that speech acts can also simultaneously take up "all the particular functions that an utterance can assume in specific contexts."[24] The system of rules which communicatively competent subjects must have mastered can be reconstructed, according to Habermas, in a "general theory of speech actions." This would provide an integrated account of components of language such as deitic expressions of time and space, personal pronouns and performative verbs, which are used by speakers to take up the three general pragmatic functions of language.[25]

As an initial effort in this direction, Habermas has suggested a categorization of performative verbs on the basis of how they relate to these three pragmatic functions and validity claims. These verbs generate the differentiated illocutionary force (the *doing* of something in speaking) of speech acts which allows them to take up one of the pragmatic functions and thus thematize one of the three validity claims. He distinguishes "constatives" (to assert, propose, etc.) which raise the truth claim; "regulatives" (to promise, prescribe, etc.) which raise the claim of legitimacy or normative correctness; and finally "expressives" (to wish, intend, etc.) which raise the claim of sincerity or truthfulness.[26]

Thus, if actors are to have the capacity to use their utterances in such a way as to generate the kind of understanding which is necessary to sustain ongoing interaction, they must have mastered a whole set of distinctions between performatives, modes of language use and validity claims. Or, to put it slightly differently, understanding-oriented action presupposes a range of mutual, "idealized imputations." Utterances which conform to these imputations constitute the "sphere of normal speech."[27] One can say then that Habermas's notion of formal pragmatics demarcates a certain sort of language use as "fundamental" or paradigmatic for understanding.[28] Only speech acts which clearly exhibit the mastery of the formal pragmatic rules fall into this category, for they alone have the full capacity to sustain understanding-oriented action.

This notion of a formal pragmatics contains a formidable number of highly controversial claims and categorial distinctions. From the viewpoint of linguistics or the philosophy of language, one could contest this project on a variety of grounds. How persuasive is the categorization of performative verbs versus other possible categorizations? Should the pragmatics of language be pursued more inductively, that is, in a less formal and theoretically guided way?[29] Although these are undoubtedly important questions, which would bear on any ultimate judgement of Habermas's scheme, I want to keep the focus on problems with a somewhat broader philosophical significance, especially ones bearing on moral, political and social theory.

One persistent criticism that has been made of formal pragmatics revolves around the justification for setting off some language uses as "normal" and others as (in some sense) secondary or derivative.[30] Speech acts which raise all three validity claims, and thus conform to standards of normality, are characterized by a relative straightforwardness, seriousness and clarity of meaning. What has disturbed critics about this picture of normality in language is whether it can "do justice to the imaginative and creative character of language use." Within such a picture what treatment can one expect of poetry, humor, multivocity, irony and so on?[31]

Now at first sight this sort of criticism might seem to raise a problem without much broad philosophical significance of the sort I just mentioned. This is not the case, however, as post-structuralism has so acutely shown in recent years. The tradition of Western metaphysics has persistently reconstituted itself by means of unambiguously marking out fundamental categorial distinctions. But, as post-structuralists have pointed out, these distinctions never support the heavy philosophical weight placed upon them. Hence the suspicion which surfaces whenever distinctions such as "normal/abnormal" are proposed is that they have less to do with an economy of reason than they do with an economy of power.

Habermas's marking out of a sphere of normal language raises just such a suspicion. His privileging of serious, straightforward, unambiguous usage can be seen as diverting our attention away from precisely those aspects of language which have the capability of sensitizing us to the oppressiveness of whatever categorial distinctions are dominating our thought and social interaction in any given historical period. Humor, irony, metaphor, and aesthetic expression in general are what give us breathing space and weapons in this ongoing struggle to prevent closure in the way we see ourselves, others and the world. And if one follows Foucault in his account of the ever-growing "disciplinary" character of modern life, one can see even more vividly the potential ethical–political implications of what might initially appear as a relatively innocuous set of choices about categorial distinctions in the philosophy of language.[32]

Habermas has tried to defend his scheme from attacks along this line by arguing both that his central categorial distinction is "harmless" if understood within the context of its theoretical purpose, and that at least some of the forms of expression which are accorded derivative status are, in fact, best understood when they are treated that way. In relation to the latter argument, he asserts that irony, humor and fiction, for example, "rest on *intentionally* using categorial confusions" which we can "see through as category mistakes" precisely because we have the competence to distinguish the three universal validity claims and the accompanying distinctions between "being/illusion, is/ought, essence/appearance."[33]

A problem with this strategy, which emerges quickly, is that it appears to tie meaning more closely to intentionality than perhaps is warranted. Do speech acts have an ironic meaning only when it is intended by the speaker? What if I were to assert a philosophical position in a series of particularly abrasive and arrogant speech acts, concluding with the statement that: "I remain, however, fully open and sensitive to entertaining impartially the claims of alternative positions." Would there not be irony here which is wholly unintended?

Perhaps Habermas might admit that he has overstressed the role of intentionality here, but still defend the key aspect of his scheme by claiming that the quality of irony in the foregoing example can be recognized only to the extent that *hearers* have mastered the system of validity claims and corresponding distinctions. Moreover, it is precisely here that charges of "systematic distortion" of communication can begin to be levelled at the speaker.[34]

As I have already mentioned, Habermas would also defend his overall classificatory scheme by reference to its ultimate purpose. Although he still sometimes uses phrases like "the inherent telos of human speech," which have distinctly foundationalist connotations, he nevertheless quite clearly admits that he is privileging certain sorts of usage only *in order to* clarify how it is possible for ordinary language to play its distinctive coordinating role in human interaction.[35] From this perspective, Habermas argues, his selectivity is harmless, since those forms of expression, both verbal and non-verbal, which seem so essential to human creativity – fiction, poetry, music, painting etc. – "do not as a rule take over functions of co-ordinating action."[36]

But what about other forms of language use that seem more directly involved with action coordination, although they do not rely upon the differentiated scheme of validity, for example the ritual or sacred use of language? Habermas contends that this category must be explained "in developmental–logical terms," that is, as a not-yet-fully-differentiated way of using language. And in *The Theory of Communicative Action,* he does attempt the kind of developmental–logical sketch which would be necessary to make this claim plausible.[37] And yet, as critics have remarked, Habermas's treatment of ritual and myth in primitive societies is too brief and overly formal to be persuasive, at least given the very strong claims he wants to make about the privileged status of modernity.[38]

Nevertheless, it does appear at first glance that his assertion about more purely aesthetic forms of expression is generally correct. One does not usually think of them as being directly involved in action coordination. A moment's reflection, however, can render this conclusion problematic. Whether this reflection emerges from the post-structuralists' work or that of Adorno, it leads one to entertain the idea that, although aesthetic expression may not directly coordinate action, it may have (at least potentially) substantial power *to erode* the effectiveness of some types of action coordination.

Now Habermas would actually accept this insight about the "singularly illuminating power [of aesthetic expression] to open our eyes to what is seemingly familiar, to disclose anew an apparently familiar reality."[39] In fact, he refers rather hopefully to this capacity in his prescriptions for modernity's ills (as will be shown in chapter 6). But the acceptance of this insight does not in his opinion entail the revamping of his analysis of language. Anticipating my discussion in later chapters, one can represent Habermas's position here as follows. The capacity of aesthetic expression to have a radical world-disclosing effect on thought and action is dependent upon the aesthetic sphere's having attained a relative autonomy in the *modern* world. Autonomy here is meant in the sense that the validity of a work of art in the modern world is evaluated in different terms from the validity of a claim about a norm's legitimacy or a proposition's truth. Moreover, this three-fold differentiation has been institutionalized in modern societies where the corresponding "cultural value spheres" of science and technology, post-conventional law and morality, and modern art and art criticism have been separated out.[40] All of this capacity to differentiate is ultimately traceable to what distinguishes us from pre-moderns: our "rationalized lifeworld" which makes the system of differentiated validity claims socially available to us in a way it is not in pre-modern society. The implication of all this, at least in Habermas's eyes, is that his classification of language usage is justified, because the action-related role of aesthetic expression can be explained only *after* having assumed the correctness of that classification to begin with.

Although the general point Habermas makes here about the aesthetic sphere is a good one, it is not so clear that it sits entirely comfortably with his classification of speech acts. This can be seen if one correlates validity claims with the cultural spheres of value in modern society, as Habermas seems to suggest: truth claim/modern science and technology; normative legitimacy claim/post-conventional law and morality; and truthfulness or authenticity claim/art and art criticism. If one recalls that the claim to truthfulness or authenticity was originally explained in terms of whether or not an utterance truthfully expresses an actor's intentions or feelings, one can see that art is here being understood on the same model: as an expression of one's self, with its validity revolving around the questions of whether it authentically represents that self's inner nature.

Using such a model, however, means according to art a rather restricted sense of validity or "truth." It is to be evaluated solely in terms of its relation to its author or creator. Habermas has, in fact, agreed that this is inadequate as a general account of art.[41] For this model would make it hard to comprehend the "world-disclosing" [*Welterschliessenden*] potential of aesthetic expression mentioned above, except in the narrow sense of opening the author's inner world to the public. Accordingly, Habermas has given a different account of this world-disclosing potential, which I will take up further in chapter 6. At this point, what is important to note is just that the original classification of validity claims and speech acts does not provide much direct heuristic light on the new account.

It is useful at this point to return to an earlier argument and ask again why, in light of the difficulties I have alluded to, Habermas thinks it so important to stick with his original categorization of speech. The general reason, as I said above, is that the usage he has delineated as normal performs a direct coordinating role for actions in a way which aesthetic expression does not (whether the fictive usage of language or non-verbal forms of expression). A closer appreciation of what Habermas means by this will prepare the ground for my discussion of "communicative action" in the next section.

In directing our attention to the role of language in coordinating action, Habermas is indicating that what animates his classificatory efforts is the problem of theory construction in the social sciences.[42] Putting it most simply, he is asking what precisely is the contribution of ordinary language to the coordination of action which is necessary to the very possibility of social life?

This orientation emerges clearly when Habermas surveys the controversy between John Searle and Jacques Derrida. At issue is the latter's assault on the Austinian tradition in general, with its persistent distinctions between normal/non-normal, serious/non-serious or fictive language usage. Habermas, of course, realizes that such an attack engages his own work and he tries to provide a justification for his use of such distinctions.

What is seminal about Austin's work and what constitutes the link with Habermas's is that it discovered "a mechanism of action coordination in the illocutionary binding force [*Bindungskraft*] of linguistic utterance." For this binding force to take hold in everyday practice, speech must be subjugated to certain limitations which do not apply to, for example, fictive speech. "These limitations, under which illocutionary acts develop an action-coordinating force and release action-relevant consequences, define the sphere of normal speech."[43]

In Austin's account, these limitations took the form of conventional conditions for the success of speech acts. From a deconstructionist point of view, however, such conventional conditions are inexhaustibly open-textured, a fact which implies that the sphere of normal speech can never be clearly delineated. Habermas argues that his own position is not open to this problem, since, on his account, the relevant conditions are not conventional, but rather those "idealized imputations" which characterize even "institutionally unbound speech actions." And these shared idealizations are part of the basic structure of a rationalized lifeworld; thus their being in force is not something which wholly results from an individual's intentions.[44]

It is the underlying, mutual expectation between actors that they can, if challenged, defend the specific claims they raise, which in turn creates the "binding force" for the coordination of action. But in fictive speech this system of validity claims brought into play by illocutive acts is at least partially suspended. This

> neutralization of the binding force unburdens the disempowered illocutionary acts from the decision pressure of communicative everyday practice; it suspends the sphere of ordinary speech and empowers [speech] for the playful creation of new worlds – or rather: for the pure demonstration of the world-disclosing power of innovative linguistic expressions.[45]

In this remark, one can see precisely how Habermas wants to begin thinking about language in terms of its "problem-solving capacity for interaction" and then show how to understand its world-disclosing capacity.[46] Of course, this particular proposal for constructing the normal/non-normal or serious/non-serious distinction would hardly satisfy a Derridean, since, in general, one point of deconstructing basic distinctions such as these is to show that all of them will *necessarily* collapse on close analysis and that actually the reverse of what they try to establish is true. For example, serious speech can always be shown to be a special case of non-serious speech.

I have no doubt that a clever Derridean could discover a way to deconstruct Habermas's position.[47] But, on the other hand, there are also good reasons for suspecting that deconstructionism, rather than being simply the revealer of all forms of metaphysics, is itself a concealed form of metaphysics.[48] If this is so, perhaps the most sensible way to make some headway in this dispute over the distinction "serious/non-serious" is simply to ask: from which side of the distinction is one able initially to get both a better account of the *other* side as well as heuristically stronger insights about social action? On the first half of this question, one would have to admit, as was indicated earlier, that Habermas's classificatory scheme does not provide effortless insight into the realm of aesthetic expression. On the second half of the question, though, he does substantially better. The deconstructionist's "aestheticization of language," which starts from its world-disclosing capacity, makes it extremely difficult to account for the reproduction of social life in general and the occurrence of learning processes that take place within it. The focus on world-*disclosing* gives one no clear way of appreciating the fact that "linguistically mediated processes such as the attainment of knowledge, identity formation, socialization and social integration master problems *within the world.*" Linguistic interaction "makes learning processes [in these dimensions] possible thanks to the idealizations" built into it. And it is within such learning processes that the world-disclosing power of language "must be *confirmed.*" In the deconstructionist model, "the renewing process of linguistic world-disclosing no longer has any *counter-pressure* from the confirming process of practice in the world."[49]

Habermas's general point here is a good one, although much still depends on the account he gives of learning processes (a matter I will take up later). I will try to bring this point to bear in a specific way in chapter 6, but it will be brought to bear against Foucault rather than Derrida, since the latter has not had much to say directly about social and political theory. My claim against Foucault will be that his focus on the power of aesthetic expression, although it is immensely provocative, nevertheless pushes him in a direction from which it is not clear how he can offer a coherent outline of an ethically legitimate form of acting collectively in the world – an outline which, at the end of his life, he apparently did want to develop.[50] Handling the problem of collective action is what Habermas means by the term "social integration" in the passage quoted in the preceding paragraph. Thus, if my specific argument against Foucault proves to be correct, it would help lend some credence to Habermas's general claim about where to begin an account of language.

III. Models of action and rationality

We have seen that Habermas focuses on language as a medium for coordinating action that is, for producing subsequent patterns of interaction. Action, however, can be coordinated in more than one way. So the central question is how precisely Habermas sees coordination coming about. The kind he is interested in occurs, as we have seen, only when actors are oriented "to reaching an understanding." It is this orientation which constitutes the category "communicative action."[51] The best way to get some initial illumination of what is intended by this notion is to contrast it with other competing notions of action. Proceeding in this way will allow me to link up the present discussion with the themes of chapter 1.

There I drew a connection between conceptions of rationality and corresponding conceptions of action. Habermas argues that this kind of connection is in fact a necessary conceptual one. As he puts it, when a social scientist chooses a conception of action he also necessarily establishes the framework for a conception of rationality. This link is a result of the fact that, in the choice of a conception of action, a social theorist implicitly makes certain "'ontological' assumptions" about the possible "relations between actor and world." And the "world relations" the theorist imputes to the actor establish, in turn, a particular framework for the "possible rationality of . . . actions."[52] Habermas demonstrates this by analyzing three different conceptions of action and the corresponding frameworks they establish for rationality. This analysis prepares the ground for his argument that each of these conceptions is inadequate on its own as a framework for fully comprehending the cooperative dimension of action. An adequate perspective can, he argues, only be constructed around his communicative model.

Two of the three alternative conceptions Habermas considers (the teleological and the norm-guided) have already been introduced in the first chapter. His arguments about their inadequacies and what must be done to remedy them will link up with those presented in the first chapter, thus showing the points at which Habermas's work offers a contribution to current debates about action and rationality.

A.   *The teleological model.* According to Habermas, this model of action presupposes a relation between the actor and a world of "states of affairs," either presently existing or producible through action. The actor relates to this world both cognitively, through opinions about it, and volitionally, through intentions to intervene in it. These two possible relations to an *objective world* can be rationalized, respectively, according to criteria of *"truth"* and *"effectiveness"* or success.[53] The former criteria demarcate epistemic rationality while the latter demarcate practical rationality in the purposive sense. This purposive sense refers both to non-social action and its corresponding "instrumental rationality," as well as to social action and its corresponding "strategic rationality."[54] In the latter case, the objective world includes not only physical objects and naturally occurring events, but also the intentions, strategies, decisions etc. of other individuals, to which the actor relates in an "objectivating" manner, that is, solely in terms of their bearing on the success or failure of that actor to manipulate states of affairs.[55]

B.   *The norm-guided model.* In this model the actor can relate not only to an objective but also to a *social world.* "A social world consists of a normative context that establishes which interactions belong to the body of justified interpersonal relations."[56] Insofar as actors share such a context, they share a social world. Now this normative context exists as a categorically distinct world only when it is *recognized as valid* by actors; that is, it maintains an "ought" quality for them. (Otherwise this context simply becomes another feature of the objective world.)

The relation of action to social world allows rationalization in two senses, both of which Habermas subsumes under the concept of *"normative correct-ness"* or normative legitimacy.[57] On the one hand, an action can be assessed in regard to how well it conforms to or deviates from an intersubjectively valid role or other norm. On the other hand, the validity of these normative expectations may itself be called into question. Criteria for a rational assess-ment in this sense would appear to have no other possible source – as was pointed out in chapter 1 – than some other set of normative expectations which are already socially prescribed as having a validity superior to that of the ones being called into question. Habermas, however, wants to argue that the legitimacy of social norms can always be called into question in a more radical, less socially defined, way. Ultimately, the validity of any social norm can be assessed by considering its consistency with an agent's intuitive sense of what ultimately gives any norm its "ought" quality: whether it incorporates interests which are "generalizable" to all who are affected by that norm.[58] This appeal to an intuitive sense of normative validity which every individual gains as he develops his competence for speech and action, is crucial to Habermas's attempt to demonstrate that the intersubjective–contextual motivation exhibited in norm-guided action has a core which is linked in a conceptually necessary way to certain universal, rational moral standards. In his discussion of the norm-guided model, however, he does not make it sufficiently clear that this is not an idea internal to that model but rather is derived from his own views about communicative competence and normative legitimacy.

C.   *The dramaturgical model.* In addition to the teleological and norm-guided models of action, there is a third one which is somewhat less prominent in the social sciences, the dramaturgical. Habermas attributes the initial development of this model to Erving Goffman.[59] Here the focus is not specifically on how an individual pursues a strategy or follows a set of nor-mative expectations, but rather on how the performance of any action reveals something about the actor's subjectivity. More particularly, in the performance of actions, an individual *represents* his *subjective world* in a specific way to an *audience* of other actors. This subjective world is "defined as the totality of subjective experiences" to which the individual actor "has privileged access."[60] This world of subjective experiences includes wishes, feelings, hopes, needs, etc., to which the subject can reflectively relate and selectively represent to others.[61] One way in which this actor-subjective world relation is open to objective judgements of rationality is by assessing the degree of consistency which exists between what a subject expresses about himself in an utterance and his ensuing action; that is, "whether he *means* what he *says*, or whether he is merely feigning the experience he expresses." Rationalization here is thus measured in relation to a subject's "truthfulness" [*Wahrhaftigkeit*] or deceptiveness in relation to others. There is, however, another sense in which a subject's presentation of self can be rationally assessed: in terms of its "authenticity" [*Authentizität*].[62] Here the assessment of consistency is directed primarily to the possibility of self-deception, that is, whether the feeling or need expressed is what one really feels or needs.

D. *The communicative model.* The foregoing survey of the major alternative conceptualizations of action has brought to the surface a correlation between the three types of validity claims mentioned earlier and the different actor–world relations implied in these alternatives. Presumably Habermas would consider this fit between his scheme of validity claims and the predominant models of action to be no accident, but rather one sort of evidence supporting his argument about the universality of these claims.

What distinguishes the communicative model of action is that ordinary language competence is now envisioned as giving actors the capacity to use this *entire* system of world relations and validity claims in a distinct fashion for the purpose of coordinating action. As I have said before, communicative action is action oriented to reaching an understanding. And what Habermas is specifically interested in is how language can function as "a medium of unhindered understanding."[63] Within this model, actors are conceived of as seeking an understanding in regard to some practical situation confronting them, in order to coordinate their actions consensually. Reaching an understanding requires "a cooperative process of interpretation aimed at attaining intersubjectively recognized definitions of situations."[64]

For this process to go on as it in fact does, one must assume a more complex competence on the part of actors than is postulated in the other models of action. Within the communicative model, actors are envisioned as being able to relate simultaneously to *all three* of the aforementioned worlds (objective, social and subjective). Moreover, they can relate to them *reflectively*, in the sense that they have the competence to differentiate the three types of relations and select one or the other as the most appropriate for interpreting a given situation and working out an agreement on a common definition of it. Thus, the three modes of world relations together constitute a "commonly imputed system of coordinates," which actors have at their mutual disposal to aid them in understanding one another.[65]

Actors within the communicative model are not only accorded the competence to dispose reflectively over the three world-relations, but also the competence to assess the rationality or irrationality of one another's actions according to all three of the respective sets of criteria (truth/success; normative legitimacy; and truthfulness/authenticity) which are implied by the different possible world-relations.

Thus, in the model of communicative action, speech acts are the medium in which actors who are oriented toward a cooperative coordination of their different plans of action "mobilize the potential for rationality" inherent in ordinary language. This potential is only partially identified in the other models of action, since they each focus on only one validity claim and one world relation.[66] The communicative model, on the other hand, can fully illuminate the "rational internal structure" of the process of coming to an intersubjectively valid agreement. And it is only such an agreement that can, in turn, constitute the basis of a form of cooperation, the rational motivating force of which is reducible neither to its accordance with strategic calculations nor to its fit with a normative structure whose validity is socially prescribed.[67]

From what has been said so far, it should be evident that much of the philosophical weight associated with the concept of communicative action rests upon what is packed into the ideas of understanding and rationally motivated agreement. When considering the concept of understanding, it is useful to recall that Habermas's formal pragmatics aims at giving an account of what is required in order to understand the meaning of an utterance or speech act rather than a sentence. If sentential meaning is understood when one knows the truth conditions of a sentence, the meaning of "*an utterance* – that is, a sentence employed communicatively" – is understood only when certain other conditions are known which make that utterance acceptable to a hearer. "*We understand a speech act when we know what makes it acceptable.*" And from the standpoint of the speaker, such "conditions of acceptability are identical to the conditions for his illocutionary success."[68]

These conditions are specified by Habermas as follows: "A hearer understands the meaning of an utterance when, in addition to grammatical conditions of well-formedness and general contextual conditions, he knows those *essential conditions* under which he could be motivated by a speaker to take an affirmative position" on the claim raised by the speaker. These last conditions are broken down into two further categories: conditions of fulfillment, which refer to the sort of succeeding orientation or action a given speech act typically requires, and "conditions of . . . agreement" which refer to the conditions under which the claim raised in the speech act *ought* to be agreed to.[69]

If these conditions are satisfied, a hearer can be said to understand the utterance. But Habermas also sometimes uses the phrase "reaching an understanding" in a way which makes it synonomous with reaching an agreement, more specifically an agreement that the relevant claim is *in fact* warranted. This "maximal" level of understanding is necessary if communicative action is to continue, but not if someone simply wants to understand a speech act. Habermas has tried to clear up this ambiguity, but at least one critic still inappropriately accuses him of claiming that understanding in the weaker sense somehow ultimately produces understanding in the stronger sense.[70]

Before turning to what is meant by this stronger sense, I want to consider a significant problem which does in fact arise from his analysis of the weaker sense. Habermas actually makes another claim about what is implicit in simple understanding which I did not elucidate in the preceding discussion. It is this claim which causes the real problem. The difficulty revolves around his argument that the question of rationality arises unavoidably for social science, not just at the *metatheoretical* level (when one chooses a conception of action), but also at the *methodological* level when one gives an account of the logic of understanding a subject matter which is symbolically structured.[71] This claim is elaborated in the following way. It was shown above that, in order to understand an utterance, an interpreter would have to know the conditions under which he could be motivated to say "yes" to the claim raised by that utterance. But an interpreter cannot understand what would so motivate someone without "*bring[ing] to mind the reasons* with which a speaker would, if necessary and under suitable conditions, defend the validity of his claim." The interpreter is thus "*himself* drawn into the process of assessing validity claims. For reasons are of such a nature that they cannot be described in the attitude of a third person, that is, without reactions of affirmation or negation or abstention." An interpreter thus must assume, like an actor, a performative attitude and actually "take a position" on the validity of the claim raised in the utterance.[72] He does not have to evaluate it in any *one* way, but he does have to evaluate it as either sound or unsound, or perhaps as not yet decidable.

This has been called one of Habermas's "most basic and challenging theses."[73] Nevertheless, I think it is incorrect or at least overstated. Thomas McCarthy has explained the difficulty very precisely. It may be true, he argues, that our ability to understand any given reason depends on our communicative competence, because it provides us with the sense of what it means "to act on reasons in general." But

from the fact that we cannot understand reasons as reasons without relying on our own competence to judge validity, cogency, soundness and the like, it does not

41

follow that we have to actually or implicitly "take a position" on [particular] reasons in order to understand them. Interpreters raised in pluralistic cultures and schooled in cultural and historical differences are quite capable, it seems, of understanding symbolic expressions without taking a position on their validity – not, to be sure, as ideally neutral observers, not as interpreters without a language, and standards of their own to serve as a hermeneutic starting point, but as individuals whose primary and professional socialization have schooled them in appreciating differences of belief and practice, "bringing (other people's) reasons to mind" while suspending judgment on them.[74]

The upshot of this line of criticism is that, although Habermas's general approach to understanding utterances – its focus, that is, on conditions of acceptability – may be plausible, the specific assertion he makes about the necessity that a hearer/interpreter actually "take a position" in order to understand is not.

I want to turn back now to Habermas's "maximal" sense of understanding: the idea of a kind of rational agreement which must be achieved if a communicative coordination of action is to take place. The key question here is the exact source of the motivation to agree, remembering again that it cannot be reduced to either strategic complementarity of interests or to the coherence of a possible course of action with a conventional context. Or, to put it another way, what creates the "illocutionary binding (or bonding) effect" that will motivate the hearer to coordinate his subsequent actions with the speaker? The source of this effect, Habermas maintains, is ultimately "*the warranty*" [*Gewahr*] that the speaker offers: "namely, to redeem, if necessary, the validity claim raised with his speech act."[75] What gives this warranty its peculiar power is its "rational basis," its attachment to validity claims which are "cognitively testable."[76]

Knowledge of how one tests the different claims is, according to Habermas, something which is intuitively available to communicatively competent speakers. In other words, they have an intuitive sense of what the proper guidelines would be for testing claims and coming to a consensus on whether given claims are warranted or not. For the truthfulness or authenticity claim, the proper test is constituted by comparing a speaker's expressed intentions with his ensuing actions. For truth and normative legitimacy, however, the test requires a suspension of normal constraints of action and the initiation of a mode of communication Habermas calls "discourse": "theoretical discourse" for truth claims and "practical discourse" for legitimacy claims. In discourse, actors orient their communication to the sole purpose of coming to a "rational consensus" on whether or not a specific claim is supportable.[77] The intuitive knowledge of discourse thus functions as a non-conventional, but intersubjectively shared, "court of appeal," within which the speaker can attempt to make good his claim if it is challenged by the hearer.[78]

Here one sees what ultimately inspires Habermas's particular way of envisioning how reason binds actions together. The concept of communicative rationality, he tells us,

carries with it connotations based ultimately on the central experience of the unconstrained, unifying, consensus-bringing force of argumentative speech, in which different participants overcome their merely subjective views and, owing to the mutuality of rationally motivated conviction, assure themselves of both the unity of the objective world and the intersubjectivity of their lifeworld.[79]

Habermas has attempted to sketch the outlines of what would constitute well-formed argumentation for both the theoretical and practical spheres.[80] Since the concept of theoretical discourse has been subjected to some telling criticism and since the focus of this book is moral and political theory, I will lay this concept aside and direct my attention exclusively to practical discourse.[81] This topic will be taken up in detail in the next two chapters. For the moment, it is only important to get a sense of how the appeal to an intuitive, discursive knowledge fits into Habermas's overall project.

The intuitive sense of the foundations of a rational consensus constitutes, for Habermas, the ultimate source from which any norm derives its "ought-ness" or legitimacy for a particular group of actors. While conformity to a given norm may involve many factors (for example, habit or strategic considerations), the capacity of that norm to provide the kind of agreement and action coordination Habermas is talking about must derive from a conviction on the part of actors subject to that norm that it is legitimate. Now Habermas is of course aware that, historically, societies have put forward quite different ideas about the ultimate sources of legitimacy for basic norms. He claims, however, that such variation can be explained either as having an ideological basis or as indicating differences in the level of social evolution. In other words, Habermas wants to interpret much of this variation as the result of different types of constraints on the capacity of given historical agents to put their intuitive knowledge to a thorough-going use in assessing the legitimacy of norms to which they are subject. To anticipate my later discussion somewhat, one can now begin to see the way in which Habermas takes modernity to be a process of rationalization in something more than a purely purposive–rational, Weberian sense. In particular, the processes of modernity have expanded the degree to which individuals can test the norms they conform to by criteria they learn as they become communicatively competent. In this sense modernity has helped to make more available that "potential for reason encapsulated" in the linguistic reproduction of social life.

IV.   Communicative action and strategic action

The aspect of the communicative model which has been stressed so far is its ability to account for a particular kind of action coordination which Habermas claims is central to social life. The strategic model, on the other hand, seems incapable of giving an account of such coordination or cooperation. The ability to draw a sharp distinction between these two models would thus appear to be crucial to Habermas's project. And yet it has been persistently argued that he is not able to establish this distinction in a satisfactory way. In this section, I want to take up two variants of this criticism.

A.   The distinction between strategic and communicative action was preceded in Habermas's early work by a similar distinction between "labor" and "interaction." The latter was intended to denote two basic categories of human self-formation which Hegel first differentiated in his Jena writings. Hegel later abandoned this distinction, and the unfortunate effects of his decision ultimately surfaced in Marx's thought in the form of a tendency to reduce human self-formation or *praxis* to labor. More specifically, Marx's thought is beset by a tension between this reductionist tendency and contrary indications that he meant *praxis* to be a broader concept. This tension was seen by Habermas as a key source of latent positivism in Marx's thought. It made it easy for later marxists to claim that practical, historical questions of action could be reduced to strategic ones.[82]

In this early categorial scheme, "labor" was closely associated with monologically working on nature, and "interaction" with the dialogical process of interpretation and decision-making between actors. And in discussions of Marx, this distinction sometimes seemed to coincide closely with the distinction between "forces of production" and "relations of production." This line of thinking led Habermas into several sorts of difficulties. The most important for present purposes is that in proposing a division of action into the two real types (as opposed to analytical or ideal constructions) he suggested, his scheme led to a rather implausible way of thinking about actual processes of production. For "all concrete processes of labor . . . are social," that is, they involve interaction and cannot be comprehended on a model which construes them monologically.[83]

Another disturbing problem which seemed to arise from Habermas's original reading of interaction was that it appeared to "reduce interaction to communication and norms." The effect of this was a significant blindness to the role of power in interaction. Power, in Habermas's model, seemed to enter only as ideology or "distorted communication."[84]

These difficulties, which adhered to the distinction between labor and interaction, are, I think, substantially alleviated when that distinction is recast in the form of communicative/strategic action in *The Theory of Communicative Action*. The latter distinction does not get any of its sense from other distinctions like forces and relations of production. Rather it is defended as separating two real or "genuine types" of action, with "genuine" here meaning that any actor can, at least upon reflection, recognize, "however vaguely and intuitively," which sort of action orientation he/she is pursuing in a particular situation. One recognizes, in other words, whether one is adopting "a success-oriented attitude or one oriented to reaching [or sustaining] understanding" (in the sense of agreement).[85]

Of course, here again Habermas is laying a heavy burden on intuition. But this would actually seem to be the most initially plausible of his appeals to intuition, for it is one which has been reflected in a broad range of moral and political thinkers. It is simply a way of reading the difference between treating another person as something like an object versus treating him/her as something like an end in itself, worthy of some sort of respect.

The new distinction also opens conceptual space for the role of power in coordinating interaction, since now one can distinguish between understanding-oriented interaction and "linguistically mediated strategic action." In the latter case, it is such things as the employment of sanctions which coordinate interaction, not the attainment of a consensual agreement.[86]

This distinction between the coordination provided by understanding-oriented speech versus that provided by "consequence-oriented speech" is useful and Habermas gives it a clearer character by associating it with Austin's distinction between illocutionary effects and "perlocutionary" effects. The latter notion was used by Austin to distinguish what is done in what is said (illocution) from what effects in the world are caused by what is done in what is said (perlocution).[87]

This plausible distinction is, however, pressed into service in order to make a further, less plausible argument, namely, that one can not only distinguish the two kinds of speech usage, but also show understanding-oriented speech usage to be the "original mode" [*Originalmodus*] and consequence-oriented speech to be somehow "parasitical."[88] Habermas does in fact succeed in showing a derivative status for some kinds of consequence-oriented speech usage, but is forced to admit that others, such as imperatives, do not fit the model. And if this is the case, the distinction between "original" and "parasitical" does not carry the necessary weight.[89] But I really do not see why this distinction is so crucial. Habermas should just admit that both forms of interaction coordination are necessary to social life, and simply argue that in the final analysis a social theory in which the central theoretical emphasis is given to communicative coordination will be more adequate.

B.   If Habermas's shift from work and interaction to communicative and strategic action makes his project less susceptible to some of the foregoing criticism, other issues can still be raised relating to the same underlying problem of adequately separating an orientation to consensus from an instrumental orientation. What disturbs one usually sympathetic critic is that apparently the more you scratch the concept of communicative action, the more it begins to resemble strategic action. The link between the two, according to Fred Dallmayr, arises from the fact that both are ultimately teleological or goal-oriented.[90] In communicative action, there is simply a different goal from that in strategic action.

Habermas does in fact argue that the "teleological structure is fundamental to *all* types of action."[91] So far, I have stressed the understanding-oriented character of communicative action. Dallmayr, however, wishes to draw attention to the fact that such an orientation is taken up by actors who are concerned "to pursue their individual goals."[92] From Dallmayr's point of view this implies that Habermas is still too tied to a subject-centered philosophical orientation. For language is thoroughly instrumentalized for making individual claims and pursuing individual goals.[93] This criticism reflects Gadamerian and Heideggerian insights which stress that we must understand the "passive" quality of action and the non-instrumental quality of language.[94]

It is perhaps easiest to see what is at issue here if one looks briefly at the alternative scheme of "communicative modes" Dallmayr offers. He distinguishes "conversation," "everyday talk" or "chatter," "discourse" and "poetry." The notion of "conversation" is seen as the "broadest or most ample type of communication – a general background category." In conversation the emphasis is on attempting to achieve mutual understanding on "matters of joint concern," and this commonality of endeavor leads to a "relative 'I-lessness' of communication." Moreover, conversation is characterized by an openness to the other and "strangeness."[95] Conversation, in sum, embodies precisely the qualities of passivity and non-instrumentalization.

Certainly this is an admirable way of thinking of what something like "genuine" communication can be about, but one wonders whether this can very usefully be interpreted as the "broadest" or "background" mode of communication, at least from the point of view of social theory.[96] Dallmayr's account is constructed with a deep practical concern in mind, and it is a concern Habermas shares. But Dallmayr's account is, I think, *too immediately* under the influence of this concern (as is the poststructuralist position examined in Section II). This is evident in his viewing conversation as the central mode of linguistic interaction. For conversation, although it is distinguished from "poetry," is defined by Dallmayr in a distinctively poetic way. The stress is laid on openness to what is strange or unfamiliar, and on the "potential for renewal," although poetry in its pure sense is seen as offering the most "distilled challenge or antidote" to communicative ossification and closure " – an antidote particularly significant in an age governed by science and practical needs . . ."[97]

As I said, this practical concern about the contemporary world is also central to Habermas's work. But that is not the point. The point is whether it makes good sense to give the broadest theoretical category of linguistic interaction such a poetic cast, rather than thinking of something like Dallmayr's genuine communication as a practical ideal for which we need to make more space in our everyday life.

If Dallmayr's claims can be rebutted in this way, then perhaps Habermas's concept of communicative action does not look quite so deficient. Perhaps, from the point of view of social theory, the teleological quality of action should not be as thoroughly submerged as it is in Dallmayr's account.[98] Moreover, it should be emphasized again that language is not simply an *instrument* in Habermas's account but also a pre-existing *context* in which commonality emerges in specific situations only in relation to a broader common orientation to the shared validity basis of speech.

This emphasis on context leads directly to the question of the lifeworld. Habermas would argue that one of the crucial advantages of his analysis of communicative action is that it can be integrated with the concept of lifeworld in such a way that it provides a far more adequate approach to gaining insight into the problem of modernity and rationalization than analyses based on the concept of strategic action.[99] I will return to this question in chapter 5.

3

Justice and the foundations of communicative ethics

A "communicative" or "discursive" ethics is a formalistic ethics "that consistently works out the independent logic [*Eigensinn*] of normative questions:" that is, "that works out the idea of justice." Such an ethics sharply distinguishes

> *moral questions* which, under the aspect of universalization or *justice*, can in principle be decided rationally, from *evaluative questions* . . . which present themselves under their most general aspect as questions of the *good life*, and which are accessible to a rational discussion only within the horizon of a historically concrete life form or individual life history.[1]

The conceptual framework which gives communicative ethics its particular character is, as I have indicated, constituted by the ideas of communicative action and the rationalization of the normative claims raised therein.

Communicative ethics stands or falls, Habermas argues, with two propositions. First, "normative validity claims have a cognitive sense" [*Sinn*] and can therefore be "treated *like* truth claims." Second, the validation of a claim that a norm is just requires "a real discourse and is not possible in the form of a monological argumentation carried through in a hypothetical manner."[2] In this chapter I will analyze the first of these two propositions (Sections I, II and III), as well as Habermas's claim that the insights of the Piaget–Kohlberg tradition of cognitive developmental psychology lend support to the idea of a communicative ethics (IV). The second proposition will be examined in chapter 4.

I.   The principle of universalization

The sort of cognitivist position which Habermas wants to defend is one which follows the Kantian tradition in arguing, first, that valid norms are ones which have the quality of fairness or impartiality; secondly, that this quality can be expressed by some version of the principle of universalization; and finally, that this principle itself can be rationally justified.[3] This last argument is, of course, what the non-cognitivist would contest, on the grounds that an individual choice to abide by any such fundamental moral principle has the logical status of a decision.[4] Reason, on this view, may be used only to justify particular judgements or actions chosen *after* this initial decision.

In recent years, numerous interpretations of the principle of universalization have been offered, some of which have been accompanied by cognitivist arguments and some of which have not.[5] Habermas finds none of these cognitivist arguments or interpretations of universalization to be completely adequate. The interpretation he offers is as follows: a norm is justified only when

the consequences and side-effects for the satisfaction of the interests of *every* individual, which are expected to result from a *general* conformance to [that] norm, can be accepted *without compulsion* by all.[6]

Before turning to Habermas's argument that this principle can be rationally justified in a way which refutes the non-cognitivist, it is necessary to offer some initial explanation as to what exactly is implied by this particular interpretation of universalization and why he considers it an adequate way of accounting for our intuitions about fairness or impartiality.

The simplest way to draw out what is distinctive about Habermas's universalization principle is to contrast it with Kant's.[7] For Kant, the categorical imperative constitutes a test which each individual can monologically carry out; that is, each asks himself if he can will a proposed norm to be a universal law. For Habermas, on the other hand, the test is whether or not a proposed norm is acceptable in an actual argumentation to all who are potentially affected by that norm, and "acceptable" is taken to mean that the norm satisfies the interests of each participant in the argument. Justifiable norms, then, are ones which incorporate "generalizable interests."[8]

Clearly, the notion that interests, and the needs on which they are based, ought to be taken into account in a formulation of universalizability runs contrary to Kant. Like Rawls, Habermas finds the Kantian formulation unacceptable partly because it cannot account for why anyone would be motivated to follow just norms and partly because he wishes to argue that there are criteria in accordance with which some interests and needs can be rationalized in a non-strategic sense and others cannot.[9] Habermas differs from Rawls, however, on the questions of exactly how interests can be rationalized and how this rationalization connects up with determinate principles of justice. I will examine this issue more closely in the next chapter. For the moment, it suffices to refer to critiques of Rawls which have focused on the fact that his framework for structuring the choice of the two principles of justice not only incorporates a theory of primary goods which is of questionable impartiality, but it also does not really represent a collective process of choice, as he implies; rather it represents a single agent's thought experiment. For Habermas, these sorts of problems will inevitably accompany *any* attempt to derive *determinate, universal* norms of justice. The most that can be expected from a "philosophical ethics" is a clarification of *what justice is*, in the sense of universally valid procedural criteria appropriate to judging the justness of proposed norms; it cannot go further and tell us with the same certainty *what justice demands*, in the sense of picking out determinate norms for guiding action.[10] What justice demands in given social and historical settings cannot be legitimately decided in advance of an *actual* argumentation or discourse among all concerned.[11]

For the moment, I want to take as given both Habermas's understanding of the limits of a "philosophical ethics" and his view that the function of just norms is to provide some legitimate ordering of the satisfaction of interests.[12] These views are what give Habermas's interpretation of universalizability its particular cast. If this interpretation can be tentatively accepted as plausible, then I can return to the prior question of whether this or any other variant of universalizability can be put forward in a way which answers the non-cognitivist skeptic.

The strategy Habermas chooses is a "transcendental–pragmatic" demonstration that every communicatively competent actor who takes up a normative argumentation already presupposes the validity of the principle of universalization. Such an actor cannot reject this principle without falling into a "performative contradiction."[13] This transcendental–pragmatic argument is laid out in two stages.

II. The "speech-act-immanent obligation"

In ongoing communicative action, subjects coordinate their behavior on the basis of a mutual recognition of validity claims. This reciprocal recognition does not necessarily rest on the actual testing of a specific claim, but rather on the basis of a supposition by the hearer of the speaker's accountability. This reciprocal supposition of accountability involves two expectations: that the other's actions are intentional and that he could, if called upon, justify the claims he raises in interaction.[14]

What is important about this necessary reciprocal supposition is that it allows Habermas to commence an argument about the "normative force" inherent in communicative action.[15] The kind of argument Habermas has in mind here is somewhat similar to Alan Gewirth's attempt to derive a basic

principle of morality by analyzing the "structure of action" and the normative constraints it necessarily requires an actor himself to acknowledge.[16]
Habermas asserts that an actor who refuses to acknowledge such constraints
is guilty of a "performative contradiction." A contradiction occurs because
the speech act in which he announces his refusal "rests on non-contingent
(thus in given contexts unavoidable) presuppositions whose propositional
content contradicts the propositional content of the speech act itself."[17]
Although Gewirth and Habermas share this mode of argument, their
positions are sharply divergent because the former thinks only in terms of a
teleological model of action and its associated conception of strategic
reason. As I have argued elsewhere, Gewirth's efforts fail and probably do
so unavoidably, given this conception of action and rationality.[18] Habermas's
conception of communicative action, on the other hand, implies a structure
of *intersubjectivity* from which one can derive a mutual "speech-act-
immanent *obligation to provide justification*" for the different sorts of claims
which are continually raised in understanding-oriented action. This obligation is one which every actor has "implicitly recognized," simply by virtue
of having engaged in communicative action.[19]

Two questions arise immediately about such claim. First, is this normative
obligation really a necessary one, in the sense of being unavoidably implied
by the communicative structure of action? And secondly, what exactly are
the normative implications of the obligation "to provide justification?"

As for the necessity of the obligation, what Habermas wants to argue is
that every agent has "grown up and reproduced" himself as a person within
contexts of communicative action where subjects interacted on the basis of a
common orientation to validity claims and a reciprocal supposition of
accountability. These orientations are a necessary part of "the *Sittlichkeit* of
human relations," and their normative implications cannot be denied in the
same way that one might deny a particular principle of morality.[20] An agent
who is part of ongoing contexts of communicative action commits a performative contradiction if he denies that he is accountable for the normative
claims his actions raise.

Against this sort of argument, the standard response of the non-
cognitivist would be that Habermas is simply committing one variant of the
naturalistic fallacy.[21] If there is any obligation flowing from engaging in communicative action, then it is an obligation which one *chooses* to take on; one
could just as easily choose to avoid communicative action altogether in the
future and orient oneself exclusively toward strategic action, thereby avoiding any normative obligation. This choice to renounce systematically *all*

communicative action could be defended by the skeptic and opted for by actors whose behavior falls into categories such as the first-person dictator or systematic free rider.

Now Habermas would admit that a choice to avoid systematically any future communicative action and its implicit obligation does not necessarily imply inconsistent behavior in any purely logical sense. If this is so, however, what kind of argument is Habermas making about the necessity of the "speech-act immanent obligation?" At this point, we are back to the problem of intersubjective–contextual orientation discussed in chapter 1 and the idea that it simply makes good sense to call into question the rationality of an individual who exhibits no such motivation. Now the proper way to interpret Habermas's arguments about the necessary implications of communicative action is, I think, to see them as helping to explicate (from the perspective of a new theory of action) that sense of rationality one feels is lost when the concept is reduced to strategic calculations of purely self-interested subjects. Habermas's notion of communicative action and its implicit obligation constitutes an account of why and how an agent's rationality is assessable not only from a subjective but also an intersubjective perspective.

Questioning the rationality of a radical strategic actor on such an intersubjective basis does not, as I have indicated, amount to a direct defeat of the argument that this actor's decision has, in a strict sense, the logical status of a decision. It does, however, provide a way of understanding a categorical difference between, on the one hand, a decision to reject all future communicative action and, on the other hand, a decision to, say, choose one political party or moral system over another. The former decision (like that of Berlin's pin-pusher) cuts against the concept of rationality without, however, violating any principle of logic.

The difference might best be described as one between those decisions which cut against a certain conceptual necessity (but not logical necessity) and those which do not.[22] Decisions of the latter type are perfectly understandable in terms of our concepts of rationality, agency and social life. Decisions of the former type, on the other hand, take us toward the limits of these concepts, such that we do not clearly comprehend what the structure of human life would be after these choices.[23] It is instructive here to compare Habermas with Hobbes and H.L.A. Hart.[24] Both Hobbes and Hart in similar ways find that certain basic facts about human beings– their desire to survive and their rough physical and mental equality – have a decisive effect on what counts as legitimate in normative relationships. Were these facts no longer to hold true, says Hart, then "whole ways of thinking and talking which constitute our present conceptual apparatus, through which we see the world and each other, would lapse."[25] Habermas wants to rely on this kind of conceptual argument but, unlike Hobbes or Hart, he is drawing attention to the basic fact that humans reproduce their social and cultural life through the medium of speech in which validity claims are necessarily raised and in which subjects make the reciprocal supposition of accountability. Such a conceptual claim is what Habermas intends when referring to his argument as "transcendental." A transcendental argument in this weak sense relies on what is implicit in a competence for speech and action which is "so general that [it] cannot be replaced by functional equivalents."[26]

The second question raised above relates to the problem of what normative implications are entailed by an obligation "to provide justification." Clearly justification is going to have to be interpreted in a fairly inclusive sense, if it is supposed to be implicit in communicative action in widely varying social and historical settings. But if this is true, how can Habermas use such an inclusive notion of justification for the purposes of deriving his specific version of the principle of universalization? Actually, he does not claim to be able to do this directly. Something else must be added to the argument in order for the derivation to work, as I will show in a moment. At this point, however, it is important to inquire about whether there is any normative orientation at all to be derived simply from the reciprocal suppositions of communicative action.

Habermas certainly thinks there is and, although he does not use the term "universalization" to cover this minimal normative content, it does appear that the speech-act-immanent obligation requires conformity with a minimal or "first stage" demand for universalization: the requirement that an agent must be "ready to apply [a norm he proposes] equally to himself and to others, and to go on applying [it] in interpersonal situations when the roles are reversed."[27] This requirement means that our normative judgements must be general in the sense of not allowing the kinds of special exceptions made by first-person dictators or systematic free riders.

For the moral skeptic, such a requirement could obligate an agent only if he were to choose to allow morality to have some relevance for his life; or, as it is sometimes put, if he were to choose to speak "within . . . the institution" of morality.[28] For Habermas, however, this choice is not open to a rational agent, because an obligation to normative argumentation or justification is already "rooted" in communicative action itself.[29] Hence first-person dictators or systematic free riders must either reveal the irrationality of their position when they try to justify it, or they must systematically avoid any understanding-oriented action. However, the latter option provides no satisfactory escape: it throws their claim to rationality even more radically into doubt, since it eliminates one of the two minimal motivational assumptions which are an inherent part of the concept of rationality as it applies to human action.

Thus, one significant normative implication of the obligation to provide justification is that it allows one to resolve the problem posed in the first chapter, which arises from within a purely strategic conception of reason, that is, our feeling that somehow it is *not* rational for an agent invariably to ride freely on collective arrangements (whenever he can get away with it), which even he himself would endorse as legitimate.

The resolution of this problem of the systematic free rider is certainly a significant step for a conception of rationality. It does not, however, take one very far in regard to distinguishing different conceptions of justice, as more or less adequate. A further step in this direction comes with Habermas's claim that the speech-act-immanent obligation is incompatible with all "traditional ethics;" that is, with any ethical system which keeps "a dogmatized core of basic convictions" away from the demand for justification.[30] This is a rather sweeping claim which Habermas does little to explain. It would, for example, render illegitimate any notion of natural law, on the grounds that it is ultimately tied to certain basic Christian articles of faith.[31]

Perhaps the point Habermas wants to make here is that, although the obligation to provide justification may be compatible with such an ethical system when basic convictions are unquestioned, the compatibility dissolves when some adherents, for whatever reason, begin to change their beliefs. At that point their demand for justification is radicalized and it cannot be adequately responded to simply by continued reference to the previously shared set of convictions and the world view from which they draw their power to convince.

Such an extension of the obligation to provide justification seems questionable. Although a refusal by the first-person dictator or free rider to justify himself required a systematic renunciation of communicative action which threw his rationality radically into question, there is no such consequence entailed when an adherent to some type of "traditional ethics" refuses to open his basic convictions up to fundamental criticism. His refusal takes him in no way toward the limits of our concepts of rationality, agency and social life. In short, his behavior clearly exhibits that element of social motivation which the free rider lacked, for his normative claims have a demonstrable coherence with an intersubjectively shared context of norms and beliefs. His decision to break off communicative action with those who radically question the validity of those norms and beliefs in no way throws his rationality into doubt.

To sum up the preceding discussion, one can say that Habermas's reconstruction of the know-how of communicative competence reveals a supposition of reciprocal accountability by anyone engaged in communicative action. Furthermore, this supposition can be interpreted as a speech-act-immanent obligation to provide justification for those claims that are raised, whenever they are questioned. And insofar as communicative action itself cannot be systematically avoided by an agent, without throwing his rationality radically into doubt, this obligation would appear to be one which is universally binding on all rational agents. But, as I have also shown, such an obligation (which can be formally stated as a minimal demand for universalization) does not have a very deep normative bite, in the sense of sorting out types of ethical positions as more or less rationally justifiable.

In order to deepen the normative bite of communicative ethics enough to be able to provide justification for his interpretation of universalization in its full sense, Habermas must turn to a second stage of transcendental–pragmatic argument. More specifically, he must turn to what he calls "discursive rules," which are not necessary presuppositions of *all* communicative action, but rather of the *modern* concept of *argumentation.*[32] For agents who share the horizons of a modern lifeworld, Habermas wants to argue that communicative competence presupposes further requirements on anyone who is called upon to justify their normative claims. This level of Habermas's argument about communicative competence introduces, as I will show, some difficulties for his position. But first, I must lay out how this link in his case for communicative ethics is constructed.

III.   The presuppositions of argumentation

The intuitive knowledge of "competent members of modern societies" as to what constitutes a valid argument can be reconstructed, according to Habermas, in the form of an explicative representation of the propositional contents of the "unavoidable [pragmatic] presuppositions" of argumentation.[33] These contents can be laid out as "rules of discourse" or argumentation which collectively describe our intuition about what it means to be in a speech situation in which a conflict would be resolved solely by the "force of better argument." In this regard, Habermas speaks of an "ideal speech situation" in which a "rationally motivated agreement" or "consensus" could be attained.[34] The discourse rules must ensure that all other motives of the participants in argumentation must give way when they clash with the motive of cooperatively reaching a consensus.[35]

Habermas actually distinguishes different sorts of presuppositions of argumentation which, when formulated as rules, put various logical and normative constraints on participants.[36] For present purposes, though, the rules of discourse are the most important since they express what he takes to be the normative core of the modern idea of argumentation: the notion of reciprocal recognition by each participant of the other as an autonomous source of both claims which have equal initial plausibility and demands for justification which must be addressed. The rules, which are constitutive of an ideal speech situation, are as follows:

1 "Each subject who is capable of speech and action is allowed to participate in discourses."
2 a) "Each is allowed to call into question any proposal."
    b) "Each is allowed to introduce any proposal into the discourse."
    c) "Each is allowed to express his attitudes, wishes, and needs."
3 "No speaker ought to be hindered by compulsion – whether arising from inside the discourse or outside of it – from making use of the rights secure under [1 and 2]."[37]

The first two discourse rules are fairly straightforward criteria for fair argumentation. The third rule, though, implies further rules for eliminating the effects of deception, power and ideology. The most important of these rules pertain to the *action* context from which argumentation might be taken up. They are intended to prevent barriers (created by deception, power and ideology) both to the initiation of discourse and to its being carried through in a way which allows no subject matter to remain immune from questioning.[38] What Habermas is arguing for here is the idea that the fulfillment of the conditions of ideal argumentation implies that the action context must have congruent normative qualities, that is, qualities which do not undermine the autonomy of each as a source of claims which have equal initial plausibility and of demands for justification to which others are obliged to respond.

Habermas proposes two rules defining "pure communicative action." The first prevents actors from taking up a discourse with hidden intentions or motives, or in a way in which the true attitudes, feelings and needs of some would be unlikely to find expression. It requires both a reciprocal openness of actors about their true intentions and motives and an equal chance to express their attitudes, feelings and needs. With the latter part of this requirement, Habermas wants to ensure especially that "traditional interpretations of needs" can be thrown into question.[39] The second rule defining pure communicative action ensures that any theoretical or practical validity claim can be effectively called into question; in other words, there will be free access to the test of argumentation. This rule requires that there be an equal distribution of opportunities "to order and resist orders, to permit and forbid, to make and extract promises, and to be responsible for one's conduct and demand that others are as well."[40]

If one can accept as plausible the foregoing reconstruction of the normative core of the modern idea of argumentation, then Habermas can proceed to the second stage of his transcendental-pragmatic derivation of a strong universalization principle. He asserts that:

A. Whoever engages in argumentation must presuppose the validity of the discourse rules; and
B. that when that argumentation concerns normative claims – that is, ones about alternative orderings for the satisfaction of interests – the participants must, "on pain of performative contradiction," admit that universalization is the only rule under which norms will be taken by each to be legitimate.[41]

I will examine Habermas's interpretation of universalization as requiring "generaliz*ability* of interests" in greater detail in the next chapter.[42] For the moment, I am only concerned with the success of his effort to establish his case for cognitivism. In this regard, the basic question is: is the second stage of the transcendental–pragmatic argument as successful as the first in refuting the skeptic? In other words, does Habermas's strong interpretation of universalization have the same rationally necessary character as the minimal one implicit in the supposition of reciprocal accountability? This appears doubtful because, in the face of the second stage of the transcendental–pragmatic argument, the skeptic could avoid a performative contradiction simply by refusing to engage in normative argumentation in its specifically modern, "post-conventional" form. He has an escape route in the form of a choice of taking up an argumentation in its less reflective, conventionally bound sense – which, as we have seen, satisfies the supposition of accountability.[43] Thus argumentation in its modern sense has a "functional equivalent." And if this is so, then the universal validity of a post-conventional normative argumentation with a correspondingly stringent interpretation of universalization, such as Habermas proposes, cannot be unequivocally established on the basis of a transcendental–pragmatic argument. Any further support for such a claim must be sought in developmental-logical arguments worked out in a psychological theory of the Piaget–Kohlberg variety or in a theory of the rational superiority of modern structures of consciousness. It is in the context of such theories that Habermas makes his case that the post-conventional mode of justifying normative claims is somehow the realization of a rational potential which is always present in all communicative action but only realized in the modern world. Without such added support, Habermas's reconstruction of normative argumentation is at best a plausible hypothesis about the deepest normative context, in relation to which normative claims can be adjudicated among those who share a modern life-world.

Having pointed out the limits of a transcendental–pragmatic argument, one needs to emphasize, on the other hand, what it has achieved. This can be succinctly stated: the escape route alluded to above, which remains open for avoiding an acknowledgement of the presuppositions of postconventional argumentation, is not an avenue a skeptic can take *without abandoning his skepticism,* at least to the extent of having to renounce the rationality of first-person dictators and systematic free riders. In other words, even if Habermas has not shown decisively that his own interpretation of universalization must be accepted by all rational agents, he has shown that such agents must reject at least some value orientations.

IV. Moral development and interactive competence

In this section, I want to examine Habermas's attempt to bolster the case for the universality of a discursive ethics by drawing upon the insights of cognitive developmental psychology. As Habermas himself acknowledges, this attempt is, by its very nature, limited in the sort of confirmation it can provide for a discursive ethics. For my purposes, Habermas's foray into this area is actually important, not so much for the limited support it provides for the universality claim of a discursive ethics, but rather for what it reveals about the role of reciprocity in interaction and moral judgement. Understanding this role is crucial to comprehending the second of the two basic claims of discursive ethics enumerated at the beginning of this chapter: that the appropriate test of normative legitimacy is "a real discourse."

The general attraction for Habermas of the Piaget–Kohlberg tradition in psychology results from a shared interest in the investigation of the structure and acquisition of human competences.[44] Habermas considers Piaget's work on cognition, Kohlberg's on moral judgement, Chomsky's on language, and his own on universal pragmatics as all contributing to the broad goal of understanding universal competences in the interrelated dimensions of cognition, language and interaction. Kohlberg's work on the development of moral judgement is of particular importance because Habermas sees it as a potential source of corroborating evidence for his discursive conception of ethics. Of central interest are Kohlberg's assertions that there are *universal forms* beneath the surface of substantively different moral judgements; and that these forms can be ordered as a set of *stages* in the development of the individual's capacity for moral judgement. The most advanced stage requires judgements to conform to postconventional, procedural criteria similar to those elucidated in Habermas's reconstruction of practical discourse.[45]

Before turning to Habermas's attempt to use some of Kohlberg's insights, it will be useful to summarize briefly what the latter claims to have established in his research. For Kohlberg, the capacity of the individual for moral judgement passes through stages, each of which entails a new, more adequate set of cognitive operations than the preceding one. Such stages or structures of thought are not simple responses on the stimulus–response model of learning, but are both adaptations and active constructions of the subject. And these stages, it is claimed, are both culturally universal and sequentially invariant, although progress through the stages varies across, as well as within, societies.[46] The six-stage, three-level model in the appendix is the result of Kohlberg's findings over two decades of research.[47]

From a psychological perspective, the child moves from one stage to the next and sees the higher stage as more adequate, because it puts him in greater equilibrium with his environment. The psychological criteria of adequacy can be explained as the increased "integration" and "differentiation" of moral consciousness at each higher stage.[48] "Differentiation" refers to the degree to which the structure of thought at a given stage allows one to separate out specifically moral judgements from other value judgements of practical reason. For example, at stage 1, the child does not differentiate between doing X because of fear of punishment and doing it because it is "fair" or "right." "Integration," on the other hand, refers to the degree to which the individual can integrate conflicting claims in such a way as to resolve conflicts. The structure of thinking at higher stages allows the individual a proportionately increased capacity to assume imaginatively the role of others involved in the conflict. The more roles or points of view a structure of thought can accommodate, the more moral judgements derived from it will bring the individual into equilibrium. As Kohlberg says, "a moral situation in disequilibrium is one in which there are unresolved conflicting claims."[49]

Kohlberg contends that his work supports the claims of philosophers in the "formalistic tradition . . . from Kant to Rawls."[50] Specifically, he argues that his *psychological* explanation of why a child moves from one stage to the next "maps into" a *philosophical* explanation as to why a higher stage is more adequate in the sense of a more rational moral scheme.[51] "Differentiation" can thus be seen as a process of sorting out the categorical "ought" of moral autonomy from the other "oughts" of practical reason. "Integration" becomes an interpretation of the idea that moral judgements must be universalizable in the sense of taking account of the claims of all others.[52] Specifically, Kohlberg finds that his (highest) stage 6 is well illustrated by Rawls's theory, in which the choice of just principles takes place behind a "veil of ignorance" which requires the agent to take hypothetically the role of all others before making his decision.

In the following chapter it will become clear why Habermas thinks that Kohlberg is mistaken in considering Rawls's theory to be an illustration of the most adequate, postconventional structure of moral judgement. For the present, though, I want to examine why Habermas thinks he can enhance the plausibility of Kohlberg's theory by providing a stronger argument for the claim that the different conceptions of moral judgement demarcated by that theory actually constitute *stages*. Kohlberg's analysis has not made sufficiently clear the necessary developmental–logical connection between these conceptions. His efforts to demonstrate such a connection have taken the form of an argument that each conception corresponds to the maturing individual's mastery of increasingly differentiated "social perspectives." Thus, at the lowest moral stage, the individual has a purely "egocentric point of view" and relates to the world purely in terms of its potential for gratification or punishment. At higher stages, the perspectives of others are increasingly taken into account in different and more complex ways.[53]

Habermas finds Kohlberg's attempt to establish the developmental–logical character of his model to be deficient. Specifically, the social perspectives, which constitute the social–cognitive building blocks for moral judgements, are not sharply enough separated analytically from the types of moral judgements Kohlberg differentiates. Better analytical clarity can be achieved, Habermas argues, only if the notion of social perspectives is reconceptualized from a distinct theoretical viewpoint. The theory of communicative action offers just such a viewpoint.[54] This theory focuses, as shown earlier, on situations where the actor's faculties are called upon to repair or establish a level of understanding, which can then form the basis of cooperative interaction. From this perspective, an interaction situation is

equally a speech situation, in which the actors alternatively take up the *communication roles* of speakers, hearers, and listeners. Corresponding to these roles are the *participants' perspectives* of the first and second person, as well as the *observer's perspective* of the third person, out of which the "I–You" relation can be observed and made conscious as an intersubjective bond.[55]

The capacity for communicative action not only assumes that an actor has mastery of this system of "speaker perspectives," but also mastery of the three "world relations" (natural, social and subjective), with their corresponding validity claims. This latter sort of mastery Habermas refers to as mastery of "world perspectives."[56] A mature actor thus has at his disposal a complex structure of *both* speaker and world perspectives. And it is this structure – Habermas calls it fully "decentered understanding of the world, [*Weltverständnis*]" – which is the key for achieving a developmental–logical justification of Kohlberg's moral stages.[57]

Habermas wants to use the insights of his theory of communicative action to construct a scheme for a developmental–logical ordering of *types of interaction.* These stages of interaction fit into the general framework of preconventional, conventional, and postconventional levels. Now these stages are differentiated along several dimensions, such as the ways in which behavioral expectations are structured, and how concepts like reciprocity, authority and motivation are construed. What specifically grounds the *developmental–logical* differentiation of stages, however, is the way in which they progressively manifest the complex structure of perspectives just mentioned.[58] Partial mastery of these perspectives allows the child to participate only in simpler types of interaction (e.g., interactions directed by external sanctions). As mastery increases, the maturing individual attains the social–cognitive qualifications "for taking part in increasingly complex systems of actions" (e.g., role behavior, argumentation). Full mastery indicates what Habermas calls "interactive competence." (See the discussion in chapter 2 for how this competence is related to communicative competence.)[59]

I will not attempt to examine the proposed stages of interaction in any detail, because Habermas still seems to be in the process of working out a satisfactory formulation of them.[60] On the other hand, the general direction he wishes to take in regard to making the connection between interactive competence and moral stages seems clear. As I have already mentioned, one of the dimensions along which types of interaction are developmentally differentiated is the structure of behavioral expectations. At the preconventional level, only expectations about *particular actions* and their consequences are part of the symbolic world; at the conventional level, *roles* and *social norms* which integrate systems of roles are incorporated; and finally, at the post conventional level, *principles* for choosing between role and other normative expectations are incorporated. These three levels, Habermas says, "are distinguished by degrees of reflexivity: the simple behavioral expectations of the first level become reflexive at the next level – expectations can be . . . expected [roles and norms]; and the reflexive behavioral expectation of the second level becomes reflexive at the third level – norms can be normed [principles]."[61]

As I have also already mentioned, interactions are further differentiated by Habermas in relation to the concept of reciprocity; that is, in relation to the completeness or incompleteness of reciprocity that exists in a type of interaction. When the two dimensions – structures of behavioral expectations and reciprocity – are integrated, one can see *how the forms in which reciprocity appears in interaction structure the different conceptions of rightness* which inform Kohlberg's stages of moral judgements.[62] This relationship works out as follows. At the preconventional level, stage 1 (Kohlberg's punishment–obedience orientation), there exists only incomplete reciprocity between actors in regard to particular actions, based typically on fear of punishment or desire for gratification on the part of the child. At level I, stage 2 (instrumental hedonism), there is complete reciprocity in regard to particular actions, based on exchange of equivalents. This reciprocity, although "complete," is inadequate as a basis for ongoing social life, since it relates only to equivalence between concrete actions and objects. (Kohlberg himself provides a good example of this kind of inadequacy: his young son thought that if Eskimos killed and ate seals, it was right to kill and eat Eskimos.) Only at the conventional level, where norms and roles become part of the child's symbolic universe, does reciprocity begin to refer to the expectations of subjects. Reciprocity in this sense is, however, only incompletely realized at this level. At stage 3 ("good boy" orientation), incomplete reciprocity is exhibited in the relation of the child to the parents; typically the child acts according to what, say, the father expects of a "good boy." At stage 4 (law and order orientation), a similarly incomplete reciprocity is exhibited in relation to sets of norms, which require an actor to act without question as another actor in authority directs. Finally, at the postconventional level, complete reciprocity is realized as principles become the basis of interaction between legal subjects (stage 5: social–contractual legalism) or all subjects in general (stage 6: ethical–principled orientation).[63]

The forms in which reciprocity appears at the different stages of interaction constitute, for Habermas, "*the naturalistic kernel of moral consciousness.*"[64] What this means is, first, that the viewpoint of reciprocity arises *naturally*, as the maturing individual learns to take part in increasingly complex forms of interaction; in other words, "the point of view of reciprocity belongs *eo ipso* to the interactive knowledge of speaking and acting subjects."[65] This is because

In communicative action a relationship of at least incomplete reciprocity is established with the interpersonal relation between the involved parties. Two persons stand in an incompletely reciprocal relation insofar as one may do or expect x only to the extent that the other may do or expect y (e.g. teacher/pupil, parent/child). Their relationship is completely reciprocal if both may do or expect the same thing in comparable situations (x = y) (e.g. the norms of civil law). In a now-famous essay Alvin Gouldner speaks of the norm of reciprocity that underlies all interactions ... This expression is not entirely apt, since reciprocity is not a norm but is fixed in the general structures of possible interaction.[66]

Reciprocity is thus a viewpoint not tied to any particular culture or historical period, but rather is available to *all* actors, and, as such, it can always provide a potential *consensual* standard for the resolution of conflict. The post-conventional conception of morality simply raises this viewpoint to full consciousness. Hence "the moral point of view" is characterized as requiring the *conscious* application of reciprocity to the problem of norming norms.[67]

If this is so, then one key question which must be asked of a discursive ethics is how its conceptualization of the requirement of reciprocity is more adequate than conceptualizations provided by other types of post conventional ethics. At first Habermas argued that, from the theoretical vantage point of interactive competence, he could justify the portrayal of discursive ethics as a new stage 7, in addition to the Kohlbergian, postconventional stages 5 (social–contractual legalism) and 6 (principled–ethical orientation). However, Habermas has since retreated from this kind of claim. He has admitted (as has Kohlberg) that the whole idea of *stages within* the post-conventional level is misconceived.[68] The reason for this is that the concept of *natural* stages of development is inappropriate at level III. Once a subject reaches this level of *reflective* moral consciousness, the psychologist can no longer claim the role of an expert who separates further stages, as if they still followed one another in the same natural way as they do for subjects at the two lower, pre-reflective levels. To say that one "stage" is "superior" to another at the postconventional level represents nothing more than a claim that, through philosophical argument and reflection, such superiority can be recognized by the subject. In this process theorist and subject are both participants and neither has any inherently privileged position.[69] The upshot of this is simply that whatever superiority one kind of postconventionalism can claim over another will be gained by the normal means of philosophical argument.

The following chapter will examine the kind of philosophical arguments Habermas offers for the superiority of discursive ethics over other forms of postconventional ethics. This analysis will take us back to the second of Habermas's basic claims about discursive ethics (which was put aside at the beginning of this chapter), that is, his contention that the appropriate test of normative legitimacy is a real practical discourse, which offers the possibility of separating generalizable interests from particular interests. The reason this claim links up with the preceding discussion in this section is that to understand the discursive test for generalizability and the necessity for discourse being real, as opposed to monological and hypothetical, is also to understand the specific interpretation Habermas gives to the requirement of reciprocity.

Before turning to the claim of communicative ethics to be the most adequate type of postconventional ethics, it is first necessary to refocus attention on the assertion that the theory of interactive competence can strengthen Kohlberg's claims about stages of moral judgement. Here the key question is not whether a discursive conceptualization of posconventionalism is the most adequate, but rather how *any* postconventional moral judgement can justifiably claim superiority over other forms of moral judgement, which are relegated in Kohlberg's scheme to levels I and II.

Even if Habermas's project of sharply delineating stages of interaction were to be developed in detail and empirically tested, it would still not provide, as Habermas himself is aware, a clear-cut case for the universal validity of postconventional moral judgements. Certainly it is important to understand the ways in which our capacity for moral judgement is linked to our competence for interaction. Illuminating the character of such a linkage cannot, however, establish on its own the universal validity of postconventional moral judgements.

The key to Habermas's linkage is, as I have shown, the viewpoint of reciprocity, which he asserts is available to all competent actors and thus can constitute an unbiased basis for resolving moral conflicts. For Habermas, level III moral judgements simply take what is part of the implicit know-how of all actors and make conscious use of it. But this way of conceptualizing level III does not resolve the question of its superiority, for the viewpoint of reciprocity is actually mastered in level II interactions, where individuals gain the capacity for simple role behavior and more complex forms of norm-guided interaction. Clearly this makes reciprocity a viewpoint *available* to mature individuals in all societies; but just as clearly there is no natural necessity for this viewpoint being *consciously accepted as the standard* for resolving moral conflicts. The reflexive use of the viewpoint of reciprocity as a requirement in moral deliberation can only be conclusively justified when one has already assumed the superiority of the moral point of view associated with a decentered, postconventional consciousness.

Now Habermas clearly acknowledges that theoretical reconstructions such as Kohlberg's must necessarily begin with some guiding ethical assumptions.[70] Although such assumptions about what constitutes the moral point of view must guide empirical research, they do not thereby become immune from reconsideration in the light of the results of that research. Consider, for example, how some psychologists working within the Kohlbergian research program have been led by their results to assert that Kohlberg's conceptualization of the highest stage of moral judgement fails to account adequately for the moral experience of women (I will consider this question further in the next chapter).[71] But if empirical research can play this sort of corrective role in relation to the ethical assumptions underlying theoretical reconstructions, it cannot of course provide direct, conclusive evidence for or against a particular conceptualization of the moral point of view. At best, Habermas argues, a well researched theory such as Kohlberg's can provide one form of "indirect confirmation" or "coherence test."[72]

Understood in this light, Habermas's foray into developmental psychology should be taken less as a direct attempt to find the key for proving the superiority of discursive ethics and more as an attempt to increase the theoretical clarity of Kohlberg's project. And even in its programatic form, Habermas's notion of stages of interaction does indeed seem to be an improvement on Kohlberg's attempt to elucidate the developmental–logical character of his moral stages by linking them with insufficiently analyzed types of "social perspectives." If Habermas thus adds strength to Kohlbergian theory, he thereby contributes to a line of research which in turn lends support to postconventional conceptions of ethics, at least to the degree to which it stands up to empirical evidence.

Such indirect confirmation, however, is by itself a fairly slim reed on which to rest the claims of discursive ethics. It provides relatively little additional strength to the conceptual reconstruction of the normative implications of communicative action which were examined in the earlier sections of this chapter. Further support for discursive ethics must come from two directions. First, as I have indicated, there are philosophical arguments that a discursive ethics's conceptualization of the reciprocity requirement is superior to that of other forms of postconventional ethics. I will turn to these arguments directly. But it should be immediately emphasized that these arguments, like the others presented in this chapter, assume in one way or another the basic superiority of modern ways of thinking about morality. What is still lacking is a systematic defense of modernity itself.

APPENDIX: Kohlberg's moral stages

I. Preconventional level

At this level the child is responsive to cultural rules and labels of good and bad, right or wrong, but interprets these labels in terms of either the physical or the hedonistic consequences of action (punishment, reward, exchange of favors), or in terms of the physical power of those who enunciate the rules and labels. The level is divided into the following two stages:

Stage 1: The punishment and obedience orientation. The physical consequences of action determine its goodness or badness regardless of the human meaning or value of these consequences. Avoidance of punishment and unquestioning deference to power are valued in their own right, not in terms of respect for an underlying moral order supported by punishment and authority (the latter being stage 4).

Stage 2: The instrumental relativist orientation. Right action consists of that which instrumentally satisfies one's own needs and occasionally the needs of others. Human relations are viewed in terms like those of the market place. Elements of fairness, of reciprocity and of equal sharing are present, but they are always interpreted in a physical, pragmatic way. Reciprocity is a matter of "you scratch my back and I'll scratch yours," not of loyalty, gratitude or justice.

II. Conventional level

At this level, maintaining the expectations of the individual's family, group or nation is perceived as valuable in its own right, regardless of immediate and obvious consequences. The attitude is not only one of *conformity* to personal expectations and social order, but of loyalty to it, of actively *maintaining,* supporting and justifying the order, and of identifying with the persons or group involved in it. At this level, there are the following two stages:

Stage 3: *The interpersonal concordance or "good boy–nice girl" orientation.* Good behavior is that which pleases or helps others and is approved by them. There is much conformity to stereotypical images of what is majority or "natural" behavior. Behavior is frequently judged by intention – "he means well" becomes important for the first time. One earns approval by being "nice."

Stage 4: *The "law and order" orientation.* There is orientation toward authority, fixed rules and the maintenance of the social order. Right behavior consists of doing one's duty, showing respect for authority and maintaining the given social order for its own sake.

III. Postconventional, autonomous or principled level

At this level, there is a clear effort to define moral values and principles which have validity and application apart from the individual's own identification with these groups. This level again has two stages:

Stage 5: *The social-contract legalistic orientation,* generally utilitarian overtones. Right action tends to be defined in terms of general individual rights, and standards which have been critically examined and agreed upon by the whole society. There is a clear awareness of the relativism of personal values and opinions and a corresponding emphasis upon procedural rules for reaching consensus. Aside from what is constitutionally and democratically agreed upon, the right is a matter of personal "values" and "opinion." The result is an emphasis upon the "legal point of view," but with an emphasis upon the possibility of changing law in terms of rational considerations of social utility (rather than freezing it in terms of stage 4 "law and order"). Outside the legal realm, free agreement and contract is the binding element of obligation. This is the "official" morality of the American government and constitution.

Stage 6: *The universal ethical principle orientation.* Right is defined by the decision of conscience in accord with self-chosen *ethical principles* appealing to logical comprehensiveness, universality and consistency. These principles are abstract and ethical (the Golden Rule, the categorical imperative); they are not concrete moral rules like the Ten Commandments. At heart, these are universal principles of *justice,* of the *reciprocity* and *equality* of human *rights,* and of respect for the dignity of human beings as *individual persons.*

Source: Lawrence Kohlberg, "From Is to Ought," in Theodore Mischel, (ed.), *Cognitive Development and Epistemology* (New York: Academic Press 1971).

4

Toward a minimal ethics and orientation for political theory

The specific interpretation Habermas gives to the postconventional criterion of reciprocity or fairness must be understood in relation to his notions of generalizable interests and real discourse. In this chapter I will show why Habermas thinks they provide us with the most adequate form of postconventional ethics. Particular attention will be paid to the procedural character of the discursive model, and some of the criticisms which have been advanced against it— most notably the charges that it is either empty of ethical content, or, if its prescriptions do have some bite, they are nonetheless so abstracted from concrete traditions as to have no motivational support. I will also briefly examine the challenge represented by Carol Gilligan's work to any Kantian formulation of ethics, in order to see whether it undermines Habermas's position. Finally, having drawn out the moral implications of the communicative model of the agent, I will suggest some initial implications it has for how political theorists study power.

I. The discursive interpretation of the demand for reciprocity

Before I turn to a closer analysis of the discursive criteria for assessing the legitimacy of normative claims, it is necessary to explain first what constitutes "a normative claim" for Habermas. As I briefly indicated in chapter 3, Habermas defines normative claims as claims "about alternative orderings for the satisfaction of interests." Similarly, he says that "norms regulate legitimate chances for the satisfaction of needs."[1] The use of "interests" in one case and "needs" in the other need not detain us, since it seems fair to assume that Habermas would say that one has an interest in something if it satisfies one's needs.

It is important to be clear about exactly what is implied in the foregoing formulation, because it has been misunderstood by critics. Focusing on the relationship between the satisfaction of needs and the legitimacy of norms is *not* the first step toward building the following sort of argument: there are certain basic or genuine needs which *all* fully emancipated individuals would have; these needs will necessarily be discovered by anyone who sincerely enters into a practical discourse; and, finally, starting from such needs, one can derive determinate principles of justice.[2] On the contrary, Habermas has in mind no such substantive conception of needs or principles of justice. When he discusses needs, his concern almost always is to draw attention to the way in which the core values of a culture deeply structure what constitutes a "need" within that culture. In fact, Habermas usually does not refer simply to "needs" but rather to "need interpretations," a locution which expresses their cultural variability.[3] If I interpret him correctly here, what he is implying is that what is taken to be a "need" in a given society will be a function of what that culture defines as necessary to the flourishing of human life.

If this is the case, it would appear that Habermas is not wedded to some universalistic, biological model of basic needs; rather the concept of need is one which is inevitably intertwined with the social and cultural dimensions of life. And this would mean that he agrees with those who do not think that the concept of need can provide us with an unambiguous, Archimedian standpoint for moral and political philosophy. An appeal to needs simply does not have the power to provide clear-cut guidelines for establishing universal, determinate principles of justice. Even something as apparently basic as the need for nourishment cannot be made the foundation for a culturally neutral approach to justice, since a given culture may prescribe that the satisfaction of that need should give way in certain situations if it conflicts with some non-biological needs, such as religious ones.[4]

Thus when Habermas conceptually ties legitimacy to need satisfaction, he is defining the latter realm in a way which is not confined simply to material satisfactions. In this regard it makes perfect sense to claim, for example, that a citizen of a democracy "needs" information about important political issues; or that a person who holds a reverential attitude towards nature has a "need" to live in a society which treats nature in a way substantially different from that of advanced industrial societies.

It might be objected here that when one uses needs in this broad sense one is simply confusing distinct types of standards for grounding the justness or legitimacy of norms.[5] For example, it could be argued that legitimacy should be gauged by conformity to moral ideals such as natural rights or the categorical imperative, and that these have *nothing* to do with needs in any sense. This view, however, carries with it substantial problems. In its strictest Kantian version, this view can never really clarify why anyone would be motivated by such ideals. If this difficulty is to be overcome, it means that ideals of this sort must gain their capacity to move people by virtue of their place within a conception of what is important for the flourishing of human life; in saying this, one is saying that they must be tied to some sort of need interpretation.

Properly understood, then, Habermas's linking of normative claims and need satisfaction is quite defensible. The question to be addressed now is what requirements the rules of discourse put on an individual who proposes a norm as legitimate. As shown in chapter 3, one must submit not only to straight-forward rules of fair argumentation, but also to rules whose effect is to open up to critical assessment the interpretation of needs which informs a given normative claim.[6] This requirement is particularly important in that it brings into question socially dominant interpretations of needs as well as all others. In short, discourse requires a test of reciprocity in regard to how each individual interprets his/her needs in relation to others who are potentially affected by that individual's normative claim. The need interpretation which is implied in a normative claim thus must be one that can be "universalized" – that is, *"communicatively shared"* – if that claim is to withstand discursive testing and thus be acceptable to all participants.[7]

The critical conceptual space created by applying discursive rules is supposed to allow for dialogue in which participants have at least the *possibility* of reaching more "truthful interpretations of their own particular needs as well as especially of those which are common and capable of consensus."[8] On matters in relation to which participants can envision common need interpretations, they can discover a generalizable interest. And norms which incorporate such interests will be acceptable to all those involved in the discourse.

As I indicated above, Habermas is not presenting a claim about the needs and interests all would have in *the* good society, and which anyone could discover if he/she merely subjected himself/herself to the rules of discourse. Such a universalistic claim about the shape of the good society is always unwarranted, since it tries to settle once and for all what must be left open, if the requirement of reciprocity is to take into account voices which may not have been evident in any given discourse.[9]

The evolution of Rawls's theory of justice is instructive in this regard, since it illustrates the problem Habermas finds inherent in any attempt to explicate the idea of justice in terms which are both universalistic and substantively determinate. With reference to Rawls, it should also be recalled that his veil of ignorance is considered by Kohlberg to be an adequate interpretation of the requirement of reciprocity. Each individual in Rawls's original position must think out the advantages and disadvantages of alternative principles of justice from the viewpoint of different social roles, because he/she is ignorant of the role he/she will actually occupy.

In *A Theory of Justice*, parties to the original position are not, however, totally ignorant. Each is assumed to value certain primary goods. This assumption is warranted according to Rawls because any individual, regardless of the role he/she may find himself/herself occupying after the veil is lifted, will consider them beneficial, or at least not harmful. These goods include greater liberty and opportunity, and greater wealth and income. In Habermas's terms, this account of primary goods is also implicitly an account of universalizable needs. The advantage to be gained by assuming that each party to the original position has a need for these particular goods is that, with such an assumption, the deliberations of the parties will result in a determinate agreement on principles of justice. The fact that the original position does lead to a determinate choice is held by Rawls to be a major advance upon the formalism of Kant, while at the same time retaining a Kantian moral status.[10].

Rawls's approach in *A Theory of Justice* has often been attacked by critics (including Habermas) on the grounds that the list of primary goods – in particular the good of greater wealth and income – is biased toward the kind of needs fostered in a *specific* type of society, i.e., one characterized by social competitiveness and economic individualism.[11] In recent reflections on his theory, Rawls has tried to revise his account of primary goods in order to avoid this bias, but, even more importantly, he seems now to accept the overall contextualist criticism that a substantive account of justice such as his cannot claim universality. As Michael Walzer succinctly puts it: "All substantive accounts of justice are particular accounts."[12] Rawls accordingly admits that his is an account of justice which claims validity only for members of "modern democratic societies."[13]

Now Habermas would agree with this contextualist insight, at least so far as it applies to a theory such as Rawls's – that is, one which incorporates *any* substantive set of needs.[14] Such incorporation invariably violates the (discursively interpreted) requirement of reciprocity in the sense that it declares once and for all that some potential voices (and the needs they express) will not be given an adequate hearing.

While the effect of Habermas's and the contextualists' critiques of Rawls are thus similar, Habermas nevertheless thinks that the possibility of a universalist account of justice or normative legitimacy does not thereby evaporate. But the universalism of a postconventionally interpreted principle of reciprocity can be saved only if it is disconnected from the "mono-logical" conceptualization it has received in the formalist tradition from Kant to Rawls, a model which inevitably becomes entangled in the sort of particularist problem Rawls experiences.

The appropriate viewpoint from which to understand universalization is rather a dialogical, procedural one: "the communally followed *procedure* of redeeming normative validity claims discursively." It is "only through the communicative structure" of "an actually carried out discourse," involving all those affected by a proposed norm, that the necessary "*exchange of roles* of each with every other [is] forced upon us."[15]

The point which Habermas wants to bring out, with his emphasis on real discourse, can be illustrated further by considering a common criticism of it. Philip Pettit, for example, argues that Habermas's appeal to the actual procedure of discourse betrays a simple confusion between "the cognitive question of what sort of norms are just," on the one hand, and the pragmatic, "organizational enterprise" of working out the problem of basic constitutional norms, on the other.[16] Pettit's assertion of confusion on Habermas's part results, however, from his prior acceptance of a strict biological model of needs. Having accepted this rigid model, Pettit of course sees the cognitive question as one to which a sufficient answer can be given by a monological deliberator, since the justness of a norm will appear in the same light for him as for all others. But the deficiencies of such a strict biological model of needs have already been pointed out. And once the sure footing provided by this model is thrown into question, the whole conception of a monological deliberator is also thrown into question, because what he is representing to himself as the necessary character of the subjects of justice has now lost its clarity.

II.   A minimal ethics

In light of the foregoing discussion and critique of Rawls, it is not surprising that Habermas refers to his discursive project as a "minimal ethics." Its minimalness is a function not only of its restriction to questions of justice (as opposed to all evaluative questions) but even more of its admission that it cannot provide us with unambiguous, substantive norms of justice. Communicative ethics can direct us only to a particular way of thinking about fair procedures for adjudicating normative claims.[17]

A fair question to be asked at this point is whether the discursive perspective is so indeterminate as to be relatively worthless in providing any effective ethical guidance to political thought and action. I think it does provide some important guidance, and in this section I will begin to indicate exactly what sorts it offers.

On the simplest level, the "indeterminacy" question is relatively easy to dispose of. Just because Habermas does not provide substantive, fully determinate principles of justice, that does not mean his position must be completely indeterminate or empty. The procedural criteria of discourse can easily be seen as providing a form of constrained indeterminateness. What exactly this entails can be brought out most clearly by examining the specific constraints, as I will do below.

Another way of interpreting the "emptiness" suspicion might be in terms of the question of whether the demands of a communicative ethics are so abstracted from concrete social contexts as to render them incapable of actually motivating actors to conform to them. This question of whether the abstract requirements of discursive ethics could ever *effectively* motivate people is related to the question of whether it is *legitimate* to impose such abstract, "unrealistic" demands on individuals. I want to take up this latter question first. In the course of addressing it, I will be able to explain in more detail some of the specific constraints entailed by Habermas's perspective (A). Having clarified these, I will return to the question of abstractness and motivation (B).

A. It has been argued that a postconventional ethics like Habermas's or Rawls's, which incorporates very strong criteria of fairness, is unrealistic to the point of being somehow illegitimate.[18] "Strong" here means simply that a given agent may find that there is a substantial gap between what the criteria require and what he/she intitially perceives to be in his/her interest. It has been argued against such proposed criteria ("veil of ignorance" or rules of discourse) that they are so strong as to constitute an illegitimate imposition on the individual. These criteria violate the very core of individual identity by placing unwarranted constraints on what one can rightly hold onto as one's basic interests or undertake as part of one's "ground project" in life.[19]

This image of abstract, alien standards being imposed on breathing, acting, concretely situated persons does indeed have an initial air of illegitimacy about it. But this air can be at least partially dispelled in the case of communicative ethics. The reason for this lies in the way Habermas conceptualizes the relationship between practical discourse and an agent's claim to rationality. The degree of reciprocity required by discourse is not something *externally imposed* on actors, but rather something which (as was shown in chapter 3) is *internally presupposed* by them insofar as they make normative claims on one another. The rules of discourse are what actors must make their normative claims conform to if they are going to sustain the reasoned character of their speech acts. Conceptualizing the problem in this way does not of course dissolve the difficulty of clashes between the individual and postconventional demands of fairness; it does, however, indicate that the latter cannot be so easily cast into the role of an illegitimately overbearing set of abstract constraints.

One important issue which needs to be clarified here is what exactly is required of individuals when they agree to follow out the discursively inter-preted demands of fairness. As was shown earlier, when one tries to justify a normative claim, one is obligated to show that the interests underlying it are generalizable rather than merely particular. In some cases this demon-stration and an ensuing agreement might come easily. For example, traffic rules and laws against murder can be seen as resting on generalizable interests in the safety and sanctity of persons.[20] But of course most questions in ethics and politics are not so amenable to simple solution. What does communicative ethics require agents to do when agreement is not so easily reached? The rules of discourse require that agents sincerely reflect upon the different need interpretations which underlie their respective, but con-flicting, concepts of what interests are generalizable.[21] This means that they must exhibit a sort of ongoing critical flexibility: a willingness to reconsider and possibly modify their need interpretations, when they appear to manifest weaker claims to universality than alternative ones. I will analyze the implications of this constraint in a moment. At this point, however, the only thing which it is necessary to emphasize is that the result of such dis-cursive reflections on needs is not necessarily any consensus (much less any revelation about "genuine" human needs).

The demand for flexibility thus provides no magic formula for guarantee-ing that agents will come up with generalizable interests. If this is the case, however, what guidance does communicative ethics offer when agents appear to have exhibited such flexibilty and yet still fail to come to a consen-sus on interests? When interests continue to conflict – that is, they do not prove susceptible to generalization – resort must be had to compromise.[22]

Habermas's position here is usually misunderstood to one degree or another. His reference to compromise is generally viewed with suspicion, given his apparently contradictory claim that he can show us a way out of an "impenetrable" Weberian pluralism of conflicting values, needs and interests.[23] This latter claim has led critics to infer that Habermas, although he speaks of compromise, actually has a deep contempt for it, seeing it as an "eliminable imperfection" resulting from the flaws of existing individuals who have not yet developed the "genuine" human needs which members of an "emancipated" society would have.[24] I have already shown that there is no such hidden agenda in communicative ethics on the question of genuine needs, so this interpretation of Habermas is simply wrong.

But if it is wrong, how can a discursive perspective get us beyond a totally impenetrable pluralism and the resulting necessity of being resigned to say, an ethics of simple contractarianism, which looks only for workable bargains between conflicting interests? Such an alternative may seem to be the only direction in which to go if one abandons the strong universalism of Rawls's *Theory of Justice*, but still wishes to speak of some minimal universal criteria for dealing with normative disputes. J. L. Mackie, for example, has proposed just such a simple contractarianism as the only sustainable sort of minimal ethics.[25] If one contrasts Mackie's position on the subject of compromise with Habermas's, one can see at least one effect of the latter's constrained indeterminism, which provides a partial penetration of a thoroughgoing pluralism.

Rejecting strong, postconventional criteria for fair agreements, Mackie contends that we must be more modest and simply seek compromises which prove acceptable to whatever "different actual points of view" and interests are involved.[26] Although this recommendation has an attractive air of realism about it, it nevertheless gains this realism at the cost of a tacit endorsement of whatever structures of inequality might exist in a given society. Such an ethics will assign an unqualified legitimacy to compromises which solidify initially unequal bargaining positions.[27] This is because it has no way of distinguishing compromises which are acceptable *but* illegitimate from ones which are acceptable *and* legitimate. An example of the former would be an agreement which a disadvantaged person accepts on *prudential* grounds, even though that acceptance occurs under conditions of constraint. The problem, as Habermas puts it, with a perspective like Mackie's is that it cannot adequately differentiate "validity claims from power claims."[28] That is, it fails to give useful standards for recognizing when arrangements that may appear to be consensual are actually functions of power relationships. This is a crucial ethical aspect of a critical approach to the theory and practice of politics.

From a Habermasian perspective, the "basic guidelines for compromise construction must themselves be justified" in discursive terms. This alone can supply a standard for separating legitimate from illegitimate compromises. In particular, the discursive emphases on procedural equality, participation, non-deception and non-manipulation provide criteria in relation to which compromises must be called to account.[29] These discursive constraints on compromise do not, however, give us a precise formula or method for unambiguously separating legitimate from illegitimate compromises. In other words, although one can say that a given compromise must not rest on one-sided manipulation or advantages derived from an unequal bargaining position, these proscriptions must always be interpreted and applied by actors operating within a particular cultural tradition. Thus, for example, one cannot categorically assert that, because normative claims must be evaluated from a perspective of equality, actors cannot ever accept claims which entail social relations permitting different sorts of inequalities. What the constrained indeterminism does allow us to do, however, is to *shift the burden of proof* in normative argumentation from where it lies in Mackie's minimal ethics. And in shifting the burden of proof, communicative ethics shifts the responsibility for abandoning reason in favor of force. In some cases where inequality between agents exists, a framework like Mackie's will confront the disadvantaged agent with the choice of accepting a "legitimate" bargain which confirms his inequality or of breaking off reasoned dialogue and using force – that is, a choice which renounces the claim to moral legitimacy. In communicative ethics, on the other hand, it is the privileged agent who is confronted with the choice of either demonstrating to what degree his inequality can be discursively justified or of relying on coercion to defend that inequality – again a choice that renounces the claim to moral legitimacy, only this time the tables are turned.

In this line of argumentation, one can begin to see why Habermas's normative foundation leads into what Paul Ricoeur calls a hermeneutics of "suspicion."[30] He provides us with an ethical orientation toward structures of inequality such that those structures are, at least *initially*, always to be brought under interpretations which illuminate them as *possible* structures of power.

B.   Habermas's arguments about compromise come into play, as I have said, in situations where sincere reflection by participants in discourse does not lead to their discovering generalizable interests. I want to turn back now to the question of what the criterion of sincere reflection on needs actually entails. What sort of criterion is this and what sort of ethical orientation, if any, does it provide?

The rules of discourse require a reflective elucidation of the need interpretations underlying disputed norms. As each agent takes up this critical, reflective attitude toward the norms proposed by another agent, he/she forces the other to be self-critically reflective about his/her own needs and their universality. As needs are examined in the undistorted, dialogical light of discourse, agents have the possibility of reaching more truthful interpretations of their own particular needs as well as those which can be communicatively shared.[31]

The sort of need flexibility required by communicative ethics would appear to place a rather heavy demand on the personality structure of the individual. Is it really plausible to expect that such self-analysis, with its "critique and justification of need interpretations, [can] acquire the power to orient action?"[32] Such a demand is indeed implausible if one imagines an individual continually throwing his/her entire need structure – and thus his/her identity itself – into question. Unfortunately Habermas has at times lent credence to this sort of interpretation of the demand for flexibility by stating, for example, that for agents who achieve this flexibility "internal nature . . . is moved into a utopian perspective."[33] Such sweeping statements, however, must be taken in the context of others which show a clear recognition of the limits of flexibility. Individuals cannot change their basic need structures in a chameleon-like fashion. The hypothetical, discursive attitude, which agents can take up in relation to a contested norm, does indeed require reflection on the relationship between that norm and the need satisfaction it implies. But this sort of sequential questioning, brought on in situations of disputed claims, is not the same thing as a once and for all, wholesale questioning of one's entire need structure. It is simply not psychologically plausible to conceive of individuals freely willing – under the imperative of discursive reason – the latter sort of experience. Discursive ethics, Habermas admits, does not demand such a radical "hypothetical attitude" toward the "very life form and life history in terms of which [agents] have constructed their identity."[34]

In order to get a clearer idea of what Habermas does have in mind with his notion of flexible need interpretations, it is necessary to turn to what he has to say about the question of both individual and collective "identity." By "identity," Habermas means "the symbolic strucure which allows a personality system to secure continuity and consistency."[35] In an attempt to integrate research in ego psychology with his own analysis of interactive competence, Habermas postulates three basic stages of individual identity formation corresponding to the three levels of development in the domains of cognition, interaction and moral consciousness (discussed in chapter 3). He distinguishes "natural identity," "role identity" and "ego identity." The last of these is obviously the most important for present concerns, since it is the only symbolic structure within which a person can satisfy both the psychological requirements of consistency as well as the postconventional requirements of discursive ethics.

At the first level the child develops a "natural identity" based on its ability to distinguish itself from its environment; but it does not yet distinguish between physical and social objects in its environment. This natural identity breaks down when "the child assimilates the symbolic generalities of a few fundamental roles in his family environment, and later the norms of action of expanded groups." The result is a "symbolically supported role identity" corresponding to level II. In adolescence, individuals usually replace their family-bound role identity with a role identity bound to more abstract groups; "typically to definite occupational and status groups, generally in connection with membership roles, be they regional, national, political, or linguistic-cultural."[36]

Finally at level III,

role bearers [are] transformed into persons who can assert their identities independent of concrete roles and particular systems of norms. We are supposing here that the youth has acquired the important distinction between norms, on the one hand, and principles according to which we can generate norms, on the other – and thus the ability to judge according to principles. He takes into account that traditionally settled forms of life can prove to be mere conventions, to be irrational. Thus he has to retract his ego behind the line of all particular roles and norms and stabilize it only through the abstract ability to present himself credibly in any situation as someone who can satisfy the requirements of consistency even in the face of incompatible role expectations and in the passage through a sequence of contradictory periods in life.[37]

An ego expected to judge any given norm in the light of internalized principles, that is, to consider them hypothetically and to provide justifications, can no longer tie its identity to particular pregiven roles and sets of norms. *Now continuity can be established only through the ego's own integrating accomplishment.* This ability is paradigmatically exercised when the growing child gives up its early identities, which are tied to familiar roles, in favor of more and more abstract identities secured finally to the institutions and traditions of the political community. *To the extent that the ego generalizes this ability* to overcome an old identity and to construct a new one and learns to resolve identity crises by reestablishing at a higher level the disturbed balance between itself and a changed social reality, role identity is replaced by ego identity.[38]

The language of "old" and "new" identities here should not be taken in a totally disjunctive sense, but rather in a dialectical sense of supersession and preservation, whereby the old is integrated into the structure of the new. The concept of ego-identity does not refer so much to the content of the new identity as it does to the integrative capacity necessary to construct it and maintain it.

Although the symbolic structure of ego-identity first emerges in the conflictual experiences of adolescence, it roots itself solidly in the individual only to the degree that the integrative ability which resolved those conflicts does not remain dormant thereafter. In new situations of conflict, the individual must call upon this integrative capacity "to organize himself and his interactions – under the guidance of general principles and modes of procedure – into a unique life history."[39]

The reference to situations of conflict is crucial, because it draws attention to the fact that the most developed structure of self-identification does not stabilize itself purely as a result of some internal dynamic. The integrative capacity, which the structure of ego-identity makes available, is further developed only when a change in social environment creates a situation in which the substantive character of one's identity is no longer in equilibrium with that environment. Now such disequilibrium-inducing phenomena can be of many types, for example a moral dilemma which arises in one's personal life. Habermas, however, is far more interested in dilemmas which are induced by phenomena having a collective significance and thus an impact on "collective identity." The link between the individual level and the collective level is crucial, for

the characteristics of self-identification must be intersubjectively recognized, if the identity of the person is to be solidly based. That which distinguishes the self from others must be recognized by others. The symbolic unity of the person, which is produced and maintained by self-identification, rests in turn on belonging to the symbolic reality of a group, on the possibility of a localization within the world of this group.[40]

This concern for collective identity is intertwined with the problem of motivation. Unlike Kohlberg, who asserts flatly that the individual "who knows the good, wills the good," Habermas finds the connection between identity and moral insight, on the one hand, and action, on the other, to be more problematic. If no adequate, complementary collective identity exists, "then universalistic morality as well as the corresponding ego-structures must remain a mere demand; that is, they can only privately and occasionally be realized without becoming substantially determinative for social life."[41]

Given the intellectual roots of the Frankfurt School, it is not especially surprising to see Habermas focusing on the interplay of the individual and the collective in situations of conflict. The sort of thesis he wants to put forward in this regard is that the familiar bases of both individual and collective identity in advanced industrial societies are being thrown into question by phenomena associated with the systematic development of those societies.

The rapid pace of social change and the deterioration of traditions in contemporary industrialized societies is creating conditions under which the fixed points around which identity has traditionally crystallized are being thrown increasingly into question.[42] One does not have to look to Habermas's specific arguments to be impressed by the dimensions of this problem. Many others have asked: to what degree can the identity of members of industrialized societies continue to crystallize around the characteristics of "possessive individualism," when the attendant ecological costs are becoming increasingly clear? Similarly, how adequate are collective identities defined almost exclusively in terms of *nation* and *territorial* political units, when the technology of warfare and industrial processes threatens us with both rapid *global* annihiliation and long-term *global* crises (e.g., the "greenhouse effect")?

However, as the moorings for such traditionally fixed points of reference for modern identity begin to loosen, the cognitive infrastructure of modern moral, political and legal traditions does not. A postconventional moral consciousness, Habermas argues, continues to present the ego with the expectation that norms should be judged "in the light of internalized principles."[43] Given this situation, an identity which is both stable and in accordance with postconventional criteria must be one increasingly tied to the experience of continually exercising one's integrative capacity in the context of changes which cannot be brought into an easy accommodation with the familiar bases of modern identity.[44] Now part of what is involved in exercising this integrative capacity is a reflective attitude toward one's need interpretations. And from what has just been said, it is clear that one of the most important dimensions of such reflection is growing sensitivity to ways in which one's need interpretations may be internally related to forms of life which are likely to become increasingly frustrating and destructive in the future.

The significance of the foregoing for communicative ethics is that the requirement of flexibility of needs can now be seen as no mere abstract demand; rather, it is one which is intimately related to concrete difficulties individuals face in managing contemporary social and cultural pressure. This means that the appearance of motivations which support a communicative ethics has some concrete, historical basis.[45] This line of argument will be picked up again in the last chapter.

Taking stock now of what has been said in this chapter about the particular form of postconventionalism offered by communicative ethics, one can see that it appears to avoid many of the problems often attributed to universalistic moral and political philosophies. In particular, the core ideas of intersubjective recognition and equal accountability make the universalism of communicative ethics one which is not "imperialistic" in the sense of always threatening to smother the "other." This can be seen in all of its key concepts: in the emphasis on real discourse; in the connection of the criterion of generalizable interests to compromise; and finally, in the interpretation given to the requirements of a mature, autonomous ego. Openness to the "other" appears especially clearly in the last concept. In this regard it is interesting to see how Habermas contrasts the Kantian self with the structure of self compatible with communicative ethics. The former self operates in the service of a formal, universalistic ethics of duty, mastering each new situation by submitting it to the test of the categorical imperative. What remain unexamined, however, are the prevailing cultural values and the need interpretations to which they give rise. These will always influence the testing process; that is, how the categorical imperative is to be interpreted in a given situation will be at least partially dependent on the way needs are interpreted. For example, it is not difficult to see a 19th century American father forbidding his adolescent daughter from studying to become a doctor on the grounds that it is not proper for women, given their "nature," to enter professions. That father could, in good conscience, will his proscription as a universal law.

If I am not mistaken, it is precisely the threat of such a smothering of the "other" and its potential claims which animates contemporary critics of universalistic moral and political philosophies. Universalism seems inevitably to support a notion of autonomy defined in terms of the rigid independence of the ego from the situations which confront it – and thus some sort of isolation from the claims of the other, particularly when they have a radically different character. This "moral rigorism," evident in Kohlberg as well as Kant, is to be contrasted, Habermas contends, with the image of autonomy which can be derived from the notions of ego-identity and the communicative interpretation of reciprocity. The critical reflectiveness and flexibility in relation to need interpretations required by these notions cannot be realized through a monological, situation-independent style of cognition and judgement. Rather it can only come into its own in dialogue requiring

sensitivity, breaking down barriers, dependency – in short, a cognitive style marked as field-dependent, which the ego, on the way to autonomy, first overcame and replaced with a field-independent style of perception and thought.[46]

At the core, then, of communicative ethics is the image of *open* conversation, that is, a conversation in which one is obliged to listen to other voices.[47] Such conversation is ultimately to be seen as a "continual learning process' in which different experiences are shared in the processes of recognizing more clearly who we are and who we want to become.[48]

This obligation to listen, to be open, has a two-fold character. On the one hand, we have the formal openness of practical discourse. But following the rules of discourse does not by itself foster the sort of personality which is existentially open to critical reflectiveness in relation to needs. For that, Habermas says, we must look to the aesthetic dimension. Forms of communication, into which aesthetic experience and imagination flow, are not reducible to discourse. The former stand, however, in "an internal relationship" to discourse, for without them the requirement of reflectiveness and flexibility would not have much potential for throwing new light on needs and possible forms of life different from those prevailing in a given society.[49] Contrary to everyday experience, where traditional cultural values function as "stencils according to which needs are shaped," in aesthetic experience and criticism, freer access is allowed "to the interpretative possibilities of ... cultural traditions."[50] From this point of view, aesthetic experience has the potential to help avoid "a stagnation of the structures of practical discourse."[51]

At this point, Habermas's appeal to the aesthetic dimension might seem somewhat abrupt, and its connection with the themes of discursive ethics rather contrived. Once I have elucidated his conception of modernity and its problems, however, the interconnectedness of communicative reason and the aesthetic dimension will become more apparent.

III.   A different voice in the conversation

Now that some of the key ideas of communicative ethics have been fleshed out, it is important to consider what is one of the most provocative recent challenges to the Kantian tradition and to see to what extent it generates difficulties for Habermas's position. The challenge comes from the work of Carol Gilligan on the particular qualities of moral thinking in women.[52] The immediate object of her critique is Kohlberg's work. She contrasts his focus on the Kantian "ethic of justice" which emphasizes rights, fairness, balancing claims, separation and autonomy, with her own focus on the ethic of "responsibility and care," which focuses on compassion, avoidance of harm, context-sensitivity, connectedness and interdependence.[53] Kohlberg's work, and the Kantian tradition as a whole, tend to neglect this second voice of morality which speaks, Gilligan contends, more clearly in the experience of women. This onesidedness has led not only to an inadequate comprehension of moral development, in the sense that women are often judged as developmentally deficient, but also to an inadequate conception of the highest, or most mature, stage of moral judgement. Gilligan argues that such a stage should be marked by an integration of the two voices: that of individual integrity and autonomy, on the one hand, with that of care and connectedness on the other.[54]

Habermas has discussed Gilligan's research and seems to accept much of its substance, at least insofar as it provides some empirical grounds for questioning the conceptualization of the moral point of view which informs Kohlberg's reconstruction of moral development. However, when the moral point of view is reinterpreted along the lines suggested by the communicative model, Habermas thinks that Gilligan's work can then be seen as largely compatible with the way he wants to envision the progress of moral judgement.[55] As I have already shown, the communicative interpretation of the highest stage of morality renounces the "moral rigorism" and certainty of judgement associated with Kantian ethics in general and Kohlberg's formulations in particular. Much of the thrust of Gilligan's critique runs parallel to the insights of communicative ethics. This is particularly evident in Gilligan's view of a mature conception of morality in which "dialogue replaces logical deduction as the mode of moral discovery," and the procedural heart of which is "a process of communication to discuss the other's position and discern the chain of connections through which the consequences of action extend."[56]

On the basis of his communicative model, then, Habermas essentially wants to claim that the two voices of morality, represented by Kohlberg and Gilligan, can be interpreted as different aspects of a single richer voice. In this vein, Habermas casts the whole debate in terms of the "problem of the mediation between *Moralität* and *Sittlichkeit*," that is, between the part of morality which deals with universalistic criteria of justice and the abstract judging of institutional orders, on the one hand, and the part which encompasses concrete relationships and value configurations peculiar to given forms of life, on the other.[57] In a modern, "ratonalized lifeworld," Habermas argues, moral questions must, "in the first instance," be construed "as questions of justice." But this construction alone does not yield determinate solutions to moral problems which require only to be "implemented" in concrete situations of conflict. This mistake, perpetuated by Kohlberg, overlooks what is an inevitable problem: "reintroduc[ing] ... demotivated answers to decontextualized questions back into practice."[58] It is this problem which Gilligan's work, properly understood, helps illuminate. It is a problem of "hermeneutic skill" in relating abstract, general criteria to specific situations, a skill which relies essentially on "sensitivity to context."[59]

At this point, one might begin to suspect that Habermas is somehow reducing the significance of the second voice, by giving it an underlaborer's role. But this image of a superior and inferior role here is a misinterpretation of the communicative model. There is no sense in which either role can claim a superior status. This can be seen if we look at a key element of what being context-sensitive requires within the communicative model. Emotions such as caring and compassion, which are integral to the second voice, are also integral to communicative ethics, because they stand in an "internal relation" to the sort of cognitive achievements expected of discourse participants. That is, there are necessary "emotional condition[s]" for the postconventional, cognitive operations of seriously engaging others in moral dialogue, as well as of imagining the harm which alternative norms may actually entail for the needs and interests of others. In other words, a communicative ethics is crippled if it proceeds in an emotional vacuum.[60]

If one takes Habermas's arguments about compatibility to be persuasive, it is important nevertheless not to intepret them as somehow *subsuming* the insights of Gilligan into the communicative model. A communicative model can indeed identify the deficiencies of moral rigorism and in so doing identify the points at which the formalist tradition must *open up* to another dimension of moral experience (just as it must open up to the dimension of aesthetic experience, as was indicated earlier). But it cannot by itself provide us with any account of this dimension. The reason for this is that, within the communicative model, the domain of morality comes into *direct* view only as subjects confront one another's claims in speech. In other words, the model begins, as Gilligan puts it, with the experience of difference and separation, rather than that of attachment and relationship.[61] If this is the case, one has to conclude that any attempt to deepen Habermas's insights into what a communicative orientation really entails must draw heavily upon sources such as Gilligan which explore the social side of being human, not in terms of language claims and contested norms, but in terms of our character as creatures who are constituted by concrete relationships and the necessity of providing long-term attentive care for their young.[62]

IV. The communicative model and political theory: an initial link

In this chapter and the preceding ones, I have explicated the ideas of communicative action and rationality, and shown how they orient our moral reflections. In other words, Habermas's model of the subject has been sketched out along with some of its moral implications. Furthermore, it has been argued that the moral orientation derived from Habermas's position is rather close to the orientation which critics of universalism embrace, although they tend to think that it can be achieved only by breaking with all forms of universalism.

It should be emphasized again that to speak of a minimal moral orientation here is not to speak of unambiguous, substantive norms of action, but rather of a focusing of moral-political attention and a giving of priority to questions to be asked in situations of conflict. This focusing and according priority will become sharper once I have laid out Habermas's theory of social evolution and modernity, as well as the related interpretation of contemporary capitalism. Before turning to these issues, however, I want to give some sense of how the communicative model's understanding of action and reason can yield provocative interpretations of other basic concepts.

Consider the debate over the concept of power, at least as it has been carried on in Anglo-American political theory since the nineteen sixties. Originally phrased in terms of pluralist or elitist models, and decision-making and non-decisionmaking processes, this debate has since given rise to extended philosophical and methodological reflections.

Most definitions of power are conceptually related to the concept of interest. Simply stated, an exercise of power by one actor is in some way adverse to the interests of some other actor. Pluralists have argued that the only sensible way to attribute interests to an actor is if he/she expresses a preference for some available policy alternative. This way of operationalizing the concept of interest and thus also power is defended on both scientific and moral grounds.[63] Scientifically, this way of thinking about interests is more easily connected with empirically verifiable analyses of power; morally, it steers clear of the latent authoritarianism which inevitably seems to lurk behind any attempt to attribute "real" interests to people which diverge from their expressed interests – with this gap being explained in terms of ideology or false consciousness.

Critics of the pluralists have countered that the concepts of real interests and manipulated consciousness are not so easily swept under the social theorist's rug.[64] Analyses of power using these concepts can be conducted in such a way that they are empirically verifiable, at least to some degree.[65] In relation to moral implications, the critics have argued that the pluralists have simply closed their conceptual eyes to a host of ways in which interests are subtly but effectively shaped by social processes so as to maintain the *status quo* in an existing society.[66] And it is not necessary to pay this cost, critics contend, if a way of conceptualizing real interests can be found which does not lend itself to authoritarian manipulation.

It is at this point that Habermas's communicative model is particularly useful. This model provides two key components of any defensible conceptualization of real interests: some model of the agent and some criteria for thinking about conditions which foster or hinder the exercise of his rationality. Amongst the critics of pluralism, William Connolly has developed probably the best representative of this type of analysis. However, I want to argue that his framework can be given greater coherence if it is rethought in communicative terms.

Connolly argues that when we are considering collective political arrangements, we can say of an individual, A, that:

Policy X is more in A's real interest than policy Y if A, were he to experience the results of both X and Y, would choose X as the result he would rather have for himself.[67]

Now Connolly stresses that this definition is only a "first approximation," and he is aware that it could be interpreted simply as a helpful calculation rule for a narrowly self-interested political actor, concerned with being as efficient as possible in reflectively clarifying and pursuing his self-interest.[68] The way Connolly avoids this sort of interpretation is to argue that the exclusively strategic–rational model of man which it presupposes does not adequately characterize "our shared ideas about persons and responsibility." These ideas have a certain shape, which can be understood by reconstructing "the depth assumptions and commitments embedded in the language and relationships of social life." In other words, Connolly wants to claim that the way his definition of an agent's real interests is to be understood can be constrained by a "loosely bounded transcendental argument" about agents and responsibility.[69]

Amongst the specific claims he makes about how real interests should be construed, Connolly includes the notions that it is in an agent's real interest "to develop the *capacity* to act as a morally responsible" person, and to take into consideration not just his "private wants" but his "higher order interest[s] ... as a social being", that is, his interest in how alternative policies either foster or undermine forms of life which incorporate mutually gratifying human relationships.[70]

Clearly Connolly's short definition is only the beginning of a rich account of the proper conditions and criteria for deliberation about real interests. To his credit, he offers no closed normative framework from which is derived a substantive claim about real interests; rather, he carefully attempts to build into his account a dimension of normativity and intersubjectivity. Although there is much insight in this analysis, it nevertheless results in a picture of the agent and responsibility which lacks a certain coherence. One is simply not too sure how all the conceptual pieces fit together and why.[71]

It is precisely such coherence which the communicative model offers. Its core is the agent's claim to rationality in disputes about proposed collective arrangements, and how that claim makes him/her intersubjectively responsible to others. And the conditions for deliberating about interests are ones which require the agent to cultivate his reflective potential in relation to what he initially might take to be his interests and the needs on which they are based. Moreover, the normative dimension is more sharply demarcated in the communicative model, with its concept of generalizable interest. In disputes over collective arrangements, the agent who maintains his claim to reason must admit that he has a real interest in committing himself to alternatives which incorporate generalizable interests. This is one important dimension of what being morally responsible means. At the same time, however, as I have tried to show, this model does not dictate that one cannot have reflectively clarified, real interests which are particular.

Habermas's model is also useful because it interprets the conditions for deliberation about interests as a structure of *communication*. This orientation is particularly appropriate for a theoretical perspective which aims at supplementing the pluralist's exclusive focus on overt clashes between interests. If the study of power is to include the study of ideology, then one needs a general orientation from which one can begin to talk about the kinds of things which constitute direct and indirect manipulations of consciousness. The notion of an ideal speech situation constitutes just such an orientation; on its basis, one can begin to focus on the ways in which· some structures of communication are "systematically distorted."[72]

This would mean that when a theorist interprets a group's situation, one of his foci of attention will be the possible gap between the self-understanding of individuals in that group – expressed in terms of dominant symbol systems – and the theorist's own hypothetical understanding of how those individuals might interpret their social situation and interests under conditions which more closely approximate those of practical discourse.[73] Now clearly this sort of inquiry is going to be somewhat speculative. However, that does not mean that the critical theorist's imagination can run wild. As I mentioned before, there can be empirical tests for the proferred interpretations, as John Gaventa's study of power in Appalachia has amply illustrated.[74] Moreover, given the moral orientation provided by the communicative model, the researcher's attribution of interests has no stamp of infallibility and is thus not susceptible to authoritarian perversion. As Habermas has repeatedly emphasized, the validity of critical interpretations cannot be divorced entirely from the assent of those to whom the interpretations are directed:

Enlightenment which does not terminate in insight, that is, in freely accepted interpretations, is no enlightenment at all.[75]

If one keeps the foregoing constraints in mind, one can understand the sense in which Habermas continues to see a loose analogy between a psychoanalytic dialogue and a political one between the critical theorist and the addressees of his interpretations. In such "therapeutic critique," *some* assumption of greater insight, and thus authority, on the part of the theorist is inevitable; but, given the encompassing communicative–ethical framework, such an assumption cannot legitimately support any form of authoritarian politics.[76]

In this section, I have tried to show how the communicative model can illuminate the analysis of power in a way which will be useful to political theory. It should be emphasized, however, that this analysis remains limited in that it is tied to a purely action-theoretical framework. The phenomenon of power must also be linked to structural constraints operating upon social life. Grasping these requires, as the next chapter will show, that one have recourse to a systems-theoretical framework.

5

Modernity, rationalization and contemporary capitalism

In chapter 3 it was shown why a simple appeal to the intuition of competent speakers in *modern* societies is not adequate to sustain the strong universalist position Habermas wants to maintain. He is clearly aware of this fact and the search for more adequate support is what provides the philosophical impetus for his ambitious theory of modernity put forward in *The Theory of Communicative Action*. What he tries to accomplish there is a demonstration of why modernity, with its clear manifestation of structures of communicative rationality, should be seen as a *progressive* development; that is, a demonstration of why modernity represents a universally significant achievement in human learning, rather than a way of organizing social and cultural life which is *simply* different from or incommensurable with pre-modernity.

In his earlier work, Habermas tried to make this progressivist perspective plausible as part of a proposed "reconstruction of historical materialism," integrating Marxian insights with those of genetic structuralism. Toward that end he sketched the idea of a theory of social evolution which posited social learning processes not only in the sphere of productive forces, as did Marx, but also in the sphere of normative structures: world views, cultural traditions and institutions.[1] The task of making a theory of such scope convincing is immense; it claims in effect to be able to explain in a developmental–logical way changes in productive forces and normative structures from the very origins of human society to the present.[2] In *The Theory of Communicative Action*, Habermas by and large restricts his attention to problems which, since Weber, have fallen under the rubric of rationalization and modernity.

The specific goal Habermas pursues there of demonstrating why modernity represents a universally significant advance in human learning puts him into a rather uneasy relationship with his forerunners in the Frankfurt tradition of critical theory. Horkheimer and Adorno in *The Dialectic of Enlightenment* pursued an analysis which so thoroughly condemned modernity that no perspective seemed to be left open from which it could be seen as truly progressive. Although Habermas wants to do justice to this critique, he nevertheless feels that the particular approach chosen by Horkheimer and Adorno is both theoretically unfruitful and unbalanced in its assessment of modernity. The real challenge, he maintains, lies in conceptualizing modernity in a way which neither overplays its costs, nor uncritically celebrates it the way mainstream social science has done. The communicative model allows this challenge to be met, for it opens the phenomenon of modernity up to a more complex reading, one which locates both the universal, rational *potential* manifested in "modern structures of consciousness" and the "selective" or "one-sided" *use* of this potential in the societal processes of Western rationalization or modernization.[3]

In the broadest sense, Habermas's project is that of resolving what he takes to be the underlying problem of that modern self-consciousness which first emerged at the end of the eighteenth century, after the high-water mark of the Enlightenment. As the corrosiveness of modern consciousness on religion and tradition became increasingly evident, that consciousness began to experience itself as self-alienating. Modern consciousness is marked from this point on by a search for "self-assurance," or a search for some standards which are both made available by that consciousness and yet can provide some normative guide for it in modern life. Modernity, in other words, *"must create its normativity out of itself."*[4] And it is Habermas's intention to develop just those standards which will allow modernity to interpret itself in a way which is self-critical, but which gives some basis for normative self-assurance.

His intepretation of modernity will be elucidated as follows. First, I will show how the communicative model allows him to draw new insights about rationalization processes out of Max Weber's work (section I). These insights, which are derived from his perspective on action theory, must then be combined with a systems perspective into a "two-stage" theory of society (section II). Only in this way can the "pathologies" of a rationalized society be adequately illuminated. He refers here to the "colonization of the lifeworld" (section III) and the "cultural impoverishment" of society (section IV), and he links these phenomena with an analysis of new forms of opposition in contemporary capitalism (section V). With the analysis of these pathologies, and their causes and effects, Habermas's project moves down to what I identified in chapter 1 as the Hegelian-Marxian dimension of critical reflection. This is the dimension in which, first, the communicative model's positive heuristic value for concrete social analysis is demonstrated; and secondly, the normative implications of the model are formulated in interpretations which provide some minimal ethical-political orientation to social actors.

I. Modern structures of consciousness and the achievement of a "rationalized lifeworld"

In the present section, I want to examine how Habermas uses the notion of communicative reason as the key to a systematic reconstruction of the development of modern structures of consciousness, and why he thinks this development can be understood as a gain in rationality for the human species. I will indicate first why Habermas turns to Weber's account of rationalization as his point of entry into this complex question, and then show how he modifies Weber in accordance with the communicative model. Next it will be shown why the concept of "lifeworld" must necessarily be integrated into the theory of communicative action in order to get beyond Weber's understanding of rationalization and its paradoxes.

What attracts Habermas to Weber is that, although he renounced eighteenth and nineteenth century philosophies of history, with their naive faith in linear progress and the universality of Western reason, nevertheless the themes of reason, universality and modernity remain intertwined in his work in a way which is no longer typical of contemporary sociological theory.[5]

Although Weber's name is indissolubly linked with rationality and rationalization, the fact is that his ideas are "tantalizingly sketchy," scattered throughout his work, and often expressed in ambiguous ways.[6] The concept of rationalization especially is used in many senses, as Weber traces that long process of development from the breakdown of magical–mythical ways of seeing the world to the emergence of the Protestant ethic which allowed purposive rationality [*Zweckrationalität*] to be motivationally and institutionally anchored in such a way that capitalistic rationalization could finally take off. It is no simple matter to link all of Weber's statements together into a cohesive, multi-dimensional account of the different senses and degrees of rationalization which are involved in that process.[7]

Habermas does not think that such an account can be given unless significant changes are made. The root of the problem is that Weber's theoretical framework is too restricted to grasp adequately the range of phenomena he hoped to account for. The task Habermas sets for himself, then, is to rethink Weber's theory, using the communicative model's resources to overcome its difficulties. The ultimate purpose of this undertaking is, however, not simply the interpretive one of generating greater coherence; it is rather the provision of a richer account of what Weber saw as the costs of modernization or rationalization: the loss of freedom in an increasingly bureaucratized society and the loss of meaning or unity in a fully disenchanted world.[8]

Habermas characterizes his approach to Weber as "a flexible exploration and deliberate exploitation."[9] Undoubtedly specialists will find much to contest in this treatment of Weber. For present purposes, however, I am not going to be concerned with such problems, but only with giving some sense of the audaciousness of this approach and the role it plays in the overall project of a critical research program.

From Habermas's perspective, Weber's analysis of rationalizaton is interesting on three different levels. First, in his sociological study of religion, Weber analyzed that process of disenchantment, whereby the magical–mythical view of the world broke down under the influence of what he called "world religions" (Christianity, Judaism, Hinduism, Buddhism and Islam). The universal hallmark of such religious–metaphysical worldviews is that they represent the cosmos as a coherent, meaningful whole, within which an explanation for suffering is given as well as directions for the sort of life conduct which is necessary to earn salvation from that suffering. What Weber was particularly interested in was how this universal rationalization process happened, in the West, to give rise also to a process of "societal rationalization," that is, a rapid increase in the degree to which areas of social life, especially the economy and administration, were organized according to the criteria of formal, purposive rationality. It was the "Protestant ethic" which answered this question for Weber, because it allowed for Christianity's ascetic, methodical conduct of life, which had first existed only in medieval monasteries, to be turned outward to extra-religious areas of social activity.[10]

In this way, Weber connected rationalization at the level of worldviews with a second, societal form of rationalization. Since his explanatory interest was focused on the latter process, it is not surprising that he left his discussion of the former process in a relatively undeveloped state. In fact, Habermas argues, Weber's discussion of disenchantment and religious worldviews makes use of "a complex, but largely unclarified concept of rationality."[11] The concept of *Zweckrationalität*, which is the key to the analysis of societal rationalization, is simply not complex enough to comprehend the earlier process of rationalization.

This difficulty is compounded by another one which arises at a third level of rationalization: where the rationalization of world views results in a differentiation of various cultural "value spheres." The idea here is that the modern social world "is composed of a number of distinct provinces of activity, each having its own inherent dignity and its own immanent norms."[12] The emergence of these different spheres with their different "inner logics" is something Weber spoke of primarily to emphasize that the different logics were doomed to irreconcilable conflict, for example the conflict between an ethic of "brotherliness," on the one hand, and the values of art and eros, or the demands of a capitalist economic life, on the other hand. In short, this differentiation and conflict represented one aspect of what Weber saw as the irretrievable loss of unity of meaning in the modern world.

Weber's discussion of rationalization at the level of cultural spheres of value is far from satisfactory. For example, what status does the assertion of irreconcilability have? It sometimes seems as though Weber advances this proposition as a metaphysical truth. And what exactly does it mean to assert that the value spheres have an autonomy or "inner logic" [*Eigengesetz-lichkeit*]? As one recent commentator puts it, Weber's analysis here at best "defies easy characterization," and at worst "obscures rather than clarifies his diagnosis of modernity."[13]

Habermas starts his reinterpretation of the three levels of rationalization by focusing on the changes brought about in structures of consciousness by the rise of the world religions. According to Habermas, Weber's concept of rationalization at this level remained largely unclarified because he focused too single-mindedly on tracing the connection between religion and the ultimate emergence of a certain sort of economic *ethics*. He thus failed to flesh out other dimensions of rationalization at the level of worldviews. He could have, for example, directed attention to the differentiation of religious worldviews from magical ones in terms of changes in *cognitive* structures. Investigation into this dimension of rationalization might have focused on the contemplative theoretical attitude which appears first (at least in the West) in classical Greek cosmology. Moreover, Weber's investigation of the Protestant ethic's importance in fostering an ascetic, methodical orientation in social life in general could have been matched by an investigation into cultural phenomena which helped in bringing the theoretical attitude out of its purely contemplative orientation and into domains of action, resulting in the emergence of modern experimental sciences.

Fleshing out the notion of a rationalization of worldviews with speculations such as these requires that one possess a clear theoretical framework, in terms of which one systematically generates insights. Weber does not seem to have had one, and Habermas argues that the strongest candidate for this role is one which combines Piaget's genetic structuralism with the communicative model. Habermas thus sees the experience of disenchantment as structurally parallel to the shift which Piaget observed in children from an "egocentric" consciousness to a "decentered" one. Disenchantment thus signifies a breakdown of a "sociocentric" consciousness of a seamless magical–mythical world and the construction of a decentered consciousness which recognizes clear demarcations between the natural, social and subjective worlds. The demarcation of formal world concepts also means increasing recognition of the differentiated system of validity claims corresponding to the three worlds.[14]

This change can be described as a process of rationalization because it enhances the learning capacity of mankind. It does this because it provides actors with the conceptual means of constructing a reflexive or *self-critical* perspective; that is, the "categorial scaffolding" constituted by the system of three world relations and corresponding validity claims makes possible an articulated consideration and evaluation of alternative interpretations of what is the case, what is legitimate and what is authentic self-expression. It is this complex, multidimensional learning potential of modernity that Habermas wants to emphasize, not just the mastering of formal, operational modes of cognition, leading to the capacity to do science and technology. The latter, logocentric emphasis is in fact what has often led to "an uncritical self-interpretation of the modern world that is fixated on knowing and mastering external nature."[15]

In order for this enhanced learning potential, which emerges with the rationalization of worldviews, to be set free, it must be crystallized into separate, "specialized forms of argumentation" which are institutionalized in corresponding cultural spheres of action. Here one sees how Habermas wishes to reinterpret Weber's notion of cultural value spheres. Although Weber seemed to have several such spheres in mind, Habermas argues that we can only sharply distinguish three: science and technology, morality and law, and art and literature.[16] The fact that only three can be separated is a reflection of the fact that the idea of different inner logics can only be made plausible by mapping it onto the three-fold system of validity claims.

Once this is understood, one can see the narrowness of Weber's focus on only one aspect of cultural rationalization: the emergence of the Protestant ethic. That focus restricted the investigation of such rationalization in two ways. First, a similar sort of analysis of learning potential could have been carried out for the emergence of both modern sicence and modern art. And secondly, Weber's analysis of learning in the ethical sphere was directed only to uncovering the cultural pre-conditions for capitalism; his investigation could have been broadened to the question of the emergence of the structures of postconventionalist ethics in general, and their embodiment in the foundations of modern law. Habermas's overall point here is to demonstrate that Weber "did not exhaust the systematic scope of his theoretical approach."[17]

The communicative model thus gives Habermas what he thinks is a deeper understanding of that process of cultural rationalization which begins with disenchantment and comes to fruition in the institutional anchoring of specialized forms of argumentation. This institutionalization takes the form of:

(a) the establishment of a scientific enterprise in which empirical–scientific problems can be dealt with according to internal truth standards, independently of theological doctrines and separately from basic moral–practical questions; (b) the institutionalization of an artistic enterprise in which the production of art is gradually set loose from cultic–ecclesiastical and courtly–patronal bonds, and the reception of works of art by an art-enjoying public of readers, spectators, and listeners is mediated through professionalized aesthetic criticism; and finally (c) the professional intellectual treatment of questions of ethics, political theory, and jurisprudence in schools of law, in the legal system, and in the legal public sphere.[18]

It is in relation to this overall process of cultural rationalization that Habermas wants to stake his universalist claim, one which is clearly stronger than anything Weber had in mind.[19] He asserts that:

If we do not frame Occidental rationalism from the conceptual perspective of purposive rationality and mastery of the world, if instead we take as our point of departure the rationalization of worldviews that results in a decentered understanding of the world, then we have to face the question, whether there is not a formal stock of universal structures of consciousness expressed in the cultural value spheres that develop, according to their own logics, under the abstract standards of truth, normative rightness, and authenticity. Are or are not the structures of scientific thought, posttraditional legal and moral representations, and autonomous art, as they have developed in the framework of Western culture, the possession of that "community of civilized men" that is present as a regulative idea? The universalist position does not have to deny the pluralism and the incompatibility of historical versions of "civilized humanity"; but it regards this multiplicity of forms of life as limited to cultural contents, and it asserts that every culture must share certain formal properties of the modern understanding of the world, if it is at all to attain a certain degree of "conscious awareness". . . .[20]

I will elaborate more on the defense Habermas gives for this universalist claim in the next chapter. For now, what is important to see is that he wants to propose that it is only after one has adequately conceptualized this universally significant process of cultural rationalization that one can properly understand the process of societal rationalization. Now, for Weber, there was of course nothing inevitable about the former process giving rise to the latter; and in fact Weber's point was to show that only with the appearance of Protestantism was there a form of postconventional ethics which allowed the connection to take place. However, in Weber's mind, once the connection occurred, societal rationalization had only one possible course to take: the spread of spheres of purposive–rational action through society. In other words, societal rationalization was *identified* with growing purposive rationalization. But, for Habermas, such an identification is not necessary. One can, he argues, open up the question of whether purposive rationalization is only *one* possible way of developing that broader *potential* for the rationalization of action which is made available with the culture of modernity.[21] Perhaps, to put it slightly differently, Western *modernization* constitutes only a one-sided utilization of the rationality potential of *modernity*. The most important implication which would flow from such a reconceptualization is that one could now see our contemporary dilemma – loss of freedom, loss of meaning – against the background of "counterfactually projected possibilities" for organizing social action differently.[22]

In order to open up the conceptual space adequately for such lines of thought, one has to make two major theoretical shifts. On the one hand, the theory of communicative action has to be integrated with an account of the lifeworld; and, on the other, the action-theoretical frame of analysis has to be supplemented with a systems-theoretical frame.

The notion of "lifeworld" [*Lebenswelt*] must be introduced in order to link action theory more convincingly with rationalization processes. This means understanding not just how particular actions might be judged as rational, but how the rationality potential made available in modern culture is "fed into" particular actions and thus makes possible a "rational conduct of life" in general.[23]

Habermas realizes that the process of coming to an understanding in specific situations must take place against the "horizon of a lifeworld" constituted by "more or less diffuse, ... unproblematic, background convictions." From the viewpoint of understanding-oriented action, the lifeworld "stores the interpretive work of preceding generations" and thus functions as a "conservative counterweight to the risk of disagreement that arises with every actual process of reaching an understanding. . ."[24] The things which become problematic in a sequence of communicative action must thus be seen as only particular aspects which are temporarily lifted out of an unproblematic, shared horizon defining what is the case, what should be done and how authentic expressions and works of art are to be assessed.

The real distinctiveness of Habermas's account of the lifeworld enters with the introduction of the concept of a "rationalized lifeworld." The formal system of world-relations and corresponding validity claims come to constitute, in the modern world, "general structures" of the lifeworld, that is, structures which remain the same even within different "particular lifeworlds and forms of life." As these basic structures of modern consciousness are institutionalized in differentiated cultural spheres (as indicated above), a crucial change occurs in the relationship between action and lifeworld:

To the degree that the institutionalized production of knowledge that is specialized according to cognitive, normative, and aesthetic validity claims penetrates to the level of everyday communication and replaces traditional knowledge in its interaction-guiding functions, there is a rationalization of everyday practice that is accessible only from the perspective of action oriented to reaching understanding – a rationalization of the lifeworld that Weber neglected as compared with the rationalization of action systems like the economy and the state. In a rationalized lifeworld the need for achieving understanding is met less and less by a reservoir of traditionally certified interpretations immune from criticism; at the level of a completely decentered understanding of the world, the need for consensus must be met more and more frequently by risky, because rationally motivated, agreement.[25]

In a rationalized lifeworld, then, the "formal scaffolding" of modern structures of consciousness can increasingly be used by the individual as a framework in terms of which new experiences are accommodated to the stock of unproblematic, substantive background convictions which constitute his lifeworld. As this occurs, each agent's own critical capacities are increasingly integrated into the ongoing reproduction of that lifeworld. And this means an increasingly rationalized orientation to social action, for now such actions are guided less and less by normative prescriptions grounded in opaque sources of authority.[26] In sum, Habermas introduces a second dimension to societal rationalization, one that transpires "more in the implicitly known structures of the lifeworld than in explicitly known action orientations (as Weber suggested)."[27]

This insight has to be further developed, however, before one can adequately understand and rethink the costs and paradoxes of rationalization which Weber identified. In particular the relationship between communicative action and lifeworld has to be further elaborated in a way which makes a more convincing connection with a basic question of social theory: how does society reproduce itself both symbolically and materially? Within Habermas's theoretical framework, the question of symbolic reproduction is the same as the question: how is the lifeworld reproduced? And framing the issues this way also throws into relief the importance of communicative action for social theory. Attention must now focus on the role it plays in the reproduction of the lifeworld, that is, on how communicative action generates ongoing patterns of social relations and the integration of individuals into them. In short, communicative action now becomes interesting as "a principle of sociation."[28] And one of the hallmarks of modernity is the enhanced role of this principle in organizing the symbolic reproduction of society.

In order to understand this reproduction process adequately, however, the notion of the lifeworld must be further articulated. The diffuse notion of an "unproblematic background" is simply too undifferentiated as it stands. In searching for a way to elaborate this notion, Habermas finds that no existing theories of the lifeworld satisfactorily grasp the breadth of what actually constitutes the unproblematic background of action. Different thinkers have focused on the lifeworld as a *cultural* storehouse, or as a source of expectations about the ordering of *social* relations, or as a mileu out of which *individual competences* for speech and action are formed.[29] Habermas, on the other hand, wants to emphasize the fact that part of what constitutes a rationalized lifeworld is its "structural differentiation" of precisely these three dimensions: culture, society and personality. The connection of this differentiation with enhanced rationalization is explained by Habermas as follows:

In relation to *culture and society* the structural differentiation indicates an increasing uncoupling of world views from institutions; in relation to *personality and society,* an expansion of the available space for the generation of interpersonal relations; and in relation to *culture and personality,* it indicates that the renewal of traditions is ever more strongly dependent on individuals' readiness for critique and capacity for innovation. The end point of these evolutionary trends is: for culture, a condition allowing for the continual revision of traditions which have become unhardened and reflexive; for society, a condition allowing for the dependency of legitimate orders on formal procedures for the . . . justification of norms; and for personality, a condition allowing for the continually self-steered stabilization of a highly abstract ego-identity.[30]

These evolutionary trends can proceed, Habermas contends, only to the degree that communicative action functions as the medium for the reproduction of the lifeworld. What he means by this is that rationally motivated action orientations are sustained only when the different aspects of sociation are mediated by processes of understanding, in which agents take up a performative attitude toward the different validity claims raised in "cognitive interpretations, moral expectations, expressions and valuations." It is only when agents take up such an attitude, as they do when they engage in communicative action, that a rational "transference of validity" [*Geltungstransfer*] across social space and time is possible.[31]

We can see that, as a consequence of the structural differentiation of the lifeworld into culture, society and personality, we must also think in terms of differentiated processes of reproduction. These processes are identified by Habermas as, respectively, "cultural reproduction, social integration, and socialization." The first process is evaluated by the degree to which there is "a continuation of valid knowledge"; the second by the degree to which there is "a stabilization of group solidarity"; and the third by the degree to which there is "a formation of responsible actors."[32]

Each of these three reproduction processes produces resources for the maintainance, not just of the directly corresponding structural component of the lifeworld, but rather for all three components. This complex relationship is represented in Figure 1. I will make further reference to this figure later.

The foregoing development of the concept of lifeworld and of its interrelationship with communicative action is necessary, as I have said, in order for Habermas to account for the symbolic reproduction of society. Communicative action now can be understood as a medium of sociation through which this process occurs. However, in order to grasp the material reproduction of society, one must turn from action theory to systems theory, which envisions strategic actions guided by systemic imperatives. These

Reproduction processes	Structural components		
	Culture	Society	Personality
Cultural reproduction	Interpretative schemata susceptible to consensus ("valid knowledge")	Legitimations	Behavioral patterns influential in self-formation, educational goals
Social integration	Obligations	Legitimately ordered interpersonal relations	Social memberships
Socialization	Interpretative accomplishments	Motivation for norm-conformative actions	Capability for interaction ("personal identity")

Figure 1   *Resources contributed by reproduction processes to maintaining the structural components of the life-world.* (*Source:* REPLY, *p. 279, slightly modified.*)

imperatives operate through the "de-linguistified media" of money and power, as I will show later. For the moment, what is important to understand is simply that, in Habermas's view, one cannot comprehend the paradox of rationalization, without shifting the theoretical focus from the simple level of different types of action to the more complex level of different principles of sociation operating in the symbolic and material processes of social reproduction. Weber tried to explain the paradox by showing how purposive–rational action orientations increasingly began to undermine the value-rational action orientations of Protestantism, in which they were originally embedded and which first made their radical expansion possible. Habermas, on the other hand, wants to argue that the paradoxical relation exists not, as Weber thought, *"between different types of action"* orientation, but rather

between *principles of sociation* – between the mechanism of linguistic communication that is oriented to validity claims – a mechanism that emerges in increasing purity from the rationalization of the lifeworld – and those de-linguistified steering media [money and power] through which systems of success-oriented actions are differentiated out.[33]

Before turning to the introduction of the systems perspective, I want to pause and take up two issues which are raised by Habermas's introduction of the concept of a rationalized lifeworld which is reproduced through the medium of communicative action. The first problem is that both concepts, rationalized lifeworld and communicative action, seem to have an ambiguous status; they apparently both describe something about modern life and prescribe a certain way it should be lived. The significance of the prescriptive or normative role will actually only become fully evident after I introduce the systems perspective and flesh out Habermas's notion of a one-sided rationalization of modern society. That analysis will show how the logic of systems integration invades spheres of life previously integrated by communicative action. But the problem I want to address now is one which can be dealt with apart from this clash between different principles of sociation. This problem concerns the way in which communicative sociation itself functions in modern life. Habermas might be interpreted as offering a rather blindly congratulatory view. By this I mean that one might understand him to be claiming that our modern, everyday life is in fact permeated by a thorough-going criticism of all traditions and norms, since our lives are so deeply structured by the expectations of a communicative mode of action, drawing on the resources of a rationalized lifeworld. Ideal and reality, as it were, coincide. Were this Habermas's position, it would certainly gloss over many forms of domination in modern life.

This is, however, a misreading. The existence of a rationalized lifeworld does not mean that all communicative action will make equal use of its potential. Social institutions often function in such a way that communicative action operates only to reproduce "normatively secured consensus." For example, the institution of the traditional family has operated in such a way that women's roles were for a long time withdrawn from the sort of normative scrutiny that was directed toward other areas of modern society, where something more closely resembling a discursive or "communicatively achieved consensus" was expected.[34] It is this kind of consensus which is the normative ideal: one which equally respects each individual as a source of claims and opinions, and which draws fully on the resources of a rationalized lifeworld. A "normatively secured consensus," on the other hand, is one which blocks in some way the process of critical, communicative dialogue.

Understood in this way, Habermas's position is not blind to a whole range of forms of domination in modern life which are significant but are not adequately understood simply as pathologies emerging from the clash of the two principles of sociation, forms such as racism and the oppression of women. However, it is one thing to say that Habermas's position is not blind to such phenomena; it is another thing to say that it provides the grounds for a sufficient comprehension of them. For this, one must simply look to more specifically focused theories. I will return to this question and try to throw more light on it in section V, after some of the other key components of the analysis of modernity have been elaborated.

There is a second question which arises from the conjunction of the idea of the lifeworld with that of a rationalization process. In order to grasp the problem, it is helpful to think in terms of a distinction between what Dallmayr calls a "weak" versus a "strong" view of the lifeworld. The weak view draws "its inspiration chiefly from Schutzian (and Husserlian) phenomenology." Within such a theoretical strategy, the lifeworld appears as something like a symbolic network within which subjects interact. This can be contrasted with the "strong" view which traces "its roots to Gadamer (and Heidegger)," in whose work the lifeworld's pre-conscious and pre-subjective character is more heavily stressed.[35]

Habermas's account of the lifeworld possesses characteristics which would seem to make it fall into the weak category. This is most notably evident in his referring to the system of validity claims as a formal structure of the lifeworld which is increasingly at the conscious disposal of modern subjects. The significance of this for proponents of the strong view, such as Dallmayr, is that it constitutes a key place in Habermas's work where traditional, subject-centered figures of thought still dominate. Otherness again becomes simply a field which is increasingly occupied by the rational subject. In this regard, Habermas's thought allows for the lifeworld to be "steadily eclipsed and finally absorbed," as actors reproduce it in an increasingly conscious and critical way.[36]

Such a sweeping judgement is, I think, not warranted. The lifeworld is never rendered totally transparent in Habermas's view. Certainly the learning processes which he associated with modernity allow for the reproduction of the lifeworld in a more conscious way, but this process has limits. This can perhaps best be seen if one considers how communicative rationality operates upon the substantive values and need interpretations which are embodied in a shared lifeworld. As was shown in the last chapter, such values and need interpretations are constitutive of any conception of the good society. Now the communicative rationalization of normative claims between actors can put certain limits on what can count for them as a good society, but it possesses no resources itself which would suffice for the generation of a substantive ideal of the good society. In brief, normative judgements about justice cannot subsume evaluative judgements about the good society. The latter always draw on sources which can never be made fully conscious or be fully rationalized.

Habermas's position here might be faulted on a number of grounds. One might, for example, ask for a better accounting of how rational normative judgements interact with evaluative ones. But it does seem to me that he recognizes a distinct limit on the former, and that this limit illustrates that, in at least one dimension, the lifeworld is not swallowed up by rationalization processes.

II. Systems theory and rationalization

The preceding section has shown how the communicative model and the framework of genetic structuralism provide an interpretation of certain distinctive ways in which modern life is structured. By identifying modern consciousness and a rationalized lifeworld as generating an enhancement of learning capacity, Habermas stresses the *enabling* aspects of these structural phenomena for human action. This means that when he turns to systems theory as a resource for comprehending other ways in which modern life is structured, he already has a perspective which allows him to stress how these other structural phenomena can generate crucial *constraints* on the rationalization of action.[37] His analysis of these constraints takes the form of a reinterpretation of the loss of freedom and loss of meaning entailed by modernization. Habermas conceptualizes this loss in terms of systemic threats to the communicative infrastructure through which the complex process of symbolic reproduction occurs. "This communicative infrastructure is threatened by two tendencies which are intertwined and mutually reinforcing: by *systemically induced reification* and *cultural impoverishment*."[38]

When Habermas first introduced the idea of a combined lifeworld-systems perspective in *Legitimation Crisis*, he was not able to go beyond a rudimentary beginning.[39] The massive size of *The Theory of Communicative Action* is due in substantial part to his sustained effort to develop a convincing integration of these two theoretical approaches.

In one way, Habermas understands his attempt to link an action or lifeworld perspective with a systems perspective as following up Marx's analysis. The latter, with his metaphor of base and superstructure, was also struggling with the problem of how to understand the interconnection between the processes of material and symbolic reproduction. Habermas, like Marx, is especially interested in the impact of the imperatives of material reproduction on everyday life, as well as the role ideology plays in how these imperatives are understood.

Although Marx's own analysis is instructive in some ways, the tradition of Western Marxism has not added much which is directly helpful to this project. Lukács's analysis of the phenomenon of reification is somewhat useful, as is Horkheimer and Adorno's distinctive reading of the pathology of rationalization. The latter, however, were wedded, as was Weber, both to an inadequate conception of action and an inadequate way of grasping the systemic structuring of modern life. What is needed, according to Habermas, is not just a critique of instrumental reason such as Horkheimer and Adorno developed, but rather a "critique of functionalistic reason," which can be obtained only when a systems perspective is integrated with a communicative model of action. From the resulting theoretical viewpoint, the key notion of reification can then be reinterpreted as "deformations of the lifeworld" which are "*systemically induced*."[40]

When Habermas speaks of functionalistic reason, he is speaking of rationality as conceptualized within systems theory. A system becomes more rational as its complexity increases; that is, as its range of adaptation to environmental changes is enhanced. In this light, the evolutionary development of societies can be understood as an increasing differentiation of social structures which enhances the capacity for *material* reproduction. The specific problem Habermas wants to illuminate is how the development of capitalism, with its differentiated subsystems of economy and administration, can be understood both as an evolutionary *advance* from a systems perspective, but also as a phenomenon which methodically *undermines* the processes by which a rationalized lifeworld is symbolically reproduced.

The route Habermas chooses for joining the systems and lifeworld perspectives is to focus on how each throws light on the different ways in which actors are sociated or coordinated with one another. One must distinguish:

> mechanisms of action coordination which bring the *action orientations* of participants into accord with one another, from mechanisms which stabilize the non-intended connections of actions across the functional web of *action consequences*. The integration of an action system is produced in the one case by a normatively secured or communicatively achieved consensus, and in the other case by a non-normative regulation of individual decisions, which operates outside of the consciousness of actors. This distinction between a *social* integration,* operating upon action orientations, and a *systems* integration of society, which operates behind action orientations, requires a corresponding differentiation in the concept of society itself. . . Society [can be] conceived from the participant perspective of acting subjects as the *lifeworld of a social group*. On the other hand society can be conceived from the observer perspective of someone not involved as merely a *system of actions*, in which actions attain a functional value according to their contribution to the maintenance of the system.[41]

Among contemporary social theorists, Talcott Parsons was the one who focused the most attention on the problem of joining a systems with an action framework. Although he asked the right question, Habermas contends his answers were never satisfactory. In his early work, he could not develop an adequate theory of how action orientations are sociated, since he adhered to a *zweckrational* concept of action; and, in his later work, the action framework itself was submerged within his systems framework. When this occurred, there was no way in which Parsons could conceptualize pathologies of modernization, since there was no longer any way to conceptualize how the lifeworld might have structural characteristics which are *resistant* to functional imperatives.[42] Parson's later work thus shares failings which Habermas attributes to all attempts to reduce society to the model of an organic system.

Such attempts interpret the distinction between the continuity or breakdown in the life of a society in the same way as one would think about the physical survival or destruction of an organism. This analogy, however, is

---

*Habermas's terminology is a little confusing here. As was indicated earlier, he uses the term "social integration" (*sozial Integration*) to name *one* of the three aspects of communicative sociation. But he also uses the term in a broader sense, as a synonym for communicative sociation. It is this latter sense which is expressed in this quotation, as well as in *LC*, Part I. For the sake of clarity I will use the term in its former sense only from here on.

misleading, for it fails to understand that the maintenance or continuity of a society is something which is experienced by its members not only in terms of ongoing physical life but in terms of categories constituting some conception of the *good* life and collective *identity*.[43] This empirically important phenomenon can only be grasped from a non-systemic perspective. Systems of action, unlike organic systems,

> are inaccessible to observation and must be unlocked hermeneutically; that is, from the internal perspective of members. The entities which are supposed to be subsumed under systems concepts from the external perspective of an observer, must *first* have been identified as lifeworlds of socially identified groups and been understood in their symbolic structures. The internal logic of the symbolic reproduction of the lifeworld (which we have discussed under the viewpoints of cultural reproduction, social integration and socialization), gives rise to *internal limits* to the reproduction of society... The ... structures, in terms of which the identity of a society stands and falls, are structures of a lifeworld and therefore are accessible exclusively to a reconstructive analysis which is directed to the intuitive knowledge of participants.[44]

Thus, for Habermas, any social theory which submerges the action perspective within the systems perspective will be flawed. The same, however, is true of any social theory which adheres to a conceptual strategy which is purely interpretive or hermeneutical.[45] The problem is how exactly to conceptualize the relationship between the two perspectives. Basically, Habermas argues that the proper connection can be made only when "one develops the system concept out of the lifeworld concept." This methodological decision is intended to allow social theory to grasp what Habermas argues is a change in "the object itself"; that is, a change which social life undergoes in the experience of disenchantment and modernization.[46]

The process of disenchantment comes to fruition, as we have seen, in the differentiated structures of a rationalized lifeworld, where actions are increasingly coordinated by consensual agreement rather than normative prescriptions. With this progressive shift in the way actions are sociated there is, however, a corresponding increase in the potential for dissensus and instability. This problem, though, can be met because modern structures of consciousness have also delimited in a clear fashion an objectivating attitude toward both the social as well as the natural world. This sharp differentiation between success-oriented action, on the one hand, and communicative action, on the other, opens up "a free space for subsystems of purposive rational action." And the progressive generalization of such strategic orientations around the media of money and power means that action coordination can be increasingly cut off or "uncoupled" from "lifeworld contexts ... in which processes of understanding are always embedded." In other words, the scope of sociation guided by systemic imperatives can be dramatically enhanced.[47]

Thus, the emergence of a rationalized lifeworld not only sets free the "rationality potential of communicative action," but it is also a necessary condition for a new level of systems differentiation, characterized by the development of a capitalist economy and a modern form of adminis-tration.[48] These latter developments and their significance for material re-production cannot be grasped adequately unless the *internal* perspective broadens to *incorporate* an observer's *external* point of view. This shift of methodological attitude occurs by means of "a reflexive objectification of the limits ... of the lifeworld concept," which allows the latent functional connections between actions to become thematic.[49]

Habermas's theoretical strategy allows him to reconceptualize Weber's contention that the rationalization processes of modernity are deeply paradoxical. This paradox can now be seen as a result of the fact that "The rationalization of the lifeworld makes possible a kind of systemic integration that enters into competition with the integrating principle of reaching understanding and, under certain conditions, has a disintegrative effect on the lifeworld."[50] One can now understand the full sense of Habermas's remark, quoted earlier, that the rationalization paradox relates, not to dif-ferent types of action, be they value-rational or communicative–rational or strategic–rational, but to different principles of sociation.

III.   The costs of modernization: "colonization of the lifeworld"

In Marx's own thought, there is a partial understanding of the phenomenon Habermas calls the "uncoupling" of systemically integrated spheres of action from those integrated by communicative action. Marx concerned himself with the process by which the economic subsystem of capitalist society instrumentalized traditional forms of life by transforming concrete labor into units of abstract labor power. This process, as well as the reifi-cation of market relations, which ascribed to them a quasi-natural life, become in Habermas's terminology the "mediatization" of the lifeworld and the uncoupling of the economic system. Now the purpose of Habermas's framework is, of course, not simply to give us new labels for those phenomena; it is also to provide a perspective from which certain short-comings in Marx's work can be identified and from which a better understanding can be reached concerning the problems of *advanced* capitalism.[51]

Before turning attention to these differences, however, it is important to stress a key link between the Marxian tradition and Habermas's analysis. This link is that both look to class conflict as the ultimate cause for the "hypertrophic," or "imbalanced" growth of systemic integration imperatives.[52] Seeing class conflict as the basic causal factor, Marx focused his analysis on economic reification processes. This focus, Habermas argues, is the "decisive weakness" in Marx's theory, the "overgeneralization of a special case of the subsumption of the lifeworld under system imperatives." Although the cause of reification may arise in the sphere of labor and capital, the process of reification and its effects is also experienced in other spheres of life. Here Habermas draws some inspiration from Lukács, at least to the degree that the latter became aware of the importance of "class-unspecific side effects" of the process of capitalist modernization.[53] Figure 2 provides a framework within which these effects can be deciphered.

Habermas's focus on two subsystems, two media and four key roles gives him an expanded field of action which can undergo the reifying effects of the expansion of systemic integration. Marx analyzed these effects on only one role (no. 1); Weber added another (no. 3). However, in order to comprehend the true dimensions of the loss of freedom in advanced capitalism, one must take into account all four roles and their changing relationship, as well as the changing relationship between the two subsystems. I will turn to these questions in a moment, after noting the other weaknesses Habermas finds in Marx.

Two other shortcomings in Marx follow from his failure to conceptualize the advances of modernity in a way which allows them to be analytically separated from their one-sided utilization in capitalist modernization processes. This failure led Marx, first, to underappreciate the evolutionary place of media-steered subsystems as the keys to enhanced material reproduction. This underappreciation led him in turn to think that the abolition of capitalism was synonymous with a total reabsorption of these subsystems into the lifeworld. He thereby failed to understand, unlike Weber, "that *every* modern society, regardless of how its class structure is produced, must exhibit a high degree of structural differentiation."[54]

Marx's framework also provides no criteria for differentiating between "the destruction of traditional forms of life" and the deformation of "posttraditional forms of life." In the uprooting of traditional forms of life, Marx sees only the onset of a process of lifeworld reification. He has no means of conceptualizing modernity in a way which allows one to see *both* the *reification* of the lifeworld *and* its *structural differentiation*. Thus his analysis is not sensitive enough to show how the pathologies of capitalism differ *rela-*

Lifeworld: institutional orders and roles		Exchange relationships and media of exchange	Media-steered subsystems
Private sphere	1 Employee	Labor power (**P**) ⟶ ⟵ Income (**M**)	Economic system
	2 Consumer	⟵ Goods and services (**M**) Demand (**M**) ⟶	
Public sphere	3 Client	Taxes (**M**) ⟶ ⟵ Organizational achievements (**P**)	Administrative system
	4 Citizen	⟵ Political decisions (**P**) Mass loyalty (**P**) ⟶	

Key: **M** money
      P power

Figure 2   *Relations between system and lifeworld from a systems perspective*
(Source: TKH, p. 473. Slightly modified).

tive to the degree of rationalization of the lifeworld. The reification of an extensively rationalized lifeworld is to be measured only in relation to "the conditions of communicative sociation," and not in relation to "a nostalgically conjured, often romanticized past of premodern forms of life."[55]

The kind of reification Habermas wants to illuminate occurs to the degree that the expansion of systemic integration begins to undermine functions essential to the reproduction of a *rationalized* lifeworld. The mediatization of the lifeworld takes on the form of a *"colonization of the lifeworld"* when the systemic media of money and power begin to displace communicative sociation in core spheres of action within which the three processes of symbolic reproduction take place: cultural transmission, social integration and socialization. The "communicative infrastructure" of a rationalized lifeworld is constituted by understanding-oriented action which creates a rational context for the "transference of validity" through these three processes. Such a transfer of rational motivation (in the communicative sense) is only possible, as we have seen, when actors take up a performative attitude toward other subjects and their validity claims. Action which is coordinated by money or power, on the other hand, requires only an objectivating attitude and an orientation to success.[56]

It is the colonization of these processes of lifeworld reproduction which generates the peculiar pathologies of advanced capitalism. And Habermas is claiming that there is some "threshold" at which mediatization in the name of enhanced material reproduction will necessarily begin to generate pathological side-effects.[57] And that threshold has been crossed in advanced industrial societies.

In order to clarify this thesis, one needs to examine several questions. (1) Why does Habermas say that communicative sociation "cannot be replaced" by sociation through money or power in central areas of lifeworld reproduction?[58] (2) How is the pressure toward colonization linked up with an analysis of the specific qualities of *advanced* capitalism? (3) What exactly does Habermas mean by colonization of the lifeworld?

(1)   What sort of argument grounds the rather categorical assertion that the three processes of lifeworld reproduction *cannot* be thoroughly reduced to the media of money and power? It might appear that Habermas is making the claim that the lifeworld is somehow "by nature" unalterably resistant to such a process of invasion.[59] But this is not in fact the best interpretation of what he is saying. The force of the "cannot" in the sentence above is rather one which is derived from the model of the subject which forms the core of his research program. A total, systemic reduction of the lifeworld cannot occur in the sense that it would be incompatible with that program's conceptualization of the human subject. In other words, the "cannot" gets its sense in terms of the theory. The theory specifies the centrality of communicative action to the reproduction of social and cultural life. In reality, however, the continuation of this centrality is ultimately an "open question."[60]

Habermas does, of course, want to offer some evidence that the colonization of the lifeworld is a phenomenon which generates pathological effects and new forms of oppositional social movements. This means that he intends his theoretical framework to provide an interpretation of why colonization should encounter observable resistance. The ultimate fate of this resistance, though, is uncertain. But the important point is that Habermas's research program does not relegate such resistance to the status of marginal events *from the start*, as do programs based on either the strategic actor model or a pure systems functionalism.[61] The communicative model allows us to interpret such phenomena in a way which links them with crucial moral and political questions for modern actors.

As I said in chapter 1, one legitimate criterion for a research program in the social sciences is the adequacy of its model of the subject in light of our most reflective moral judgements. Habermas's approach, insofar as it helps us to perceive structural changes in and systematic pressures on the lifeworld, provides a way of interpreting the diffuse feelings of loss and displacement we experience under the impact of contemporary life. While this theoretical interpretation must, of course, be shown to "fit the facts" of contemporary social life in some sense, it nevertheless has an ineradicably *practical* – that is, moral and political – dimension. What is "really" at stake in the changes Habermas emphasizes cannot be totally divorced from actors' decisions about what kind of beings they take themselves to be.

(2) Habermas's analysis of the two media-steered subsystems in *The Theory of Communicative Action* builds on his discussion of advanced capitalism in *Legitimation Crisis*. In the latter, he focused, as do most contemporary Marxists, on the enhanced role of the political system in managing capitalism's development. One of his specific concerns is to illuminate how the political system, as it expands its sphere of action in order to avoid economic crises, finds itself increasingly subject to contradictory imperatives. On the one hand, its actions must accord with the class interests of capital in continued accumulation and, on the other, with the demand of the population that the political system express universalistic, democratic values. This dilemma is the core of advanced capitalism's legitimation problems. Moreover, this ferment in relation to legitimation, when combined with the breaking down of classical bourgeois ideology (especially the belief in the fairness of market relations), gives rise to a decline in the syndromes of motivation (achievement orientation, possessive individualism, etc.) which are necessary to a capitalist economy.[62]

In *The Theory of Communicative Action*, Habermas uses an extensively reconceptualized theory of system and lifeworld to recast his analysis of the side-effects generated by contemporary capitalism's strategies for avoiding economic disequilibrium. Colonization of the lifeworld begins when

critical imbalances in material reproduction (that is, the steering crises accessible to systems theoretical analysis) can only be avoided at the cost of disturbances of the symbolic reproduction of the lifeworld (and that means "subjectively" experienced, identity-threatening crises or pathologies).[63]

In order to understand the form which such disturbances take, it is necessary to refer back to Figure 2, which illustrates the key social roles involved in system–lifeworld relations. Habermas, like many other radical critics, argues that advanced capitalism has been relatively successful in defusing class conflict in the sphere of production, and in increasingly neutralizing the public sphere as a site of effective participation by citizens.[64] What differentiates Habermas's position is how he analyses the compensations capitalism offers in exchange for this control over the roles of *employee* and *citizen*. Compensation comes in the form of system-conforming rewards which are channeled into the roles of private *consumer* and public *client* of the welfare state. It is this shift and its effects which Habermas thinks have not been adequately comprehended by Marxists or anyone else:

> The more effectively class conflict, which a private enterprise economy builds into a society, can be dammed up and held latent, the more persistently are problems pressed into the foreground which do not *immediately* harm interests which are calculable on the basis of class.[65]

This shift constitutes a distinctively new expansion of systemic integration. It is distinctive because now the expansion is at the expense of core areas of communicative sociation, "core" because it is within these spheres of action that the reproduction processes of the lifeworld take place. Habermas is claiming, then, that the pathologies specific to contemporary capitalism arise as the media of money and power increasingly infiltrate spheres of social life in which traditions and knowledge are transferred, in which normative bonds are intersubjectively established, and in which responsible persons are formed.

(3)   In order to make this thesis more concrete, Habermas turns to the phenomenon of the increasing "juridification" [*Verrechtlichung*] of social life. This term has emerged recently in German social theory to describe the vast increase in legal regulations in the welfare state and the effects this phenomenon has on clients who are subject to such regulations. In the literature Habermas refers to, there is a growing recognition that this new extension of law, even though it often comes in the name of expanding social rights, has a seemingly inevitable tendency to create a *new sort of dependency* between the client and the system of administration.[66]

The problem that arises from the explosion of legal regulations in the welfare state is "generated out of the structure of juridification itself." As social guarantees of the welfare state are bureaucratically implemented, there is an inevitable "pressure toward the redefinition of everyday life situations." This redefinition occurs first in relation to the individual citizen, who is induced to define his public existence increasingly in terms of strategic–rational, acquisitive relationships to bureaucracies. Habermas suggests that this subjective redefinition of public life may have a deleterious effect in the long run on the propensity of citizens to engage in various forms of cooperative social and political action.[67] Yet this sort of redefinition is not as important as the objective redefining of the client's lifeworld which arises from the fact that juridification requires an incessant process of "compulsory abstraction" of everyday life situations. This is not just a cognitive necessity in order for everyday situations to be subsumable under legal categories, but a practical necessity in order that administrative control can be exercised. Juridification thus exerts a *reifying* influence on the lifeworld, which, when combined with the enhanced claims to *expertise* of social workers and other administrators in the newly redefined categories of life, produces an insidiously expanding domain of dependency. This domain comes to include the way we *define* and *norm* areas of life such as family relations, education, old age, as well as physical and mental health and well-being.[68]

As Habermas describes the threat posed by the expansion of this "net of client relations" over core areas of the lifeworld, it is difficult not to think of Foucault's work and his image of an increasingly "carceral" society.[69] Habermas's description of the role of reification and expertise in defining, categorizing and organizing everyday life bears a strong similarity to Foucault's analysis of how the "discourses" associated with the growing organization of modern life create new ways of subjugating people, while ostensibly enhancing their freedom and well-being.

There are two crucial differences here, however, between the two theorists, and they involve the viewpoint from which such forms of dependency are grasped. Foucault uses the metaphor of writing or inscription to describe the process of the elaboration of discourses. This inscription is constituted as power, not in relation to some conception of the subject, but in relation simply to the "claims" of "bodies and pleasures."[70] One problem with this conception emerges quickly when one begins to try to give an account of what those claims might be and how they could become the basis of any possible collective action in opposition to the dominant discourses of modernity. From Foucault's point of view, it seems inevitable that the very attempt to articulate the claims of bodies and pleasures must constitute the initiation of new discourse, ultimately indistinguishable from the one it is replacing.[71] Moreover, thinking of these claims in the context of possible collective action is merely preparing for a new, more insidious form of regenerating subjugation through collective self-discipline.

Foucault thus leaves us first with a normative standpoint which cannot be articulated, but toward which we can merely gesture. Secondly, he provides no way of thinking coherently about collective political action. Although he does want to praise spontaneous "local resistance," he ultimately has no way of distinguishing a Ku Klux Klan from a Polish Solidarity movement.[72]

For Habermas, on the other hand, the dependency generated by the phenomenon of reification is constituted from within the communicative model of the subject and the associated notion of a structurally differentiated lifeworld. The metaphor of colonization draws attention, as does the metaphor of inscription, to the intrusive character of what is happening. But the former alerts us to something else as well. We gain a full sense of the phenomenon Foucault and Habermas want to grasp only if we give a coherent account, not only of the strategies and organization of the colonial forces, but also of what colonization means from the viewpoint of the consciousness of those colonized. This sort of significance becomes apparent in Habermas, given his account of communicative sociation, wherein actors define and coordinate interaction on the basis of those critical, interpretative capacities at their disposal in a rationalized lifeworld. Moreover, in regard to collective action, although I have stressed the minimal character of communicative ethics, it does seem clear that it provides somewhat better grounds for making judgements about the legitimacy and illegitimacy of different social and political movements.

Even if Habermas's general framework allows for the drawing of some important distinctions, it is still not clear how he distinguishes between different forms of juridification. It would certainly not make much sense to see the expansion of written law in modernity as having *in toto* the sort of negative qualities Habermas wants to emphasize in relation to juridification in the welfare state. To address this problem, he proposes that the "freedom-guaranteeing" and the "freedom-reducing" aspects of law be distinguished by asking, in a given case, whether laws have a "regulative" or a "constitutive force" in relation to the reproductive processes of the lifeworld. Habermas is here using a familiar philosophical distinction between types of rules. Regulative ones *regulate* some pre-existing, on-going activity, e.g. rules for safe driving. Constitutive rules on the other hand, *constitute* some form of activity, e.g., the rules of chess. Habermas wants to argue that law increasingly takes on a constitutive character in contemporary society.[73]

When processes of juridification have a regulative character, "they attach themselves to pre-existing institutions of the lifeworld," in the sense that new laws "stand in a continuum with ethical norms and [merely] modify communicatively structured spheres of action; they give a binding state-sanctioned form to spheres of action which are already informally constituted." Here one might think of basic constitutional rights or criminal law. When processes of juridification have a constitutive character, however, they are following imperatives of the economic and administrative systems in constituting new spheres of action or reconstituting pre-existing ones. An example of constituting new spheres of action might be the original legislation and administrative enactments in the United States governing the construction, siting and safety of nuclear power plants. An example of reconstituting existing spheres of action would be most welfare laws and regulations.[74]

This distinction between regulative and constitutive parallels a second criterion Habermas uses, that between law which is "capable of material justification" and law which "can only be legitimated through procedure."[75] In the former case, since law is embedded in the lifeworld context, it is more comprehensible to the average individual and must be defended by elites on material grounds. In the latter case, law becomes far less comprehensible and easier to defend purely on the grounds that it has been appropriately enacted by competent and responsible elites. And behind these claims of competence and responsibility, Habermas clearly sees decisions guided by the imperatives of adminstrative control and capital accumulation.

Although Habermas uses the problem of juridification to illustrate his thesis of colonization, it is important to remember that he is referring to a process which structures not only the relationship of administration to *client*, but also the relationship of economy to *consumer*. Here the problem is the increasingly intensive commodification of private life: the growing categorization and redefinition of new areas of private life through the intrusion of exchange value. Leisure, family life, sexual relationships, and even one's sense of self and development as a human being, increasingly become targets of commodification, as we are presented with new and more extensive pre-selected packages of behavioral, psychological and sexual scripts.[76]

Here again, Foucauldian analysis can be useful at one level. For example, his discussion of the discourse of sexual liberation in contemporary society as a new, more inconspicuous form of (self-) control and dependence is quite provocative.[77] But this exposure of the popular culture of psychosexual therapy needs to be linked to an analysis of this new discourse as part of a commodification process, in which one is increasingly told that one must purchase the proper directions for the use of one's mind and body.

IV.   The costs of modernization: 'cultural impoverishment'

The theoretical companion to Habermas's reinterpretation of Weber's loss of freedom as a colonization of the lifeworld is a reinterpretation of the loss of meaning as a process of "cultural impoverishment."[78] Weber saw this loss in modernity as the *inevitable* result of the disenchantment process, leading ultimately to secularization, with its corrosive effect on traditions and its splitting up of life into different cultural spheres, each becoming increasingly divorced from the others. Habermas, on the other hand, wants to build the case that at least some of the pathological effects Weber enumerates can be interpreted differently, and in a way which can show them not to be inevitable. This alternative interpretation is summed up in the claim that it is "not the differentiation and development of cultural value spheres according to their own logic [which] leads to the cultural impoverishment of everyday life, but the elitist splitting off of expert cultures from the contexts of everyday practice." In short, it is not the differentiated structures of a rationalized lifeworld which are themselves the problem, but rather the fact that increasingly specialized forms of argumentation become the guarded preserve of experts and thereby lose contact with the understanding processes of the majority of individuals. Thus, like the process of reification, the process of insulating expertise has a deforming effect on everyday life, for now that participation in the transference of validity which a rationalized lifeworld opened up to all competent speakers is increasingly short-circuited.[79]

Although Habermas does not devote nearly the amount of attention to the phenomenon of cultural impoverishment that he does to colonization, it is not too difficult to speculate about what he has in mind. It is a common lament that science and technology as enterprises are far removed from the world of the average citizen. Likewise, art in many of its forms has become increasingly incomprehensible to those outside a relatively small circle. Finally, in the moral–legal sphere, Habermas is presumably referring to such things as the fact that professionals are almost a necessity in even the simplest of legal matters; or the fact that planners and policy "experts" make a wide range of decisions with extensive normative impact on everyday life, claiming in the process to have some sort of "scientific" justification.

If the claims associated with this thesis of the growth of expert cultures are not particularly novel, they are given an interesting turn when Habermas analyzes this phenomenon's implications for the problem of ideology. In one sense, he claims, ideology is now indeed dead. This sense of ideology is the one Marx focused upon: those global interpretations of social life which were rooted in metaphysical or religious ideas and which mystified what was really at stake in the "hypertrophic," class-driven expansion of systemic integration. Such interpretations relied on at least some categories of beliefs, especially religious ones, remaining partially immune from the corrosive effect of rational scrutiny. But as this scrutiny was increasingly turned on all beliefs, ideologies began to lose their force. Such is the effect, Habermas argues, of the persistent "logic of cultural rationalization." We live now in a "definitively disenchanted culture," in which such ideologies have no way of sustaining, in the long run, their power to convince.[80]

If ideology in this classical sense has been disintegrating, does that not mean that the opposition between social and systemic integration should become increasingly apparent? The answer, according to Habermas, is no. And here is where the phenomenon of cultural impoverishment comes into play. In advanced capitalism, this splitting off of expert cultures helps generate a "functional equivalent" for ideologies. The latter had to facilitate social integration in a positive way by providing some overall interpretive framework for core aspects of social life. Today, however, this function is performed negatively, in the sense of systematically hindering "everyday knowledge" from even reaching the "level of articulation" of an ideology. What Habermas appears to be arguing here is that, as the insulation of expert cultures grows, so does the incapacity of the average individual to make effective use of the cognitive arsenal of cultural modernity. "*Everyday consciousness* is robbed of its synthesizing power; it becomes *fragmented.*" The citizen of an advanced industrial society is indeed bombarded with greater quantities of information, but the knowledge which results from it remains "diffuse" and difficult to employ in critical ways.[81] The thrust of this line of argument is that:

In the place of false consciousness there appears today *fragmented* consciousness, which hinders enlightenment about the mechanism of reification. The conditions for a *colonization of the lifeworld* are thereby fulfilled: as soon as it is stripped of its ideological veil, the imperative of independent subsystems press in *from the outside* on the lifeworld and compel assimilation, like colonial masters in a tribal society. [And] the perspectives of the native culture are so scattered that they cannot be coordinated sufficiently to allow the workings of the metropole and world market to be deciphered from a peripheral standpoint.[82]

Given this problematic in advanced capitalism, traditional "ideology critique" loses its foothold, since it depended on beginning from the *positive* ideals projected within an ideology.[83] Ideology critique in this sense must be replaced by the critique of cultural impoverishment and fragmentation of everyday consciousness. And for this task, the communicative model and the associated idea of the rational potential of modernity provide the critical foothold.[84] These conceptions together give Habermas a comprehensive viewpoint from which he can give substance to his idea of "systematic distortions of communication." And what is to be explained under this rubric is how the organization of knowledge and practical deliberation in contemporary society systematically undermine the potential of a rationalized lifeworld.

Unfortunately, Habermas does not do anything more than abstractly sketch the problem of fragmented consciousness as a phenomenon of advanced capitalism. A host of important questions arise from this sketch, which are not very satisfactorily addressed by him. One problem is that he merely asserts that insulated, expert cultures and fragmented consciousness are "functional" for advanced capitalism. While suggestive, this claim does not, however, do much to illuminate the actual social processes by which these two phenomena are actively promoted and reproduced. Moreover, drawing attention to the enhanced role of experts would seem to require that attention be paid to questions as to precisely what role such experts play in the class structure. Do they form, for example, a "new class" of some sort?

Another major question which arises here is what relation does Habermas's new thinking on ideology and pathology have to the discussion of legitimation and motivation crises in *Legitimation Crisis*. In a general sense, the intent of his new line of thought seems clear, although the specific implications flowing from it are not. By saying that the general intent is clear, I mean that Habermas appears to shift in the direction of seeing more resiliency in advanced capitalism than he did in *Legitimation Crisis*. Capitalism is now seen as being able to block motivation and legitimation deficits more effectively.

One aspect of this shift becomes apparent if we compare Habermas's new way of thinking about ideology with his earlier treatment of that topic. In *Legitimation Crisis*, classical bourgeois ideology was also seen as undergoing an irreversible process of disintegration. And this disintegration (along with the fact that new ideology cannot be administratively manufactured to order) was one key to the appearance of a legitimation deficit Habermas forecast for advanced capitalism.[85] Although this forecast was hedged with some provisos, it nevertheless seemed to promise a future in which the contrast between class structure and universalistic, democratic values would become increasingly apparent to broad segments of the population. Now, however, this emerging critical consciousness seems more problematic. Habermas has become convinced that the development of such consciousness is seriously and systematically impeded by the splitting off of expert cultures and the resulting fragmentation of everyday thought.[86]

If this general shift in Habermas's thinking is clear, specific aspects of it are, as I have said, less transparent. He appears to want to integrate the earlier with the more recent work in the following way. In *Legitimation Crisis*, he failed to distinguish adequately between the two viewpoints from which disturbances in the exchanges between system and lifeworld (see Figure 2) can be represented. Such disturbances, which arise because of the "inflexible structures" of the lifeworld, can be represented from the system's point of view as "disequilibriums," and from the lifeworld point of view as "pathologies."[87] In the latter case, we are concerned with immediate problems arising from systemically derived deformations of the three processes of lifeworld reproduction. Since the structures of the lifeworld have a certain inflexibility, the deformations give rise to pathological symptoms. In the case of "disequilibriums," we are concerned with what effects, if any, these pathologies have on the equilibrium of the economic and political subsystems.

This new distinction between different sorts of crises can be fully developed if we apply it to the material in Figure 1. That figure represents the contribution which the three lifeworld reproduction processes (cultural reproduction, social integration and socialization) make to the three structural components of the lifeworld (culture, society and personality). If one now considers the kinds of lifeworld crises or pathologies which may appear when the reproductive processes are disturbed by the colonization of the lifeworld and the insulation of expert cultures, one can derive what appears in Figure 3.

Represented here are nine sorts of crises or pathologies which can arise within the lifeworld perspective. Any of these can be seen as a potential source of disequilibria for the economic and political subsystems. And in *Legitimation Crisis*, Habermas focused on the withdrawal of legitimation (no. 4) and motivation (no. 6) as just such potential sources. In his more recent work, however, he is interested in other pathologies as well.

Although these other pathologies now move into a position of importance, Habermas does not provide a full enough analysis to be very satisfactory. As I said before, the general thrust of his new line of thinking goes toward seeing more ways in which advanced capitalism can avoid encountering motivation and legitimation crises. When one tries to get more specific about such avoidance strategies and their implications, however, things become more uncertain. Relatively little is actually said and the things that are may not be entirely compatible.[88] In what follows I will try to

	Structural components			
Disturbances in the domain of	Culture	Society	Person	Evaluative dimension
Cultural reproduction	1. Loss of meaning	4. Withdrawal of legitimation	7. Crisis in orientation and education	Rationality of knowledge
Social integration	2. Insecurity of collective identity	5. Anomie	8. Alienation	Solidarity of members
Socialization	3. Breakdown of tradition	6. Withdrawal of motivation	9. Psychopathologies	Accountability of the person

Figure 3   *Crisis phenomena connected with disturbances in reproduction.*
(*Source:* REPLY, *p. 280.*)

reconstruct what I *think* Haberas is saying and speculate about some of its implications.

Habermas has continued to assert that potential economic crises for advanced capitalism are defused by steering performances of an expanding state. This expansion has the effect of politicizing more and more areas of social life, particularly as both pre-bourgeois traditions and classical bourgeois ideologies are increasingly debilitated. Such politicization has the potential for generating conflicts which could ultimately lead toward an anomic condition (no. 5), that is, a total disintegration of social institutions. However, long before this limiting case occurs, there will be a withdrawal of legitimation from the state (no. 4) and motivation from the economic system (no. 6)[89] This prognosis, as I mentioned earlier, was the one Habermas put forward in *Legitimation Crisis*.

In his recent work, he does not argue that such crisis tendencies are eliminated, but rather that the emergence of a critical consciousness which is especially necessary for the withdrawal of legitimacy from the political system, is more difficult to attain than he originally thought. This is because, as the processes of lifeworld colonization and insulation of expertise expand, their collective effect is one of undermining the development of critical thought and action. I have already indicated how Habermas understands the pathology of loss of meaning or cultural impoverishment (no. 1) as a functional equivalent for classical ideology. But it is important to see also that the lifeworld colonization processes have a similar role to play.

These processes have the effect of lessening the dangers of disequilibrium, which might arise from anomie or withdrawal of legitimation and motivation, by means of "the depletion of the *remaining* resources," which social integration provides for *culture* and *personality.*

Culture and personality are attacked for the benefit of a crisis-overcoming stabilization of society... The results of this substitution [are that] in place of anomic occurrences (and in place of the ... withdrawal of legitimation and motivation) phenomena of alienation and the insecurity of collective identity arise [pathologies no. 2 and 8].[90]

In order to understand what Habermas is talking about here, it is useful to refer back to Figure 1. There it was indicated that the resource which social integration provides for *culture* is "obligations," by which he means that a well integrated society is one in which strong attachments are formed to the core values of a culture. Attachment to such a set of values is what provides actors with a sense of collective identity. The resource which social integration provides for *personality,* on the other hand, is "social memberships," by which Habermas means a sense of belonging to social groups and society as a whole.[91] Disturbances in the provision of these resources by systemically induced reification take the form of the disintegration of collective identity and alienation. These pathologies result from the way in which the new dependencies of client and consumer are created. They are generated, as I have shown, by reification processes in which everyday life is increasingly brought under external imperatives of continual redefinition, recategorization and reorganization.

For Habermas, then, alienation, disintegration of collective identity and cultural impoverishment or loss of meaning are all lifeworld pathologies which help to hinder the emergence of critical consciousness and action. The effect of such pathologies would thus appear to be that the state is relieved of some of the pressure for legitimating its actions. The sort of solidarity necessary for oppositional movements is impeded by the growing experience of alienation and isolation. And the sort of cognitive changes necessary to develop interpretations which challenge the legitimacy of state action are undermined by the fragmentation of consciousness.

In *Legitimation Crisis,* the state appeared headed for difficulty because it had to implement class-based, economic imperatives and yet secure at the same time general normative acceptance in terms of universalistic criteria. Now, however, reification and fragmentation processes are seen as decreasing the necessity for the state to rely on a basis of "normatively secured and communicatively achieved agreement." The reverse side of this phenomenon is that "the scope of [systemic] tolerance for merely instrumental attitudes, indifference and cynicism is expanded."[92] And these attitudes would be the sorts one would expect to be fostered from the three pathologies just discussed (nos. 1, 2 and 8).

Unfortunately, Habermas does not do much to trace out potential implications of this change for advanced capitalism, most specifically in regard to particular ways it might increase the resilience of that system. For example, one might speculate that a renewed emphasis on instrumental attitudes like possessive individualism, when combined with a growing indifference as to whether the political order is legitimate, could point in the direction of a future of which we are already getting a glimpse.[93] The Thatcher and Reagan regimes' popularity seems to rest at least partially on a reemphasis of possessive individualism within some segments of the population, combined with a growing indifference to the plight of the bottom segment. This phenomenon, often referred to as the growth of "two Britains" (one with jobs and prospects, the other without), can now be seen as something which is increasingly acceptable to the degree to which the "first" Britain (or America) simply suspends its commitment to the basic norm that democratic values must be universalized. Moreover, people with such attitudes are unlikely to get particularly upset by the judicious use of repression against the "second" Britain (or America). If this sort of hypothesis is correct, the state in advanced capitalism is indeed gaining increasing room to maneuver and assert control.

Similar sorts of effects might also be postulated in regard to a combination of instrumental attitudes with a growing cynicism toward the legitimacy of the state or the market as a fair allocator of opportunities. One might see the growth of such things as tax evasion and the underground economy as evidence of this syndrome of attitudes. While at first glance such phenomena might seem to signal challenges to the state, it has been argued that that kind of behavior by citizens also leads to new sorts of conformity in relation to the political system. That is, as the number of those engaged in questionable activities grows, so may the number who wish to keep a consistently low public profile and avoid any radical political orientations.[94]

Speculations such as these indicate some of the kinds of foci that Habermas's research program would emphasize for social theory. He suggests a number of other areas of investigation, such as mass media and mass culture, in which new insights might be generated on the basis of his analysis of moderniztion and its pathologies.[95] Finally, he also suggests that this analysis requires us to look in new directions for the sources of possible social opposition to contemporary capitalism. Although, as I have indicated, Habermas sees the emergence of new ways in which opposition can be undermined, he nevertheless also sees some new sources of potential opposition.

V. New social movements

The phenomenon of what have come to be called "new social movements" presents a particularly good example of the heuristic value of the communicative model for concrete social and political analysis. As Jean Cohen has shown, Habermas's understanding of rationality, action and modernity provides a better framework for understanding such social movements than other existing theoretical paradigms.[96]

Since the 1960s, groups have emerged which many observers see as exhibiting characteristics distinct from those of other social movements typical of modern society. Falling into this new category are the women's movements, radical ecologists, peace activists, gays, local autonomy groups and various other counter-cultural movements. The shared characteristics of these groups which appear new are their "self-limiting radicalism" and their distinctive concern with questions of group identity.[97] They are self-limiting in that they reject the "totalizing" elements of modern revolutionary theory: collective revolutionary subjects speaking in the name of all of society and seeking to take over the economy and polity. However, they also do not follow the standard pattern of interest-group behavior. As Habermas says, for new social movements, politics is not primarily a matter

of compensations that the welfare state can provide. Rather the question is how to defend or reinstate endangered ways of life, or how to put reformed ways of life into practice. In short, the new conflicts are not sparked by *problems of distribution*, but concern the *grammar of forms of life*.[98]

It is this somewhat defensive character as well as the focus on struggling for the ability to construct their own social identities that makes these movements somewhat anomalous from the viewpoint of those theories of collective behavior whose core is constructed from strategic notions of action and rationality. Such theories are most successful in explaining offensive collective behavior (either directly influencing or seeking to control the state), which is undertaken by established groups for whom identity is less of a central, ongoing problem.[99]

On the other hand, attempts to comprehend new social movements on the basis of an "identity-oriented" paradigm are also rather unsatisfactory. For here action is reduced to being simply expressive or dramaturgical in Habermas's terms. This dimension of action is of course important in new social movements, but an over-emphasis on it in the analytical framework fails to give adequate scope to the strategic dimensions of these movements' behavior as they interact with established institutions in their attempts to secure some autonomous space for identity articulation. [100]

Habermas's communicative model provides the best available framework, not only for constructing explanations of the behavior of new social movements, but also for understanding why such movements have arisen, and for interpreting what, at a general level, is at stake in the struggles in which they engage. In terms of their behavior, the communicative model is the only one complex enough to provide some comprehension of the peculiar mix of strategic, norm-guided (especially its universalistic quality) and expressive or dramaturgical action such groups engage in. In terms of understanding why such movements have arisen and interpreting what is at stake in their struggles, Habermas directs our attention to his interpretation of modernity and modernization, more particularly to the notions of systemic versus communicative sociation and of a one-sided process of societal rationalization versus a rationalized lifeworld.

From Habermas's perspective, new social movements are reacting against the increasing colonization of the lifeworld and cultural impoverishment. [101] This perspective allows one to understand the peculiar defensive quality such movements exhibit. On the one hand, there is a defensive reaction against the encroachment of the state and economy on society, something which is similar to traditionalistic, reactive movements. On the other hand, the behavior of new social movements cannot be understood simply as a reaction against "the destruction of traditional forms of life," but rather as a reaction against the deformation of "posttraditional forms of life" made possible by a rationalized lifeworld. Protecting the conditions of possible "communicative sociation" means generating space for a more autonomous construction of group identity and political deliberation. [102]

This sort of analysis in turn allows one to draw useful distinctions between various contemporary social movements. For example, the recent revival of religious fundamentalism, especially in the United States, is in some sense new, but Habermas's model allows us to recognize why it should not be categorized among new social movements. This is because, although this fundamentalism is a reaction to the destruction of traditional life forms by big government and a corporate America dedicated to marketing a "permissive" lifestyle, the articulation of this reaction is all too smoothly integrated into new modes of internal colonization. The identity of religious fundamentalism is increasingly defined by a television-mediated corporate strategy of marketing a new "sanctified" consumption of products, services and images.[103]

Habermas's perspective also yields an understanding of the self-limiting character of new social movements. The sort of consciousness and behavior which are compatible with conditions of greater space for communicative sociation do not support totalistic revolutionary programs, either for generating a traditional revolutionary ideology or for smashing the institutions of capitalism. The problem is less that of building a collective, revolutionary ideology to combat that provided by capitalism, than it is one of overcoming the colonization and fragmentation of consciousness by creating enough slack in the system for the ongoing autonomous articulation of plural identities by the groups involved.

As for the institutions of capitalism, new social movements have an appreciation of their ambiguous character. The welfare state, for example, is both a vehicle for the universalization of rights and a threat to the ability of people to control the direction of their lives. Compare here the attitude of the women's movement to a capitalist economy. Once it is stripped of its traditionalist prejudice against women, it is a vehicle for the achievement of material independence and self-assertion; but it is also a powerful force for an externally coded homogenization of women's consciousness.

Such a sensitivity to ambiguity is precisely what is appropriate to our contemporary situation, as it is analyzed by Habermas. Many of the benefits of contemporary life have an intrinsic relationship with the differentiation and hierarchy of the structures of modern economies and states. And yet this process of systems rationalization threatens our integrity as independent, critical beings capable of shaping the direction of our collective lives in a democratic way.

These are some of the ways in which the communicative model exhibits its heuristic value for the study of a category of collective action which is only poorly comprehended from the perspective of other research programs. But, of course, this model also provides insights about these movements which have distinct normative implications for their self-consciousness and action.

In *Legitimation Crisis*, Habermas predicted the rise of a critical politics, but he really gave no sense of what shape it would take. One was left to speculate that, in some way, there would be a reemergence of a critical "public sphere," the decline of which he had traced in his first book about the development of liberal capitalism.[104] Habermas's most recent work allows these speculations to take on a little clearer shape. The clarity to be gained here is not in regard to the probability for success of a critical politics. On that Habermas is, as I have said, probably less optimistic than he was when he wrote *Legitimation Crisis*.[105] What is becoming clearer is the kind of normative self-understanding a critical politics needs.

Habermas's new thinking about a critical, public sphere of discourse and action is characterized by the assertion that there must be a clear and enduring demarcation between this sphere and the formal political system. The "political public sphere, in which complex societies gain a normative distance from themselves and are able to assimilate collectively experiences of crises," must be conceptualized as being just as distinct from the *political* system as it is from the economic system. This is because the former system must operate through the "legal–administrative medium," and that, as the colonization analysis has shown, carries an inevitable tendency toward "normalization" in Foucault's sense.[106] The creation of autonomous, critical public spheres must now be understood as the "building up of threshold impediments . . . and the building in of sensors in the exchange between lifeworld and system." The general notion of self-limitation characteristic of new social movements is developed here into a normative prescription that they understand their most fundamental task to be fighting in an unending "border conflict" [*Grenzkonflikt*] between the lifeworld and the political and economic systems.[107]

Unfortunately, Habermas has not elaborated this image of critical politics in any detail. We are left with what seems to be a thoroughly negative vision of the possibilities of politics. New social movements should continue to eschew both grand revolutionary schemes and the path of integrating themselves into the normal workings of established institutions. Moreover, they should be wary of even their own internal organization. For relinquishing the horizontal, communicative qualities of grass-roots political interactions and crossing "the threshold to formal . . . organization" entails an increase in the degree to which internal politics will inevitably be organized through a "legal–administrative medium."[108]

Habermas has been criticized for seeing only this negative, political potential in new social movements. Cohen finds it "ironic" that Habermas does not consider these movements to be "carriers of a new collective identity, capable of institutionalizing the positive potentials of modernity [which he has identified], or of transcending particularistic and expressive politics."[109] I think Cohen is wrong about Habermas's not seeing new social movements as, among other things, the potential carriers of a collective identity which partially overlaps and partially extends beyond the sphere of their more particular group identities. Even if his position here is sometimes more implicit than explicit, it is fair to say that he considers new social movements as the best hope for a more "balanced" institutionalization of the potentials of modernity. I will sketch the outlines of this more positive – if still institutionally vague – image of politics in the next chapter.

6

The two tasks of critical theory

At the end of *The Theory of Communicative Action*, Habermas suggests that critical theory has two sorts of tasks: philosophical and social–scientific. I have referred to these as the quasi-Kantian and Hegelian–Marxian faces of critical theory, or the negative and positive heuristic of a critical research program. The former task is that of developing "a theory of rationality," which constitutes a minimal model of the subject. This in turn allows for an illumination of the concept of modernity which Habermas feels can "assure the modern understanding of the world of its universality." The latter task, on the other hand, begins from the analysis of modernity in relation to Western processes of societal rationalization and proceeds to the construction of the theses of colonization of the lifeworld and cultural impoverishment. The thread to be picked up there by critical social theorists, is one which investigates the pathologies, disequilibria and new forms of oppositional movements in advanced capitalism.[1]

In this chapter I will elaborate further upon how one should understand these two tasks. The first section will consider the frequent charge that Habermas is offering a new form of philosophical foundationalism which misconstrues the proper relation between philosophy and the empirical sciences, and between philosophy and culture. This question will lead into a consideration of the difficulties of claiming that the "modern understanding of the world" has the sort of universal significance Habermas ascribes to it. The initial focus here will be on his contention that the three specialized forms of argumentation (empirical–theoretical, moral and aesthetic) and their corresponding cultural value spheres represent that organization of consciousness within which knowledge can be most effectively accumulated. This discussion of the learning potential of modern structures will then lead, in the second two sections, into an examination of Habermas's claim that such structures also allow an adequate understanding of the "processes of unlearning" which have accompanied modernization, in particular the subjugation of both "outer" and "inner" nature.[2]

I. A non-foundationalist universalism

A foundationalist position in philosophy is one which claims that philosophy can, by some method, demonstrate the absolute, universal validity of some conception of knowledge or morality. This view that there are ahistorical conceptual or moral frameworks existing, as it were, above the heads of concrete historical actors, is one which has increasingly fallen into general disrepute. Habermas's work has often been suspected of harboring some variant of foundationalism, and yet he has just as often claimed that his is a non-foundationalist position.[3]

How does the quasi-Kantian task Habermas endorses differ from the traditional Kantian foundationalism? The latter assigns philosophy the role of "usher" (*Platzanweiser*) in relation to empirical sciences, because Kant's transcendental method claims to show these sciences their place and limits in the theater of possible human knowledge. Habermas, on the other hand, envisions only a quasi-transcendental role for philosophical reflection. This means elucidating, not the conditions of all possible knowledge, but rather the "various conditions for the validity of meaningful expressions and performances." The legitimate sphere of philosophical reflection is now reduced and redefined. It extends only to the development of:

rational reconstructions of the know-how of subjects, who are entrusted to produce valid expressions and who trust themselves to distinguish intuitively between valid and invalid expressions. This is the domain of such disciplines as logic and metamathematics, of epistemology and the philosophy of science, of linguistics and the philosophy of language, of ethics and the theory of action, of aesthetics, of the theory of argumentation, etc. These disciplines all have the common intention of giving accounts of the pretheoretic knowledge and intuitive command, let us say, of the rule systems by means of which competent subjects generate and evaluate valid expressions and performances, such as correct inferences; good arguments; true descriptions, explanations, or predictions; grammatical sentences; successful speech acts; effective, instrumental actions; adequate evaluations; and authentic self-expressions.[4]

In short, the traditional sphere of theoretical philosophy is now to be taken over by "reconstructive sciences." The question which immediately arises with this shift, however, is how exactly these reconstructive sciences differentiate themselves epistemologically from philosophy, on the one hand, and "normal" science, on the other.[5]

In regard to philosophy, this question can be answered by examining what the grounds are for deciding whether a particular reconstruction is valid. Certainly Habermas wants to claim that his particular reconstructions of action and rationality have a universalistic status, but he clearly shows that this claim is not foundationalist. The validity of his reconstructions can be assessed in two ways. First, they can be assessed in a heuristic sense: how well they provide for conceptual "coherence" across a range of theories and interpretations. Secondly, they can be indirectly tested by examining how well these theories and interpretations stand up to empirical evidence.

It is important to see that rational reconstructions, like all other types of knowledge, have only a hypothetical status. They may very well start from a false sample of intuitions; they may obscure and distort the right intuitions; and they may, even more often, overgeneralize particular cases. They are in need of further corroboration. What I accept as an antifoundationalist criticism of all strong a priori and transcendentalist claims does not, however, block attempts to put rational reconstructions of supposedly basic competences on trial and to test them indirectly by employing them as input in empirical theories.[6]

The hypothetical, non-foundationalist nature of Habermas's rational reconstructions can perhaps be brought out most clearly if one thinks of them, as I suggested earlier, as constituting part of the core of a social science research program. Thus, the success or failure over time of, for example, Kohlberg's theory of moral development or Habermas's theory of advanced capitalism throws indirect evaluative light on the validity of the reconstructions of action and rationality. If the state of such theories shows the program to be "degenerating," then the core will likewise increasingly be thrown into question.[7] Interpreted in this way, it is easy to understand what Habermas means when he says that pure philosophical speculation can play nothing more than the role of temporary "place holder" [*Platzhalter*] for reconstructive projects which in turn have only a hypothetical status.[8]

If Habermas is allowed to differentiate reconstructive science from foundationalist philosophy in this way, one is still left with the question: what now differentiates reconstructive science epistemologically from normal science? This question is of some significance for Habermas, because both he and his Frankfurt School predecessors have spent much of their time defending their own philosophical reflection as a necessary activity for gaining some critical, reflective distance from what they see as the dangers of a positivistically conceived science.[9] The problem now is whether, as Habermas increasingly distances his reconstructive efforts from foundationalist philosophy, he also in the end obliterates the distinction between these efforts and those of normal science.

It seems clear that Habermas does want to maintain this distinction and somehow keep reconstructive science from being entirely absorbed within the sphere of the technical, cognitive interest which defines ordinary science. Such absorption would render his entire project just as positivistic as others that he criticized in his early works. Habermas has attempted to justify his distinction by arguing that the reconstruction of basic competences into an explicit set of rules is more purely descriptive than normal science in the sense that it does not impose a theoretical structure to the same degree. Yet this way of justifying the distinction has not proved very persuasive to critics who see no real basis for distinguishing reconstructive and normal science; both are tied ultimately to fallible hypotheses. [10]

Perhaps something like the kind of distinction Habermas wants to maintain might be established if one reflects on the nature of the core of a social science research program. As was shown at the beginning of chapter 1, the conceptualizations which constitute the core must provide a minimal model of the subject. Now the model is of course indirectly tested as the theories and interpretations it informs are tested against empirical evidence. But, as was argued earlier, it seems plausible to see such models as strongly underdetermined by such evidence. The normative implications of the model must also stand up to the standards of our most reflective moral judgments. And these judgments reflect a practical cognitive interest rather than a technical one. The implication of this for Habermas is that it might allow him some grounds for continuing to differentiate epistemologically between his reconstructive efforts and normal science, since the former cannot be envisioned as simply serving a technical cognitive interest. [11]

Even if one accepts Habermas's arguments about how philosophical reflection within his project no longer plays the role of "usher" [Platzanweiser], there is another basis for the suspicion that this project still harbors foundationalist tendencies. Here it would be argued that philosophy also cannot play the role of "highest judge" [obersten Richters] of culture. It cannot offer absolute judgments, from an ahistorical position, about what are privileged, and what are unprivileged, forms of knowledge or reason. [12] The specific problem in Habermas's case is that he would appear to be setting out an ahistorical categorization, not so different from Kant. Pure reason, practical reason and judgment are rendered in Habermas's work as three distinct validity claims (truth, legitimacy and authenticity). Moreover, it is also argued that the treatment of these specialized claims must be institutionalized in corresponding cultural spheres (which are distinct and in some sense privileged in relation to other spheres) if the rational potential of modern structures of consciousness is to be consistently realized in social interactions.

In what sense does Habermas provide some absolute philosophical grounding for the cultural constellations of the modern world? In no sense, he would argue. Philosophy brings no independent, ahistorical framework of validation here. The three cultural spheres (science and technology; law and morality; and aesthetics), representing "three moments of reason," emerged in modernity as a matter of historical fact; they "crystallized out without the aid of philosophy."[13] The philosophical task here is one of reflective illumination of this phenomenon and its implications. Part of this task will be that of elucidating the internal logic of argumentation characteristic of each of the three cultural spheres; in other words, providing the self-assurance that they do represent distinct "moments" or "complexes" of reason.

Although Habermas admits that he has not developed any such full-blown theory of argumentation out of his analysis of universal pragmatics, he has given a provisional illustration of some of the implications it would entail. These are represented in Figure 4. There he tries to integrate his own framework of formal pragmatic attitudes and formal world concepts with Weber's thinking about the distinctiveness of the three cultural value spheres. The figure is designed to illustrate those combinations of formal pragmatic attitudes and world concepts which form fertile complexes of rationality, i.e., those which are "sufficiently productive from the standpoint of *acquiring knowledge* to permit, in Weber's terms, a development of cultural value spheres with their own inner logics."[14]

In Figure 4 the knowledge-generating complexes of rationality are those within the heavier black lines (1.1, 1.2, 2.2, 2.3, 3.3, 3.1). This, of course, implies that other combinations of attitudes and world-concepts (the ones marked with "x"s) do not have distinct, corresponding forms of argumentation, capable of generating knowledge. For example, the fact that combination 2.1 is empty indicates "a skepticism concerning the possibility of giving a rational form to fraternal relations with a non-objectivated nature – for instance in the form of a philosophy of nature that could compete with the modern sciences of nature.'[15]

The foregoing framework has been met with skepticism, even from sympathetic critics. McCarthy has argued that it is not so easy for Habermas to separate clearly his privileged complexes of rationality from the other ones. Habermas's skepticism about the empty cells in Figure 4 is based largely on his claim that in the privileged ones there is an "*accumulation* of knowledge." Yet, as McCarthy points out, it is not at all clear in what sense knowledge is generated in a cumulative fashion in, for example, aesthetic argumentation. And if this is not clear, it is not so easy for Habermas to make such a sharp distinction between the learning potential of at least one of his privileged complexes and those marked with "x"s.[16]

McCarthy's remarks thus raise two key problems for the framework of

Worlds Basic attitudes	1 Objective	2 Social	3 Subjective	1 Objective
3 Expressive	Art ↓			
1 Objectivating	↑ Cognitive–instrumental rationality Science ¦ Social Technology ¦↓technologies		X	
2 Norm- conformative	X	↑ Moral–practical rationality Law ¦ Morality ¦↓		
3 Expressive		X	↑ Aesthetic–practical rationality Eroticism ¦ Art	

Figure 4   *Rationalization complexes*
(*Source:* TCA, *p. 238; cf. REPLY, p. 249.*)

privileged and unprivileged complexes of reason: 1) the possibility that at least one of the complexes marked "x," such as a new conceptualization of man's relation to nature, can be articulated in such a way as to become a vehicle of learning; and 2) the suspicion that Habermas's notion of aesthetic learning cannot be adequately articulated. Although these problems are raised in the specific context of claims associated with Figure 4, they raise issues which are at the heart of what I take to be the two most fundamental lines of criticism which have been directed against Habermas's overall account of reason and modernity. The thrust of these challenges is that the differentiated structures of modern consciousness, which Habermas links to learning potential, are far *less enabling* and far *more constraining* of human thought and action than Habermas allows. In particular, these structures blind us to what we, as moderns, have "*unlearned* [*verlernt*] in our learning processes."[17]

Such criticism proposes, on the one hand, that Western structures of consciousness, which privilege a cognitive-instrumental relation with *outer* nature, are ultimately to blame for environmental destruction.[18] It is also argued, on the other hand, that such structures are intimately involved in the subjection of *inner* nature: an atrophying of our aesthetic–expressive capacities. This sort of argument about modernity and aesthetic experience has been made quite provocatively by Foucault with his analysis of the subjugation of the body and his proposals for a new "aesthetics of existence." Both of these lines of thought thus locate the source of modernity's crisis not just in one-sided processes of modernization, but rather in the very core of the modern subject's way of learning about and relating to the world.

Although Habermas is concerned with answering these challenges, he is aware that the answers he has so far given are not overwhelmingly convincing. He is convinced, however, that these challenges have internal theoretical difficulties which mitigate their own force.[19] Actually he agrees with much of the substance of these criticisms, but he considers it absolutely essential to show that such insights can be preserved from *within* the perspective of modernity. That perspective can illuminate such pathologies as part of the "*un*learning process" of one-sided modernization, that is, as phenomena associated with an unbalanced development of modernity's potential.[20]

Before turning directly to his response to the foregoing challenges, it is necessary to become clearer about a key point. When Habermas refers to an *unbalanced* path of development in Western society, he implies some sort of ideal of what a *balanced* one would look like. Now what is at issue here is not a substantive model of the good life which is supposedly derived from the communicative notion of reason. One can only specify "certain *formal conditions* of a rational life."[21] From this formalist perspective, one can identify the outlines of a balanced or "non-selective pattern of rationalization": the

three cultural value spheres have to be connected with corresponding action systems in such a way that the production and transmission of knowledge that is specialized according to validity claims is secured; the cognitive potential developed by expert cultures has, in turn, to be passed on to the communicative practice of everyday life and to be made fruitful for social action systems; finally, the cultural value spheres have to be institutionalized in such a balanced way that the life-orders corresponding to them are sufficiently autonomous to avoid being subordinated to laws intrinsic to heterogeneous orders of life.[22]

Thus the key components of the model of balance are: the institutional securing of a differentiated transmission of knowledge; the minimization of the degree to which the knowledge generated by experts remains insulated from the critical capacities of citizens; and the achievement of a balance between the three cultural spheres which correspond to the three differentiated aspects of reason. The latter two components certainly raise the most pressing questions. As for the deinsulation of expertise, this could be said to be a goal which has been central to Habermas's work from the very beginning: "With the discourse ethic as the guiding thread, we can . . . develop the formal idea of a society in which all potentially important decision-making processes are linked to institutionalized forms of discursive will-formation."[23] Although such an idea, at this level of abstraction, raises a multitude of questions about institutional forms (as critics have often noted), it nevertheless is one which is fairly comprehensible.

The second component of the model of balance, however, raises more perplexing questions. Part of what is at issue here is how to invigorate and give more institutionalized independence to the aesthetic and moral-practical dimensions of life which have increasingly been brought within the overbearing tutelage of the cognitive-instrumental during the processes of modernization. But there is more involved here, for the problem is not just an adequate independence for each cultural value sphere. There must also be an interdependence, for the different "moments" of reason which these spheres represent are "incomplete in themselves." Differentiation must be tempered by "an equilibrated interplay of the cognitive with the moral and the aesthetic-expressive."[24] This last point complements the one relating to the problem of reconciling expert cultures with everyday communicative practice. Both seek to address the sense of loss of wholeness or unity which haunts modernity.

It is in connection with the exploration of this issue that Habermas sees a second task for philosophy (along with that of "place holder"). As we have seen, philosophy cannot claim the position of "highest judge" of culture, offering foundational justification for the differentiation of the cultural value spheres which emerges with modernity. At best, philosophical reflection can address itself to exploring how some sense of unity can be achieved within an attained level of differentiation. Thus the philosopher can only play the role of a "mediating interpreter," investigating how to get expert cultures in communication with discursive practices of everyday life and how to ensure that the different cultural spheres "communicate *with* each other," without at the same time "violating the inner logic of [that sphere's] dominant form of argumentation specialized either in truth, normative correctness or aesthetic harmony."[25]

Clearly what Habermas has in mind here is developing an account of some sense of unity or reconciliation which is compatible with the potential of modernity but incompatible with the actual course of capitalist modernization. This would allow him to save some self-assurance for modernity. The precise sense of this view of the unity of reason is, however, not made very clear. He suggests that we "always already" have a certain "intuitive knowledge" of unity in this sense, because our everyday communicative action always involves us in defining and acting within situations in such a way that "cognitive explanations, moral expectations, expressions and evaluations interpenetrate."[26]

Unfortunately, Habermas does not go much beyond this somewhat vague appeal to intuition. He offers no developed argument, as he does with his other claims about the intuitive knowledge of communicatively competent speakers. We are left simply with a notion of each actor's intuitive sense that he could distinguish between forms of life on the basis of their providing either a more or less unifying interplay of the different moments of reason. I will try to flesh this speculative thought out more in the next section, in the context of the discussion of how to address the problem of the subjugation of outer nature.

Habermas squarely admits the sketchy and relatively unsatisfactory quality of his claims about unity. But he adamantly maintains that those who try to develop alternative conceptualizations of unity or reconciliation which reach "behind" or "over" the modern understanding of the world are even more inadequate.

All this is not really an argument, but more an expression of skepticism in the face of so many failed attempts to have one's cake and eat it too; to retain both Kant's insights and, at the same time, to return to the "home" [*Behausung*] from which these same insights have driven us.[27]

The skepticism Habermas expresses in this quotation is directed against the two sorts of proposals mentioned earlier for curing modernity's ills. The first are remedies for the domination of *outer* nature and the second are remedies for the domination of *inner* nature.

II. Modernity and the domination of "outer" nature

Proposals of the former sort suggest that the only adequate way to cure modern man's destructiveness in relation to his environment is to rethink radically our way of conceptualizing non-human nature. This rethinking would involve some basic rejection of our dominant cognitive–instrumental mode of relating to nature. This might include the idea of nature itself having an ultimate purpose, or the idea of the moral status of some parts of nature, such as animals. Now, as has been indicated, Habermas admits that there is no foundationalist counterargument to such proposals. He remains skeptical, however, as to whether the proper way to treat such problems as environmental crisis is by making a radical break with the differentiated structures of modern consciousness. The burden of proof, he suggests, is on those who suggest such a break. For example, those who envision an ultimate purposiveness to nature must make clear how this idea avoids leading us "back to metaphysics, and thus behind the levels of learning reached in the modern age into a re-enchanted world."[28]

In opposition to such a charge, McCarthy has suggested that it is in fact at least possible to develop some sort of philosophy of nature that would not lead back to metaphysics.[29] This is certainly an important challenge to Habermas, for it sensitizes one to the dangers in his position. Generating distinctions between valid and invalid modes of cognition always carries with it the danger of creating distinctions which really turn on criteria of power and privilege. But unless one wants to deny any difference between the two sorts of criteria, then one is left with a continuous process of demonstrating the validity of some proposed distinctions and defending them against counterargument. In this light, McCarthy's claim is important, but the controversy can only be carried further by actually looking at the implications that would arise from a full elaboration of such a new philosophy of nature.[30]

At this point, a perhaps more fruitful avenue to pursue in this controversy would be to ask how Habermas's position allows one to address at least some of the *practical* concerns which appear to animate efforts to rethink the relationship between humans and nature. In short, can we envision the development of practices and institutions which would be both environmentally sound and more supportive of a communicative-ethical orientation without a new philosophy of nature? For example, are communities tied, say, to a commitment to decentralized forms of energy (such as solar) and political-economic decision-making possible only on the basis of such a philosophy? Perhaps this may be the case. Perhaps the sort of social-psychological changes necessary to support such institutions could only be achieved when mediated by a radically new orientation to nature, stressing more reverence or respectfulness.[31] On the other hand, the tradition leading from Marx to critical theory might make one a little skeptical about overemphasizing the role of a new *philosophy* of nature. Perhaps we do not really have to envision a totally new world view in order to imagine how a consciousness appropriate to radically new institutions might arise.

In this regard, one can think of growing environmental crises as functioning at least somewhat analogously to growing economic crises in Marx's thought, that is, as a practical catalayst for reflection on how the ways in which we currently assault nature are leading to a more and more frustrating and self-destructive form of life. In a context of growing numbers of people experiencing growing frustration in their everyday lives with the scale and organization of dominant forms of technology, the potential for interest in new practices and institutional arrangements might become more pressing. And to the extent that growing numbers of people begin experimenting with alternative forms of life and technology, and find them to be less frustrating and more empowering, one might have some social–psychological basis for widespread support for increasingly large-scale social changes.[32] Now just as one criterion for these alternative forms would be their potential for empowerment and enhancement of all citizens' critical capacities, so another would be their potential for enhancement of a sense of balance or harmony with natural systems. In this scenario, support for the latter value would not necessarily require a bold new philosophy of nature, but rather a new sense of what makes for human satisfaction and well-being, a sense which would arise out of reflective practice and embody a new appreciation of the aesthetic dimension in everyday life.[33] Imagining such an alternative form of life and the way in which it might attract widespread support is perhaps the best way to give some persuasiveness to Habermas's speculative remarks about our intuitive sense of what would constitute a more satisfactory unity of the cognitive, moral and aesthetic–expressive spheres of knowledge at the level of everyday practice. It is certainly not immediately implausible to imagine people living such a life with a high degree of satisfaction and critical self-consciousness, and doing so without having a brave new overarching worldview in which to situate their practice cognitively. Although Habermas does not explicitly elaborate the kind of alternative form of life I have suggested, it would seem to manifest some of his essential ideas, especially the emergence of alternative practices in which there is an enhancement of the *moral–practical* and *aesthetic–expressive* dimensions of everyday social life.

This image of a more balanced form of life is, of course, relevant to a range of issues, not just that of the proper relationship to "outer" nature. The model of balance is especially important for reconsidering some of the questions which were raised about new social movements at the end of the last chapter. Thus, I want to digress for a moment from the specific focus on "outer" nature. In the last chapter, it was shown how the colonization analysis shifts the normative sense of a critical, democratic politics:

The normative meaning of democracy, in a social–theoretical sense, can be expressed in the idea that the fulfilment of the functional necessities of systematically integrated spheres of action ought to find its limits in the integrity of the lifeworld; that is, in the requirements of spheres of action which are socially [i.e. communicatively] integrated.[34]

But, as was also indicated in the last chapter, critics have suggested that this image of critical opposition as an unending "border conflict" is too thoroughly negative. I suggested, on the contrary, that Habermas's political vision is not thoroughly negative. I can now make that assertion more plausible.

The source of a more positive image of politics is the general concept of a society which makes more balanced use of the potential of cultural modernity. Such a concept is utopian in obvious ways, but Habermas sees it as grounded in some of the practices and ideas of new social movements.[35] These movements have the possibility of becoming politically significant in this positive sense, to the degree that they begin to recognize that their struggle to create space for plural, autonomous group identities must link itself in a reciprocally enriching way with a broader collective identity which embodies the model of balance. That is, the struggle for autonomy by such movements must become a broad medium for political education, in which their concrete experiences and goals are reflectively interpreted in terms of the criteria of balance. That means that they must be interpreted, first, in terms of the enhancement of a new moral–practical orientation: a communicative–ethical one, associated, as I have shown, with distinctive understandings of universality, equality and tolerance. And, similarly, the search for new modes of identity must be related to that necessity for more flexible need interpretations which is associated with such an ethical–political orientation (see chapter 4). Finally, this opening up of need interpretations must be understood as part of a rebalancing of modernity which emphasizes new, aesthetic–expressive attitudes toward both outer and inner nature (more about the latter in the following section).

Now Habermas has not produced any detailed studies of the ideas and behavior of new social movements, interpreted from the perspective just outlined. However, his remarks about such movements provide certain general directions for speculation. For example, when he speaks of groups involved with "a critique of growth based on *environmental and peace concerns*," he is directing attention to experiments with alternative, ecologically sound technologies and forms of life which have the potential to make us reconsider our attitude towards outer nature.[36] And speculation about the growing effect of such movements quite plausibly raises issues of an emerging collective identity which is compatible with communicative ethics. Thus, one might suggest that, although the radical ecology movement is at present relatively small, it is nevertheless laying a foundation of ideas and practices which could, under conditions of more rapid environmental deterioration, achieve wider support and greater political impact.[37] For example, at present much of the middle-class opposition to nuclear power and the dumping of hazardous wastes has a relatively blind defensiveness to it. Although it may tap some old democratic traditions of localism and citizen independence, it hardly constitutes a radical challenge with its implicit slogans of: "Dump that chemical waste in someone else's backyard, not mine;" or "Site that nuclear reactor in the next state, not mine." Yet with advancing ecological deterioration, these forms of opposition may increasingly recognize the short-sighted and contradictory character of their positions and become more susceptible to a restructuring of their views. This might mean a greater openness to the substantive ideas and practices of those more radical, marginal groups. And, just as importantly, the openness may carry with it a recasting of their thinking about political problems in more universalistic, even global terms. It is in this context that one must understand Habermas's thoughts on the growth of new forms of collective identity (see the discussion in chapter 4). Growing recognition of potential ecological disaster could help expand the opportunities for combining localist democratic traditions with a sense that we are all members of one global community or "fictive world society," as Habermas called it.[38] The recent rise of the nuclear freeze movement in the United States helps lend some concrete plausibility to this idea of a collective identity which links local, *everyday life* concerns with *global* ones.

Habermas's perspective also provides a general framework for at least some thinking about institutions. Many recent institutional proposals of radical democrats for cutting down the power of large economic and political units are quite compatible with Habermas's thought; for example, soft energy technologies and more local control of other forms of power generation; or workplace democracy conceived, not as a cornerstone of a worker's state, but as simply a space for getting greater control of our everyday lives; or more extensive use of decentralized computer networks and video-technology for enhancing the information and capacity to act of the average citizen.[39] If Habermas does provide some general orientation in favor of this sort of decentralizing political practice, there nevertheless remains another sort of political practice which is less clearly defined. In order to bring the former sort of practices into existence, new social movements need the support, at least to some degree, of existing economic and political institutions. It is here that the guiding metaphor of an unending "border conflict" ceases to be very helpful. Habermas's view, mentioned in the last chapter, that new social movements should shy away from large, formal organizations or parties makes it unclear how such movements could gain the sort of support they need from the economic and political systems for the institutional changes they want.

What Habermas apparently believes in this regard is that the collective behavior of new social movements will exercise its influence on the political and economic system *indirectly*, through mass public opinion. This notion emerges in his discussion of the use of civil disobedience by the German environmental and peace movement. He argues that mass civil disobedience is a legitimate response only under certain conditions. The disputed policy must be one which will have relatively irreversible consequences or which involves a "confrontation of different forms of life."[40] When such conditions do justify civil disobedience, the action must always maintain a "symbolic character" and be carried out "only with the intention of appealing to the capacity for insight and the sense of justice of the relevant majority."[41]

Habermas's argument here is quite sensible, but one wonders whether the strategy behind such civil disobedience is adequate to the full range of political concerns of new social movements. What I mean is that, although civil disobedience might be an important activity for helping to turn public opinion against, say, nuclear power, it is unlikely, by itself, to be an adequate strategy for the long-term goal of promoting specific alternative policies. Even if one envisions a future of relatively decentralized, soft energy sources, that future will be structured in important ways by centralized political and economic institutions. And if one of the key characteristics of new social movements is their acceptance of many of the features of liberal, democratic systems, then they must develop ways of interacting with them to promote certain sorts of policies. Habermas's concern about the dangers of colonization which inhere in "the legal–administrative medium" must continually be taken into account; but it can be taken too far, with the result that new social movements will be less effective in achieving the changes they seek.

Thus there is a distinct gap in Habermas's positive vision of politics. The gap exists between the level of a new, broad collective identity, grounded in a balanced model of modernity, and the level of local or internal practices and institution-building. Given the "self-limiting" character of new social movements, something more in the way of a positive political repertoire must be elucidated for their interactions with the centralized institutions of the economic and political systems.

Having made this criticism, it is important to emphasize again that parts of a positive vision do exist. Habermas does not quite leave us, as Weber did, with a vision of the future in which there are merely sporadic eruptions of countercultural protest against the expanding iron cage.[42] Moreover, the notion of a collective identity grounded in a balanced model of modernity is a significant advance over the views of Foucault about resistance to the sub-jugation of modern life. Habermas's model identifies common elements in new social movements which offer at least the promise of grounds for dialogue and collective action between them which go beyond the exclusively negative one of particularistic and local resistance to normaliz-ation. (I will return to this question from a slightly different direction in the following section.)

Summing up, one can say that Habermas maintains the promise of practical guidance in the Hegelian–Marxian face of his critical theory. Its initial addresses are new social movements, for they are the ones struggling with problems of universal significance to industrial civilization. Habermas's critical interpretation of modernization is thus aimed, at least initially, at helping to orient the self-understanding of these groups in the following ways: (1) by clarifying (through the analysis of internal colonization) at least part of what is at stake in these groups' struggles; (2) by opening up a way of understanding modernity which allows such groups to be radically critical of it without having to reject it totally; and (3) by proffering the model of balance in everyday life as a minimal, formal guide for practices and ideas which can corrode the reified structures and insulated expert cultures of contemporary society.

If Habermas does indeed intend his analysis to have an enlightening effect on the self-understanding of new social movements, it is surely important to ask how the interpretations he offers are viewed by those more directly associated with the struggles and concerns of such movements. One can usefully explore this issue in regard to the women's movement, since some feminists have criticized what they see as both normative and empirical blindspots in his theory. Stated most broadly, the criticism asserts that this theory fails to sensitize us to the "gender subtext" of the key roles and institutions of contemporary capitalism.[43] Habermas's interpretation of society's ills in terms of the colonization phenomenon, it is argued, tends to occlude much that is of intense concern to women. For example, the key diagnostic distinction between system and lifeworld has the effect of playing down the fact that the family, which Habermas conceptualizes largely in terms of the medium of communication, has always in capitalism been shot through with the media of money and power. Conversely, his concep-tualization of the polity and economy largely in terms of the systemic media of money and power plays down the degree to which these subsystems are still structured by the lifeworld, more specifically by traditional norms, which make these subsystems reproduce themselves in ways which reproduce male dominance.

A number of these sorts of criticisms can, I think, be met at least in part by remembering that the problem of domination in Habermas is not just conceptualized as reification (in the sense of colonization). The communicative-ethical basis of his analysis of modernity and modernization contains resources which can certainly bring power relations in the family into the field of analysis.[44] *The Theory of Communicative Action* may be slightly misleading in this regard, for there Habermas's particular line of inquiry leads him to use the concept of power almost exclusively with reference to administrative decisions in the polity; in other words, power is the medium within which these decisions function. But the specific goals of this text should not be taken out of the context of the rest of his work, where power is more broadly conceived (see the dicussion in chapter 4, section IV).

In one sense, however, criticism of Habermas for not adequately illuminating the struggles and concerns of the women's movement is entirely on the mark. But then *adequate* illumination of these phenomena should not really be expected from a research program whose primary practical, historical focus is the crises of modernity (or "new obscurity") rather than the condition of women. To say this, though, does not of course mean that these foci are completely separate; indeed Habermas and many feminists would argue that they are not. If one sees such an overlap, then the real question becomes the degree of reciprocal illumination it is legitimate to expect from two such theoretical perspectives. From the perspective of Habermas's research program, it seems fair to have at least two expectations. First, it should be the case that the program's conceptualizations allow themselves, without distortion, to be supplemented by analyses more closely tied to the other practical, historical focus. Here I think Habermas emerges tolerably well in regard to feminist concerns, as I have indicated in the preceding paragraph and in chapter 4, section III. Secondly, some of Habermas's analyses should be able to supplement or enrich the insights generated by feminist theorists. Here I also think Habermas does fairly well. For example, in regard to the question of new social movements, his model of balance and of a thin collective identity provide a useful interpretation of a consciousness that might be shared by all such movements as they engage in their own more specific struggles. (I will develop another example at the end of the next section.)

III. Modernity and the domination of "inner" nature

I want to focus now on Foucault's thought in a more sustained way than I have done up to now. This is necessary because I agree with those who see his work as raising *the* most provocative contemporary challenge to critical theory.[45] In what follows, I want to suggest first what seems to me the most useful way to conceptualize the general relationship between Foucault and Habermas's critical theory (1). Then I will turn to the more specific question of the subjugation of "inner nature," looking first at how Foucault handles this problem (2), and then at how it might be understood within the Habermasian framework (3). I will argue that, although Foucault's attempt to treat the problem of inner nature by an aestheticization of subjectivity is provocative, it ultimately leaves one with an inadequate way of treating normative or juridical aspects of subjectivity. Habermas's approach, on the other hand, allows at least some access to the aesthetic–expressive dimension, and it can do so within a more comprehensive framework of subjectivity. An examination of this question is especially important because its implications extend beyond Foucault to cast doubt on other critics of modern society who try to achieve some normative foothold through the aesthetic–expressive dimension.

(1)   What makes Foucault's work so challenging to critical theory? At bottom, it is the fact that his genealogies, like Nietzsche's, discover power operating in structures of thinking and behavior which previously seemed to be devoid of power relations. In effect, Foucault provides us with an incisive way of interrogating the structures of culture. His specific targets are the cognitive and institutional structures of modern life. He wants to show us that structures which we take to be thoroughly *enabling* are always simultaneously *constraining*. This orienting intention of all of Foucault's work is clearly expressed in the following: "it seems to me that the critical question today [is:] in what is given to us as universal, necessary, obligatory, what place is occupied by whatever is singular, contingent and the product of arbitrary constraints?"[46]

This question and Foucault's method of analysis command the attention of critical theory because the latter has always claimed to be on its guard against mistaking new forms of mystification for enlightenment and new forms of subjugation for emancipation. This wariness, but also its *limits*, are expressed in Habermas's remark that critical theory must try "to formulate an idea of progress that is subtle and resilient enough not to let itself be blinded by the mere appearance [*Schein*] of emancipation. One thing, of course, it must oppose: the thesis that emancipation itself mystifies."[47] Put simply, critical theory cannot give up the idea of more enabling cultural structures, nor the inherently related problem of subjectivity – since the concept of enabling only has sense when one can say *for whom* those structures are more enabling.

Although the philosophical orientations implied in the two preceding quotations are different, the latter can nevertheless fruitfully attune itself to the former's insights. Foucault's genealogical method can, as I have suggested, be used to call into question a large number of new phenomena associated with the structures of contemporary capitalism.[48] Here also his rhetorical style of describing such phenomena with metaphors we associate with power and coercion can have a useful shocking effect in getting us to imagine what is initially familiar and unthreatening as actually constraining and debilitating. Moreover, such critique can be aimed directly at key ideas of critical theorists themselves, as Foucault himself did when he illuminated the negative side of a psychoanalytically conceived model of self-reflection. Here some of Habermas's early remarks about making the self "transparent" have a far more problematic and ominous ring.[49] And such questions can legitimately be pushed even to the level of asking about the potentially constraining qualities of the ideal speech situation itself.[50]

However, as these questions are played out, there comes a point where the question of *weighing degrees of constraint against degrees of enablement* must be faced. But this problem can only be faced if Foucault offers some alternative conceptions of subjectivity and normativity, in the light of which one can engage in this sort of weighing process.[51] Habermas can claim that he at least makes explicit his views in this regard. The articulation of the core of his research program lays these views open to argument and criticism. Such is not the case with Foucault.

(2)   Although Foucault sometimes hinted at "new kinds of subjectivity," he was notoriously reluctant to be very specific about these.[52] And yet in some of his last essays and interviews, there emerges the outline of a subject whose character informed, if only implicitly, all of his genealogical work. What disturbed Foucault about the rational, self-reflective, self-mastering subject of the humanist tradition in Western philosophy was that it becomes all too easily an accomplice in those modern networks of power which subjugate and provide authoritative scripts for our "bodies and pleasures." The disciplining power of authoritative discourses on, for example, mental or sexual health, can be substantially enhanced if the subject is easily drawn into modes of *self*-discipline or *self*-policing.[53]

From the Foucauldian point of view, the self-reflective, responsible,

Habermasian subject shares this danger. Not only is its developmental genesis one of distancing itself from "inner nature,"[54] but it is also easily drawn into networks of "normalizing" "bio-power."[55] In both these ways, the Habermasian subject apparently shows itself to be inhospitable to its own pre-rational, embodied otherness.[56]

What model of the subject could avoid such a fate? In answer to this question, Foucault offers a model in which the reflective self is more open to the body and pleasures. This subject is one which is oriented, not around making the body and its needs the object of *knowledge* or *judicial regulation*, but rather the object of an *aesthetic self-formation*. Foucault finds some elements of such a conception of the subject among the early Stoics who began to distance themselves from the classical Greek *techne* of life focused on the city to a different sort of *techne*, one focused on "the *bios* as a material for an aesthetic piece of art," in short, "an aesthetics of existence." In addition to this aesthetic focus on the *bios*, Foucault is also attracted to the associated Stoic idea of a "strong structure of existence without any relation with the juridical *per se*, with an authoritarian system, with a disciplinary structure."[57]

This theme of an aesthetics of everyday life finds a modern counterpart, according to Foucault, in the nineteenth century idea of "*dandyism*." In fact, he finds in this idea of Baudelaire's the best point of departure for thinking about what is distinctive in "the attitude of modernity." The dandy is the individual "who makes his body, his behavior, his feelings and passions, his very existence a work of art." And again, this "elaboration of the self" is produced exclusively by attention to the body, pleasures and aesthetic form, not by attention to the social or political realms.[58]

Foucault thus provides us with hints toward a different way of thinking about subjectivity, one which is constituted so as to give a central place to the body, spontaneity and expressiveness. The questions now are: does Habermas's work provide any mode of access to such an idea of subjectivity, and, if so, how adequate is it? In order to answer these questions, it is necessary to turn to a closer consideration of the aesthetic dimension in Habermas's work. This analysis will make it possible to appreciate both the insights and the limits of Foucault's work.

(3) Habermas's treatment of the aesthetic dimension is relatively undeveloped. Nevertheless, some general contours are clear. Several key questions will help guide my remarks. How does the aesthetic dimension relate to the validity claim Habermas call truthfulness or authenticity? What sort of rationality or learning process is manifested within the aesthetic

dimension? And finally, in what sense is this learning process one which is peculiarly open to what has been suppressed, denied or "unlearned" in modern life?

The validity claim of authentic self-expression appears to have a two-fold meaning. On the one hand, it has the straightforward sense of the speaker's sincerity or non-deceptiveness toward the hearer. As was pointed out earlier, this is not a claim which is tested directly by argumentation. Rather it is demonstrated by ongoing action, which shows whether the speaker's declared intentions or motivations have been truthfully expressed or not.

On the other hand, an authentic self-expression is one which expresses a speaker's real or true needs. As was pointed out in chapter 4, there is no philosophical device by which "true" needs can be unequivocally separated from "false" needs for any given person. As with sincerity, it would appear that one can only examine ongoing behavior for clues as to whether someone has truthful interpretations of their own needs or not. Clues would be constituted by evidence that, say, a person's need interpretations are, or are not, self-debilitating or self-deceptive. However, such substantive criteria are, of course, notoriously difficult to apply and they involve a substantial assumption of authority on the part of the observer. There is nevertheless a procedural criterion which, while hardly unambiguous, also gives some basis for evaluating the authenticity claim. As Habermas says, "We call a person rational. . . if he can adopt a reflective attitude to the . . . [cultural] value standards through which desires and feelings [*Bedürfnisnatur*] are interpreted."[59] (This criterion is involved in the kind of problematic the political theorist faces when considering the interrelated problems of power and real interest discussed in chapter 4.)

Now how does this notion of truthful or authentic self-expression connect with the aesthetic dimension and some sort of associated learning process? The idea of such a learning process is crucial to Habermas's claims about the universal significance of modern structures of consciousness. But, as was shown earlier in this chapter, critics have questioned whether any sense can be given to the idea of aesthetic–expressive learning.

There appear to be two aspects to this claim about learning. First of all, Habermas emphasizes a distinctive characteristic which only *modern* aesthetic consciousness shares with experimental science and post-conventional morality. They all manifest a

hypothetical approach to phenomena and experiences, which are isolated from the complexity of their life-world contexts and analyzed under experimentally varied conditions. This is equally true for the states of an objectified nature, for norms and modes of acting, and for the reflective experiences of an "unbound" subjectivity set free from the practical constraints of life.[60]

The second aspect involves the precise sense in which there is some accumulation of knowledge in the aesthetic sphere. One way to imagine such a learning process is to think of a progressive accumulation of epistemic contents in works of art, the way such contents are said to accumulate in theories. Habermas, however, suggests something different:

what accumulates are not epistemic contents, but rather the effects of the inner logical differentiations of special sorts of experience: precisely those aesthetic experiences of which only a decentered, unbound subjectivity is capable.[61]

In order to understand Habermas's meaning here, one must understand his interpretation of what is implied in the process by which the aesthetic dimension became an autonomous cultural sphere in the modern world. Already in the eighteenth century, idealistic aesthetics began the separation of "the beautiful and the sublime, on the one hand, from the useful and the desirable, on the other." In the course of the nineteenth century, there emerged out of this romantic spirit the radicalized consciousness of "aesthetic modernity." And Habermas, like Foucault, sees the work of Baudelaire as the first clear manifestation of this consciousness. Baudelaire was the first to radicalize the distinctiveness of aesthetic experience, divorcing it completely and unequivocally from the claims of tradition, morality and society. The distinctly *modern* aesthetic experience is thus seen as emerging when "the categories of the patterned expectations of organized daily experience collapse, ... the routines of daily action and conventions of ordinary life are destroyed, and the normality of foreseeable and accountable certainties are suspended." Implied in such experience is an "unbounding of subjectivity," a willingness to transgress the normal, a playfulness, imaginativeness and inventiveness.[62]

This distinctiveness of aesthetic experience, this radical questioning of everything, even other shibboliths of modernity, both cognitive and juridical, must nevertheless be recognized as itself dependent upon modern structures of consciousness *in general*. What ties the ethos of "aesthetic modernity" to "cultural modernity" as a whole is that the "reflective experiences of an 'unbound' subjectivity" partake of that general experimental or "hypothetical approach" to phenomena and experiences which a decentration of consciousness first makes possible.[63] A radicalized aesthetic consciousness is thus, like scientific thinking and post-conventional ethical consciousness, something *socially* available only to the modern subject.[64] This point must always be kept firmly in mind whenever an appeal to the aesthetic sense is used by critics of modernity.[65] Briefly, this means that the aesthetic sense cannot be employed as the basis of a critical perspective which claims to observe modernity's problems from the *outside*, as it were.

To return to the original question of learning, what exactly is there in the modern aesthetic experience which allows the accumulation of some sort of insight? Apparently, the key is greater fluidity and flexibility in modes of access to our desires and feelings. The radical decoupling of the aesthetic sense from the imperatives of society and tradition has the potential for informing consciousness about how we normally interpret our desires and feelings in ways which unreflectively mirror the prevailing value standards of the culture around us. The modern aesthetic sense thus has the potential to make us more reflective in relation to who and what is actually structuring the interpretation of our *Bedürfnisnatur*.

This aspect of insight, while important for Habermas, would hardly be adequate for someone like Foucault. For here, one finds the subject engaged in a discipline of self-interrogation, and it is just such a procedure that Foucault is always wary of. However, this ambivalent aspect of insight is only one side of what is made available in the modern aesthetic experience. The other side conforms less to a model of interrogation and more to one of unexpected discovery of things which exceed the confines of any rational, methodical, self-disciplining interrogatory framework. It is this sort of insight which has at least the potential for generating more sensitivity to the subordination of inner nature: the pre-rational and embodied aspects of human being. One thing which links the modern aesthetic consciousness from Baudelaire to the avant-garde in the twentieth century is its inextricable involvement with the shocking, the unexpected, the unknown, with what shatters normal patterns of seeing, thinking and feeling.[66] A central feature of this consciousness is thus its

increased sensitivity to what remains unassimilated in the interpretive achievements of the pragmatic, epistemic, and moral mastery of the demands and challenges of everyday situations; it effects an openness to the expurgated elements of the unconscious, the fantastic, and the mad, the material and the bodily, thus to everything in our speechless contact with reality which is fleeting, so contingent, so immediate, so individualized, simultaneously so far and so near that it escapes our usual categorial grasp.[67]

Hence one way to think about the value of a modern work of art is in relation to its capacity to keep the rational, reflective consciousness exposed to what is pre-rational or what is left out or unassimilated in any given categorical framework or set of cultural standards. In short, it leaves the rational subject with an awareness of the irony of its own achievement: the structures within which this subject moves are *always constraining* in potentially serious ways, *even* when they appear on balance to be the *most enabling ones available.*[68]

One can now see that what is crucial about aesthetic learning is the openness it offers to awareness of the unlearning that necessarily accompanies the other dimensions of cultural modernity and their institutionalization in modern society. If this is true, the practical problem – as both Habermas and Foucault are aware – is how to extricate this potential from the hermetic closure of expertise and infuse everyday life with its effects. Foucault's remarks about an "aesthetics of existence" constitute a proposal for doing just this.[69] However fragmentary his remarks, they are more substantive than anything Habermas has said. Actually Habermas might find Foucault's proposal provocative. And yet, it is clear that he would also find it too limited in certain ways.

Habermas's framework allows for an understanding of subjectivity within which cognitive, juridical and aesthetic dimensions each have a place. Leaving the cognitive aside, a crucial question for Foucault is how he can link up his aesthetic subject with some notion of ethics and politics – in short, the juridical. This question is crucial because, although Foucault is eager to avoid juridical conceptions with a normalizing potential, he does want to endorse certain ethical–political positions. Numerous times he expresses support for some of the same new social movements Habermas endorses. And he clearly wants to establish a coherent link between this support and his ideas on aesthetic subjectivity. In discussing his aesthetics of existence, he states rather explicitly: "Recent liberation movements suffer from the fact that they cannot find any principle on which to base the elaboration of a new ethics."[70]

Foucault clearly sees his "aesthetics of existence" as having ethical implications. It has at its core, he says, an idea of self-control, of "the kind of relationship you ought to have with yourself, *rapport a soi.*" What Foucault means by this is an ongoing formation and articulation of the self according to aesthetic criteria. The primary criterion apparently is the will to "live a beautiful life and to leave to others memories of a beautiful existence." Such an ethics, Foucault hopes, could in no way be implicated in "an attempt to normalize the population."[71]

What is striking about Foucault's ideas here is that he defines ethics simply as this activity of self-formation: "*rapport a soi,* which I call ethics." Thus any reference to *other subjects* and even the possibility of more liberating or consensual forms of common life seems problematic from the start. Foucault speaks of the process of aesthetic self-formation as involving "asceticism in a very broad sense." He intends this phrase to call attention to the practice of self-control which is part of any ethics; but in the case of his own aesthetics of existence, the phrase seems also to have the unavoidable connotation of solitude.[72] Ironically, in the process of constructing such a provocative mode of access to the *self's own* pre-rational, embodied *otherness*, Foucault seems to have simultaneously cut off access to *intersubjective otherness*. At this point it becomes difficult to see how Foucault could possibly bring his aesthetics of existence into any coherent relationship with his endorsement of some forms of collective political action. His antipathy to anything juridical leads him inexorably into a conceptual *cul de sac* in relation to ethics and politics.[73]

Even if Foucault himself is not very helpful in showing how one can move from aesthetic to juridical aspects of subjectivity, one can try to speculate about how such a link might be established. One might point out, for example, that an aesthetics of existence could not literally be a private activity any more than speaking a language. What constitutes art must always be related to some public, shared understanding of style and form.[74] Although true, this insight does not take one very far toward any normative conceptions.

Another possible avenue might be the one hinted at by Adorno, whose totalistic critique of modern society and its cognitive and juridical forms of consciousness was also accompanied by an appeal to aesthetic conscious-ness.[75] What attracted Adorno to aesthetic consciousness was the non-grasping, non-dominating way it related to its object. Thus he found in the aesthetic dimension a model of intersubjective reconciliation, of a com-munity which allows intersubjective otherness to flourish.[76]

Perhaps Foucault's aesthetics of existence could be thought through in a similar fashion. I doubt, however, if this would really be possible. The prob-lem with thinking that the aesthetic dimension can be a *model* for community has been clearly stated by Albrecht Wellmer:

the aesthetic synthesis represented by the work of art, even if we concede to Adorno that it contains a *promesse du bonheur,* can hardly be understood as a model of dialogical relationship *between* individuals, who recognize each other in their individuality, as equals and as absolute others both at the same time. If beauty is a promise of happi-ness, of reconciliation with our internal and with external nature, the work of art would be a *medium* of this transcending experience rather than a *model* of reconcili-ation itself. For at least the *moral* "synthesis" of a dialogical relationship can only be *mediated,* but not be brought to *appearance* by the aesthetic synthesis of the work of art. Even if, as Adorno stresses, the subject, which comes to speak in the work of art, is a "we" (and not the individual artist), this collective subject speaks with *one* voice, speaking to itself, as it were; i.e., the rules of "synthesis" of this trans-subjective speech cannot possibly prefigure the open rules of a dialogue with *many* voices. Aesthetic synthesis is no possible model for a state of society free from repression.[77]

If we use this distinction between model and medium we might be led to think in ways which build on both Foucault and Habermas. Foucault's image of an aesthetics of existence might be interpreted as a provocative way of thinking about the process of self-formation, in which aesthetic criteria might come to have a constitutive significance for the way a subject thinks and acts in general. Thus, Foucault might be seen as giving us a way of conceptualizing how the aesthetic dimension's potential for tapping into the self's pre-rational, embodied otherness can be released in such a fashion that its effects infuse all aspects of everyday life. By this I mean that the aesthetic sense can be seen as permeating not only our need interpretations, but also our moral–political judgments about the kinds of social institutions and technological infrastructure we find satisfying and self-empowering, as well as our judgments about what sorts of knowledge we find worth seeking.

Taken in this light, it is likely that Habermas would find Foucault's ideas suggestive, since his own speculations about aesthetics and everyday life have a similar ring. He argues that when aesthetic experience is infused into everyday life, it then

no longer only affects our evaluative language or only renews the interpretation of needs that color our perceptions; rather it reaches into our cognitive interpretations and normative expectations and transforms the totality in which these moments are related to each other.[78]

But as Wellmer suggests, and Habermas is aware, such a role for aesthetic subjectivity cannot replace an at least partially independent elaboration of juridical subjectivity. A useful way of clarifying this point is to look at recent feminist thought. A recurrent theme there, as in Foucault, is how modern society and consciousness deny our character as embodied creatures and suppress our aesthetic–expressive capacities. Women's experience in this society is seen as making them especially sensitive to these problems. An important question for feminist thinkers is therefore how this sort of gender-based sensitivity can inform everyday life in a transformative way. Part of this inquiry involves asking what this means in terms of how we might reconceptualize moral and political life.

Some feminists have argued that the different experience of women can be used as a *model* for this reconceptualization. Thus "mothering" and "attentive care" become new models for the moral–political community.[79]

This view has been countered, correctly I think, by other feminists who, while not denying the importance of an emphasis on embodiment, aesthetics and expressiveness as a *medium* for reconceptualizing the substantive qualities a community might have, nevertheless feel that the general character of moral–political relationships among equals cannot be modeled on maternal thinking.[80]

IV. Concluding remarks

Throughout this book I have argued that Habermas's recent work should be taken as a sketch for an alternative research program in the social sciences, with the communicative model of reason and action as its core. Now that the particulars of this project have been examined, it is useful to stop for a moment and ask: What does it mean for critical theory to embrace such an overall theoretical strategy? It might be objected that this orientation constitutes an illegitimate appropriation of the original Frankfurt School's intentions. After all, were its aims not inextricably tied to the "power of negative thinking" or critique? And thus does the whole idea of a research program for critical theory not harbor within it a positivistic urge to grasp its subject matter in a way which implies subtle forms of domination?[81] Such questions emerge quite naturally from texts written during and after World War II, such as the *Dialectic of Enlightenment* and Adorno's *Negative Dialectics*. For his new project, however, Habermas harks back to the Frankfurt School of the 1930s for inspiration. There he finds the beginnings of a promising "interdisciplinary research program" for the social sciences. That initial program foundered, though, because its normative basis was too entangled with an unsupportable "objective teleology of history" derived from Marx's view of the dialectical relation between forces of production and relations of production. The communicative model Habermas offers is designed precisely to remedy this normative difficulty in critical theory.[82] With this shift accomplished, Habermas sees the prospects for fruitful social research along some of the same lines taken by earlier critical theorists: the forms of social integration and pathologies of contemporary societies; family socialization and ego development; mass media and mass culture; and strategies by which capitalism mutes some sorts of protests and stimulates others.[83]

Thus, for Habermas, global objections inspired by Adorno's later work cannot be accepted as automatically fatal to his project. Neither, however, are they to be ignored. Rather they constitute a source of perennial concern about what the concepts central to Habermas's project leave unsaid and marginalized. Indeed Habermas's attention to precisely this problem, whether emphasized by Adorno or Foucault, is one of the things I have tried to stress throughout the book.

* A related problem which I have also struggled with in this text is the status and intention of Habermas's universalism. Although I have tried to show that his views here are more plausible and defensible than some of his critics have implied, it nevertheless seems clear that such arguments are not likely to elicit mass conversions among contextualists and relativists, any more than the reverse is likely to occur. But this should not really be surprising, because what is at issue is one of the key questions of contemporary philosophy; and it is likely to be answered only in a piecemeal way over a long period of time. This question, at its simplest, is what it means to create some legitimate commonality among different forms of life, with "legitimate" here carrying the sense of reciprocity and mutual respect. What I would argue is that both contextualists and universalists can shed different, but complementary, light on such a question.

It is important to stress that the creation of some legitimate commonality is not the self-willed project of philosophical or social science elites. Rather it arises, as Clifford Geertz puts it, because we increasingly live in a world where "nobody is leaving anybody else alone and isn't ever again going to."[84] The project then in one which we are *practically* confronted with on a global scale. The contextualist contribution to this problematic is to explore alternative forms of life and help build communicative links between them by fostering interpretive practices which take the form of "reciprocal commentaries, mutually deepening."[85] The universalist contribution might accordingly be envisioned as drawing out one of the implications of this task: in particular, how it is premised upon motivations involving inter-subjective recognition and equal respect; and how we (at least some of us) feel deeply that such motivations can somehow be supported by good reasons whose force is not exhausted within only one form of life.

Notes

Introduction

1 Richard Rorty, *Consequences of Pragmatism* (Minneapolis: University of Minnesota Press, 1982) pp. 158, 208; Clifford Geertz, *Local Knowledge: Further Essays in Interpretive Anthropology* (New York: Basic Books, 1983) p. 234; Michael Walzer, *Spheres of Justice: A Defense of Pluralism and Equality* (New York: Basic Books, 1983) pp. xii, 314; and Jean-François Lyotard and Jean-Loup Thebaud, *Just Gaming*, translated by Wlad Godzich (Minneapolis: University of Minnesota Press, 1985), pp. 66–7.

2 *REPLY*, p. 253. Emphasis mine.

3 "The New Obscurity: The Crisis of the Welfare State and The Exhaustion of Utopian Energies," *Philosophy and Social Criticism* 11 (Winter 1986).

4 "Modernity versus Postmodernity," *New German Critique* 22 (Winter 1981), pp. 11–12; "Neo-Conservative Cultural Critique in the United States and West Germany," *Telos* 56 (Summer 1983); *PDM*, pp. 11–12; and *TCA*, p. xli.

5 *PDM*, p. 11; *TCA*, part II, ch. 1, and p. 221; and "Modernity versus Postmodernity."

6 *PDM*, pp. 16, 26; "The New Obscurity," pp. 3–5; *TKH*, ch. 8.

7 *PDM*, p. 7.

8 "Consciousness-Raising or Redemptive Criticism," *New German Critique* (Spring 1979) p. 56. I have corrected a translation error in this text. In the last sentence, "enlightenment" was incorrectly inserted in place of "emancipation."

9 *PDM*, p. 27.

10 *PDM*, pp. 344–6.

11 *TKH*, pp. 138–41, 556, 560–2; *TCA*, pp. xxxix–xl, 273–4, 278.

12 J. Donald Moon, "The Logic of Political Inquiry," in Fred Greenstein and Nelson Polsby, eds., *Handbook of Political Science*, vol. 1 (Reading, Massachusetts: Addison Wesley, 1975); and Terence Ball, "From Paradigms to Research Programs: Toward a Post-Kuhnian Political Science," *American Journal of Political Science* 20: 1 (Feb. 1976); Moon, "Values and Political Theory: A Modest Defense of a Qualified Cognitivism," *Journal of Politics* 39 (Nov. 1977), p. 900; Moon and Brian Fay, "What Would an Adequate Philosophy of Social Science Look Like?," *Philosophy of the Social Sciences* 7: 3 (1977), p. 222; and Imre Lakatos, "Falsification and the Methodology of Scientific Research Programs," in Lakatos and Alan Musgrave, eds., *Criticism and The Growth of Knowledge* (New York: Cambridge University Press, 1970).

13 Lakatos, "Falsification," pp. 133ff.
14 Cf. John S. Dryzek, "The Progress of Political Science," *The Journal of Politics* 48 (May 1986).

1 Rationality, social theory and political philosophy

1 Lakatos, "Falsification and the Methodology of Scientific Research Programs," in Lakatos and Musgrave, eds., *Criticism and The Growth of Knowledge* (New York: Cambridge University Press, 1970).
2 See the literature cited in the Introduction, n. 12, especially Moon, "Values and Political Theory: A Modest Defense of a Qualified Cognitivism," *Journal of Politics* 39 (Nov. 1977).
3 I am not, of course, arguing that if our moral judgements diverge from what appear to be enduring features of social life, we are *obliged* to change them.
4 On how historical contingency affects the evaluation of social science research programs, see Dryzek, "The Progress of Political Science," *Journal of Politics* 48 (1986).
5 See especially *TKH*, pp. 561 ff, 583–4; "Interpretive Social Science v. Hermeneuticism," in Norma Haan *et al.*, *Social Science as Moral Inquiry* (New York: Columbia University Press, 1983); and "Die Philosophie als Platzhalter und Interpret," *MKH*.
6 See, for example, John O'Neill, "Critique and Remembrance," in O'Neill, ed., *On Critical Theory* (New York: Seabury Press, 1976).
7 *REPLY*, pp. 221–5. A term like "model of the subject" is one which critical theorists have traditionally been leery of, given its potential for serving as the cover under which characteristics particular to a given historical period are presented as characteristics which are universal. Cf. Habermas's own early article on "Philosophical Anthropology," in *KK*.
8 Peter Winch, "Understanding a Primitive Society," *American Philosophical Quarterly* 1 (1964). Reprinted in Winch, *Ethics and Action* (London: Routledge and Kegan Paul, 1972), p. 34. On some of the problems with contextual rationality, see Steven Lukes, "Some Problems about Rationality," in Brian Wilson, ed., *Rationality* (New York: Harper and Row, 1970).
9 The classic works in this area for political theory are Anthony Downs, *An Economic Theory of Democracy* (New York: Harper and Row, 1957); Mancur Olson, *The Logic of Collective Action* (Cambridge, Massachusetts: Harvard University Press, 1971 ed.); and Brian Barry, *Sociologists, Economists and Democracy* (University of Chicago Press, 1978 ed.). Useful overviews of this research program are Dennis Meuller, *Public Choice* (New York: Cambridge University Press, 1979) and Brian Barry and Russell Hardin, eds., *Rational Man and Irrational Society* (Berkeley: Sage Publications, 1982).
10 Some rational choice theorists *define* a rational choice as one based on the assumption of self-interested motivation. See, Meuller, *Public Choice*, p. 1. The view that self-interest is simply the most methodologically fruitful assumption to make is represented by Hardin, *Collective Action* (Baltimore: Johns Hopkins University Press, 1982), p. 11; cf. also, Jon Elster, *Ulysses and the Sirens* (Cambridge University Press, 1979), p. 142.
11 Elster, *Ulysses*, pp. 141–2.

12 Cf. Barry, *Economists*, pp. 1–6, 165–72.
13 See, for example, Downs, *An Economic Theory*, pp. 12, 23.
14 For an explanation of "collective" or "public goods," see Olson, *Logic*, pp. 14–16.
15 See the discussion of Downs's analysis of voting in Barry, *Economists*, ch. 2.
16 Olson, *Logic*, ch. 1.
17 In regard to voting, see John A. Ferejohn and Morris P. Fiorina, "The Paradox of Non-Voting," *American Political Science Review* 68 (June 1974). More generally, see Robert Axelrod, *The Emergence of Cooperation* (New York: Basic Books, 1984).
18 Olson, *Logic*, p. 51.
19 Hardin, *Collective Action*, chs. 6–7, 10–13. Although Hardin admits the importance of "extra-rational motivation," he tries to extend the strategic model further than is really plausible. See his discussion of the emergence of norms of cooperation among backpackers, pp. 174–5. Contrast the interesting discussion of the limits of rational choice in Claus Offe, "The Two Logics of Collective Action," in *Disorganized Capitalism: Contemporary Transformations of Work and Politics* (Cambridge, Massachusetts: MIT Press, 1985).
20 See William Riker and Peter Ordeshook, *An Introduction to Positive Political Theory* (Englewood Cliffs, New Jersey: Prentice-Hall, 1973), p. 63; also James Q. Wilson, *Political Organization* (New York: Basic Books, 1973), ch. 3.
21 Stanley Benn, "Rationality and Political Behavior," in Benn and G.W. Mortimore, eds., *Rationality in The Social Sciences* (London: Routledge and Kegan Paul, 1976), pp. 255–6.
22 See Winch, *The Idea of a Social Science* (New York: Humanities Press, 1958).
23 The term "thick description" is used by Clifford Geertz in "Thick Description: Toward an Interpretive Theory of Culture," in Geertz, *The Interpretation of Cultures* (New York: Basic Books, 1973).
24 *KHI*, pp. 175–6.
25 *TCA*, p. xxxix.
26 *CES*, p. 41.
27 An interesting recent attempt to take account of this dimension of motivation is Howard Margolis, *Selfishness, Altruism and Rationality* (New York: Cambridge University Press, 1982). Using an evolutionary theoretical framework, he argues that humans have a two-channel genetic program which causes them to have both the motivation of self-interest and that of "group interest." Different types of situations will call forth one or the other of these motivations. Although Margolis hopes to develop a model with analytical power comparable to those employing only self-interest, it is difficult to see how this could be achieved. It seems likely that prediction as to such things as the precise points of trade-off between self- and group-interest will be heavily dependent on particular knowledge of social and historical background.
28 Max Weber, *Economy and Society: An Outline of Interpretive Sociology* (Berkeley: University of California Press, 1978), pp. 24–5. Rational choice theorists sometimes, as an aside, refer to "value rationality" as another possible category of rationality in addition to the strategic; see, for example, Barry and Hardin, *Rational Man*, p. 383.

29 Cf. the discussion of this kind of difference in Benn, "The Problematic Rationality of Political Participation," in Peter Laslett and James Fishkin, eds., *Philosophy, Politics, and Society* (New Haven: Yale University Press, 1979), pp. 310–11.
30 Weber does admit that traditional behavior may "shade over" into behavior which is "value-rational." What I am claiming is that this shaded area is what is crucial to developing a philosophically and sociologically useful conception of rationality which is distinct from the strategic conception.
31 Isaiah Berlin, "Rationality of Value Judgments," in Carl J. Friedrich, ed., *Rational Decision* NOMOS VII (New York: Atherton, 1964).
32 Colin Turnbull, *The Mountain People* (New York: Simon and Schuster, 1972).
33 Turnbull, *The Mountain People*, p. 135.
34 Steven Lukes comes close to seeing this point in "Relativism: Cognitive and Moral," *Supplementary Proceedings of the Aristotelian Society* (1974); reprinted in Lukes, *Essays in Social Theory* (London: Macmillan and Co., 1977).
35 Turnbull, *The Mountain People*, pp. 283–6.
36 Cf. Olson, *Logic*, p. 64.
37 Winch, "Understanding a Primitive Society;" and *The Idea of a Social Science* (New York: Humanities Press, 1958).
38 For a balanced view of Winch and his critics, see A.I. Dirksen, "On an Unnoticed Key to Reality," *Philosophy of the Social Sciences* 8 (1978).
39 From this perspective, it might become irrational to vote if, say, the electoral process exhibited undemocratic characteristics of some blatant sort.
40 Winch, "Understanding a Primitive Society."
41 See Dirksen, "On an Unnoticed Key."
42 Winch, "Understanding a Primitive Society," pp. 33–5.
43 Susan Hekman has argued recently that Gadamer's interpretive framework overcomes such problems. See Hekman, *Hermeneutics and the Sociology of Knowledge* (Notre Dame University Press, Indiana, 1986), pp. 117–55. Although Hekman makes some interesting observations, her argument about Gadamer is not completely convincing. See my review of her book in *The Journal of Politics* (forthcoming, 1987), and my "Post-Structuralism and Political Reflection," *Political Theory* (forthcoming, 1988).
44 For critiques of Winch on the foregoing points, see Karl-Otto Apel, *Analytic Philosophy of Language and the Geisteswissenschaften* (New York: Humanities Press, 1967), p. 56; Alisdair MacIntyre, "The Idea of a Social Science," in B. Wilson, ed., *Rationality* (New York: Harper and Row, 1970), p. 118; and especially John Thompson, *Critical Hermeneutics: Paul Ricoeur and Jurgen Habermas* (Cambridge University Press, 1981), chs. 4–5. For an attempt to use a contextual model to understand changes in constitutional law, see John Brigham, *Constitutional Language* (Westport, Connecticut: Greenwood Press, 1978).
45 See, for example, Samuel Popkin's analysis of peasant movements in *The Rational Peasant: The Political Economy of Rural Society in Vietnam* (Berkeley: University of California Press, 1979), pp. 18, 22, 27.
46 For example, Popin's rational choice approach to the study of precapitalist peasant society illustrates this sort of overall perspective. He sets out to

critique the "moral economy" approach to such societies, which focuses on the normative structures of village society and the meaning and protection they give to a peasant's life. Popkin is concerned to expose such structures as instruments which maintain or promote inequality and domination, and to argue that capitalist penetration of such structures provides an enhancement of individual peasant welfare. Cf. also Barry, *Economists*, pp. 162–4, 173–4.

47 Winch does argue that he is not an extreme relativist. For example, he sees a common significance accorded by all societies to matters of "birth, death and sexual relations." The limitation on moral relativism offered by such a position, at least as it has been worked out so far by Winch, are, however, not substantial enough to satisfy those who seek something closer to the traditional universalism of Western moral and political philosophy. For Winch's position, see "Understanding a Primitive Society," "Introduction," and "Convention and Human Nature," in Winch, *Ethics and Action*.

48 See, for example, MacIntyre, *After Virtue* (Notre Dame, Indiana: University of Notre Dame Press, 1980); and Michael Walzer, *Spheres of Justice* (New York: Basic Books, 1983).

49 Stuart Hampshire, "Morality and Convention," in Amartya Sen and Bernard Williams, eds., *Utilitarianism and Beyond* (Cambridge University Press, 1982), p. 148.

50 John Rawls, *A Theory of Justice* (Cambridge, Massachusetts: Harvard University Press, 1971). Another prominent adherent of the universalist position is Ronald Dworkin. This comes out most clearly in his review of Walzer's *Spheres of Justice*, in *The New York Review of Books*, April 14, 1983, pp. 4–6.

51 Rawls, "Kantian Constructivism in Moral Theory," *The Journal of Philosophy* 77 (Sept, 1980). Rawls does not explicitly endorse ethical relativism, but leaves the question open as to the validity of his theory in a "wider context," (p. 518).

52 Richard Rorty, *Consequences of Pragmatism* (Minneapolis: University of Minnesota Press, 1982), pp. 158, 208.

53 Walzer, *Spheres of Justice*.

54 Walzer, *Spheres of Justice*, pp. xii, 314.

55 *LC*, p. 120.

2 Communicative action and rationality

1 "Interview with Jürgen Habermas." Interviewed by Detlev Horster and Willem van Reijen. Translated by Ron Smith, *New German Critique* 18 (Fall 1979), p. 43. Cf. *TCA* pp. 140–1.

2 Max Horkheimer and Theodor W. Adorno, *Dialectic of Enlightenment* (New York: Seabury Press, 1972). Cf. also Max Horkheimer, *The Eclipse of Reason* (New York: Seabury Press, 1947); and the interview cited in n. 1.

3 For an overview of this problem, see my "The Normative Basis of Critical Theory," *Polity* 16 (Fall 1983). Cf. *TCA*, pp. 373–99.

4 "The Analytical Theory of Science and Dialectics" in Adorno *et al.*, *The Positivist Dispute in German Sociology*, translated by Glyn Adey and David Frisby (New York: Harper and Row, 1976), p. 143; and "A Positivistically

Bisected Rationalism," in the same volume, pp. 198–9, 219. Cf. *TCA,* p. 10.

5 "Positivistically Bisected," pp. 198–9, 221 ff.

6 "Analytical Theory," p. 149.

7 "Analytical Theory," p. 162.

8 See esp. Horkheimer, "Traditional and Critical Theory," in Horkheimer, ed., *Critical Theory: Selected Essays,* translated by Matthew J. O'Connell and others (New York: Seabury Press, 1972).

9 *TP,* pp. 8–9; *KHI,* pp. 194–5 ff.

10 "Analytical Theory," pp. 153–5.

11 *KHI,* p. 176; "Positivistically Bisected," pp. 215, 220–1.

12 Habermas's arguments as to what in a strictly logical sense is entailed by positivism have a number of difficulties; see Russell Keat, *The Politics of Social Theory: Habermas, Freud and Positivism* (University of Chicago Press, 1981), ch. 1.

13 See, for example, Keat, *The Politics of Social Theory,* chs. 3–4; and McCarthy, *The Critical Theory of Jürgen Habermas* (Cambridge, Massachusetts: MIT Press, 1978), ch. 2.

14 "A Postscript to *Knowledge and Human Interests," Philosophy of the Social Sciences* 3 (1973); *TG,* p. 178; *REPLY,* pp. 232–3; *TCA,* p. xxxix.

15 *REPLY,* p. 221; *TCA* pp. xii, 140.

16 *TCA,* pp. xi; *REPLY,* p. 232–3.

17 *CES,* pp. 1 (and n. 1), 13.

18 J.L. Austin, *How to Do Things with Words* (Cambridge, Massachusetts: Harvard University Press, 1975 ed.); John Searle, *Speech Acts* (New York: Cambridge University Press, 1969).

19 *TCA,* pp. 99, 329; *CES,* p. 29.

20 *TCA,* pp. 69–70, 137, 287; *CES,* p. 3; *REPLY,* pp. 236–7; *PDM,* p. 232.

21 *TCA,* pp. 8, 9, 15.

22 *TG,* pp. 121, 123.

23 I have developed this schema from several sources. See *KK,* pp. 196–7; *CES,* p. 89; and "Notizen zur Entwicklung der Interaktionskompetenz," in *VET.* The three competences can be analytically separated, but the development of each one is closely dependent on the development of the others.

24 *CES,* pp. 27–9, 33, 58, *TCA* p. 275.

25 For Habermas's ideas on formal pragmatics, see "Toward a Theory of Communicative Competence," in Hans Peter Dreitzel, ed., *Patterns of Communicative Behavior* (New York: Macmillan, 1970); *TG,* pp. 101–4; *CES,* pp. 1–68; and *TCA,* pp. 273–336.

26 *CES,* p. 58. This classification is made somewhat more elaborate in *TCA,* pp. 325–6, 329.

27 *PDM,* pp. 230–1.

28 *CES,* p. 1.

29 For Habermas's attempt to try to meet these and other criticisms, see *TCA,* ch. 3.

30 John B. Thompson, "Universal Pragmatics," in John B. Thompson and David Held, eds., *Habermas: Critical Debates* (Cambridge, Massachusetts: MIT Press, 1982), pp. 125–8.

31 Thompson, "Universal Pragmatics," p. 128.

32 Foucault's ideas on the "disciplinary" character of modern society are taken up in chs. 5 and 6.
33 *REPLY*, p. 271; *TCA*, pp. 331–2. My emphasis.
34 *TCA*, p. 332.
35 *TCA*, p. 287.
36 *REPLY*, p. 270.
37 *TKH*, ch. 5.
38 Cf. the criticism by David Rasmussen, "Communicative Action and Philosophy: Reflections on Habermas' *Theorie des kommunikativen Handelns*," *Philosophy and Social Criticism* 9 (Spring 1982); and Anthony Giddens, "Reason Without Revolution? Habermas' *Theorie des kommunikativen Handelns*," in Richard J. Bernstein, ed., *Habermas and Modernity* (Cambridge, Massachusetts: MIT Press, 1985), p. 100.
39 *QCQ*, p. 237.
40 See chs. 5 and 6.
41 *QCQ*, p. 237; *PDM*, p. 366.
42 As was shown in ch. 1, this task has both a normative and a theoretical–explanatory dimension.
43 *PDM*, pp. 230–1.
44 *PDM*, pp. 231–2; *CES*, pp. 38–40.
45 *PDM*, pp. 236–7.
46 *PDM*, p. 241.
47 It might be rather persuasively argued that non-serious or fictive speech does have an important role in action coordination, which Habermas overlooks. Think of the importance for political and economic actions of metaphors embedded in the lifeworld: mechanical metaphors in the eighteenth century and systems mataphors today.
48 Cf. *PDM*, pp. 197 ff; and Gillian Rose, *The Dialectic of Nihilism: Post-Structuralism and Law* (Oxford: Blackwell, 1984), ch. 8.
49 *PDM*, pp. 240–2. My emphasis.
50 On the general theme of "aestheticism" in Foucault, see Allan Megill, *Prophets of Extremity* (Berkeley: University of California Press, 1985), pp. 2–3, and ch. 5. Megill's discussion however, does not include some of Foucault's last essays, which are crucial to my interpretation in ch. 6.
51 *CES*, p. 1.
52 *TCA*, pp. 75, 84.
53 *TCA*, pp. 87–8.
54 *TCA*, p. 285; *REPLY*, p. 263.
55 *TCA*, p. 88.
56 *TCA*, p. 88.
57 *TCA*, pp. 85, 88–90.
58 *LC*, pp. 104 ff.; *TG*, pp. 121, 123; *TCA*, p. 89.
59 *TCA*, p. 90. Cf. Goffman, *The Presentation of Self in Everyday Life* (New York: Doubleday and Co., 1959).
60 *TCA*, p. 91. Habermas limits the subjective world to "*intentional* experiences" (hopes, wishes, etc.) and avoids the much disputed problem of utterances reporting sensations.

61 *TCA*, pp. 92–2. Utterances which express opinions about the objective world and intentions to intervene in it can also be taken to be part of the subjective world; they, however, have an internal relation to the objective world which pure subjective experiences do not. Thus the latter are not open to rationalization according to the criteria of truth or success.

62 *TCA*, p. 93.

63 *TCA*, pp. 94–5, 285–6.

64 *TCA*, pp. 69–70, 86.

65 *TCA*, pp. 69–70, 95, 98, 101.

66 *TCA*, pp. 94–5, 99.

67 *TCA*, pp. 94–5, 99.

68 *TCA*, pp. 282 ff.

68 *TCA*, pp. 297–8.

69 *TCA*, pp. 298–300.

70 Keat, *The Politics of Social Theory*, p. 196.

71 *TCA*, pp. 102ff.

72 *TCA*, p. 115.

73 Richard Bernstein, "Introduction," in Bernstein, ed., *Habermas and Modernity* (Cambridge, Massachusetts: MIT Press, 1985), p. 10.

74 Thomas McCarthy, "Reflections on Rationalization in *The Theory of Communicative Action*," *Praxis International* 4 (July 1984), pp. 184–5. Reprinted in Bernstein.

75 *TCA*, pp. 294, 302.

76 *CES*, p. 63.

77 *WAHR*, *TCA*, pp. 17, 23ff.

78 *TCA*, p. 17.

79 *TCA*, p. 101.

80 See especially *WAHR* and *MKH*.

81 Habermas's consensus theory of truth has been subjected to penetrating criticism by John B. Thompson in *Critical Hermeneutics: Paul Ricoeur and Jürgen Habermas* (Cambridge University Press, 1981), pp. 198–213. See also Mary Hesse, "Science and Objectivity," in Thompson and Held, *Habermas*, pp. 98–115. It should be emphasized here that Habermas could admit that these criticisms are correct without having to modify his consensus theory of normative legitimacy.

82 *TP*, pp. 142–69.

83 Anthony Giddens, "Labor and Interaction," in Held and Thompson, *Habermas*, p. 156.

84 Giddens, "Labor and Interaction," pp. 158–60.

85 *REPLY*, p. 266; *TCA*, pp. 285–6.

86 *TCA*, p. 295. Actually Habermas prefers to use the concept "*Gewalt*," translated as "force," in this context. But since the connotations of "force" do not make it really any more appropriate here than "power," I will stick to the latter term and simply distinguish this case as one sense of "power." See *REPLY*, p. 269.

87 *TCA*, pp. 288–95. Cf. J.L. Austin, *How to do Things with Words*, pp. 101–8.

88 *TCA*, p. 288.

89 *TCA*, pp. 287–305.
90 Fred Dallmayr, *Polis and Praxis: Exercises in Contemporary Political Theory* (Cambridge, Massachusetts: MIT Press, 1984), pp. 239–40.
91 *TCA*, p. 101.
92 *TCA*, p. 286.
93 Dallmayr, *Polis and Praxis*, p. 240.
94 Dallmayr, *Polis and Praxis*, Introduction and ch. 7.
95 Dallmayr, *Polis and Praxis*, p. 214.
96 Dallmayr does try to link up his scheme with political theory, but the result remains impressionistic at best (pp. 217–23).
97 Dallmayr, *Polis and Praxis*, pp. 214–17.
98 *TCA*, pp. 274 ff.
99 *TCA*, pp. 279, 284, 328.

3 Justice and the foundations of communicative ethics

1 "Über Moralität und Sittlichkeit – Was macht eine Lebensform 'rational'?" in Herbert Schnädelbach, ed., *Rationalität* (Frankfurt: Suhrkamp, 1984), p. 225; *LC*, p. 89; *MKH*, pp. 54, 113–14; *REPLY*, p. 251.
2 *MKH*, p. 78.
3 *MKH*, pp. 53, 73; *LC*, p. 108.
4 See, for example, J.L. Mackie, *Ethics: Inventing Right and Wrong* (Harmondsworth: Penguin Books, 1977), pp. 99–100, 105.
5 For other interpretations, see *MKH*, pp. 73–5.
6 *MKH*, p. 103; *REPLY*, p. 257.
7 McCarthy draws this distinction out very clearly in *The Critical Theory of Jürgen Habermas* (Cambridge, Massachusetts: MIT Press, 1978), p. 326.
8 *MKH*, pp. 75–7; *LC*, pp. 111–16.
9 *LC*, pp. 89, 108. Rawls, *A Theory of Justice* (Cambridge, Massachusetts: Harvard University Press, 1971), pp. 18, 130–5; and "Kantian Constructivism in Moral Theory," *Journal of Philosophy* 77 (1980), pp. 515–72. Rawls uses the term "reasonable" to express this sense of rationalization.
10 Adina Schwartz, "Moral Neutrality and Primary Goods," *Ethics* 83 (July 1973), pp. 302–7; Jean Hampton, "Contracts and Choices: Does Rawls have a Social Contract Theory?" *Journal of Philosophy* 77 (June 1980), pp. 332–5, 337. I borrow this way of distinguishing between "what justice is" and "what justice demands" from Philip Pettit, "Habermas on Truth and Justice," in G.H.R. Parkinson, ed., *Marx and Marxisms*. Royal Institute of Philosophy Lecture Series: 14. Supplement to *Philosophy* 1982 (Cambridge University Press, 1982), pp. 217 ff.
11 *MKH*, pp. 4, 103–4, 108.
12 Both of these topics will be taken up in more detail in the following chapter.
13 *MKH*, pp. 90–4, 96–7, 110–11; Cf. *CES*, pp. 21–6.
14 *TG*, pp. 114–20; Cf. *MKH*, p. 110.
15 *LC*, p. 120 *RHM*, p. 339.
16 Alan Gewirth, *Reason and Morality* (University of Chicago Press, 1978), esp. ch. 2.

17 *MKH,* p. 90. Habermas borrows the concept of "performative contradiction" from Karl-Otto Apel, *Towards a Transformation of Philosophy,* translated by Glyn Adey and David Frisby (London: Routledge and Kegan Paul, 1980), pp. 262 ff.

18 Stephen K. White, "On the Normative Structure of Action: Gerwirth and Habermas," *The Review of Politics* 44 (April, 1982).

19 *CES,* p. 64; *RHM,* p. 339.

20 *MKH,* pp. 109–10.

21 Cf. Friedrich Kambartel, "Wie ist praktische Philosophie konstruktiv moglich?" in Kambartel, ed., *Praktische Philosophie und konstruktiv Wissenschaftstheorie* (Frankfurt: Suhrkamp, 1974).

22 See the discussion of "conceptual necessity" in Kant and Hegel by Charles Taylor, *Hegel* (Cambridge University Press, 1975) pp. 95–6.

23 Taylor shows how conceptual necessity in this sense is not simply a question of the meanings of words. *Hegel,* pp. 95–6.

24 Thomas Hobbes, *Leviathan* (New York: Macmillan, 1962), ch. 13; H.L.A. Hart, *The Concept of Law* (Oxford University Press, 1961) ch. 9, esp. pp. 189–91; also Hart, "Positivism and the Separation of Law and Morals," *Harvard Law Review* 71 (1958), p. 593, reprinted in R.M.Dworkin, ed., *The Philosophy of Law* (London: Oxford University Press, 1977), pp. 35–6.

25 Hart, "Positivism and the Separation of Law and Morals," pp. 35–6.

26 *MKH,* p. 94; Cf. *CES,* pp. 21–6.

27 Mackie, *Ethics,* pp. 84–5.

28 Mackie, *Ethics,* pp. 97–100.

29 *MKH,* p. 110.

30 *MKH,* p. 98.

31 For Habermas's use of the category "traditional societies," see *LC,* p. 19; *TRS,* p. 94.

32 *MKH,* pp. 97–9.

33 *MKH,* pp. 100–3; *REPLY,* p. 253. Cf. Apel, *Towards a Transformation of Philosophy,* translated by G. Adey and D. Frisby (London: Routledge and Kegan Paul, 1980), ch. 7.

34 *MKH,* p. 98; *WAHR,* pp. 252–60.

35 *MKH,* p. 99.

36 *MKH,* pp. 97–8.

37 *MKH,* p. 99. This particular formulation of the rules constituting an ideal speech situation was suggested by a sympathetic critic; see Robert Alexy, "Eine Theorie des praktischen Diskurses," in Willi Oelmüller, ed., *Normenbegrundung und Normendurchsetzung* (Paderborn: Schöningh, 1978), pp. 40–1. For Habermas's original formulation, see *WAHR,* pp. 255–7.

38 *WAHR,* p. 257.

39 *WAHR,* pp. 251–6. Although this rule might seem to be relevant only to practical argumentation, Habermas claims that theoretical argumentation, at its most radical level, cannot be sharply separated from practical argumentation; and thus this rule is relevant for argumentation in general. Cf. McCarthy, *The Critical Theory,* pp. 305–6.

40 *WAHR,* p. 256.

41 *MKH,* pp. 54, 103.

42 *LC,* p. 108.

43 The terminology "post-conventional" and "conventional" follows the Piaget–Kohlberg tradition in cognitive developmental psychology. See, for example, Lawrence Kohlberg, "From Is to Ought: How to Commit the Naturalistic Fallacy and Get Away with It in the Study of Moral Development," in Theodore Mischel, ed., *Cognitive Development and Epistemology* (New York: Academic Press, 1971).

44 It is Kohlberg's work on moral judgement which bears most directly on the topics I will take up in this chapter. His most relevant texts are: "From Is to Ought;" "The Claim to Moral Adequacy of a Highest Stage of Moral Judgement," *The Journal of Philosophy* 70 (Oct. 1973); and "Justice as Reversibility," in Peter Laslett and James Fishkin, eds., *Philosophy, Politics and Society* Fifth series (New Haven: Yale University Press, 1979).

45 *REPLY,* p. 259; *MKH,* pp. 127–30.

46 Kohlberg, "From Is To Ought," pp. 163–80.

47 See Kohlberg for a summary of this research.

48 Kohlberg, "From Is to Ought," pp. 154, 180–6.

49 Kohlberg, "The Claim to Moral Adequacy," p. 633. An illustration of how, say, stage 4 leaves a disequilibrated situation can be seen in one of the hypothetical dilemmas Kohlberg presents his subjects. In "Heinz's Dilemma," Heinz's wife has a disease from which she will die, unless she gets a new medicine which has just been discovered by a particular druggist. The druggist, arguing that he should profit from his discovery, asks a price for the drug which is far beyond Heinz's means. The question is, should Heinz break the law and steal the drug to save his wife's life or not? A stage 4 orientation, in which all "oughts" are subordinated to the "ought" of maintaining the legal system, cannot accommodate the claim of a right to live on the part of the wife. More generally put, it cannot accommodate certain situations where we feel that extreme injustice would be done by following the letter of the law. "From Is to Ought," pp. 156–7, 198–9.

50 Kohlberg, "The Claim to Moral Adequacy," p. 633.

51 Kohlberg, "The Claim to Moral Adequacy."

52 Kohlberg, "From Is to Ought," pp. 184–5.

53 *MKH,* pp. 138–40.

54 *MKH,* pp. 140–3.

55 *MKH,* p. 146.

56 *MKH,* p. 142.

57 *MKH,* pp. 148–50.

58 *MKH,* p. 143.

59 Rainer Döbert, Jürgen Habermas and Gertrud Nunner-Winkler, "Zur Einführung," *Die Entwicklung des Ichs* (Köln: Keizenheimer, 1977), p. 20; *CES,* pp. 82–3.

60 For different attempts to formulate the notion of interactive competence, see *KK,* pp. 196–7; *VET,* sec. II; *CES,* pp. 69–94; and *MKH,* pp. 127–206. Haber-

mas's latest formulation draws on Robert L. Selman's work on perspective taking in *The Growth of Interpersonal Understanding* (New York: Academic Press, 1980).

61 *CES*, p. 86.
62 *CES*, p. 88; *MKH*, p. 182.
63 *KK*, pp. 215, 218–9; *CES*, pp. 88–90.
64 *MKH*, p. 182. My emphasis.
65 *CES*, p. 88.
66 *CES*, p. 88.
67 *CES*, pp. 78, 88; *MKH*, p. 174–5.
68 *CES*, p. 78; *REPLY*, pp. 259–60. Also see Kohlberg, "A Reply to Owen Flanagan and Some Comments on the Puka–Goodpaster Exchange," *Ethics* 92 (April, 1982), p. 53.
69 Thomas A. McCarthy, "Rationality and Relativism," in Thompson and Held, eds., *Habermas: Critical Debates* (Cambridge, Massachusetts: MIT Press, 1982), p. 74.
70 *MKH*, pp. 127–30.
71 Carol Gilligan, *In a Different Voice: Psychological Theory and Women's Development* (Cambridge, Massachusetts: Harvard University Press, 1982). Habermas argues that one advantage of his own discursive conceptualization of postconventional morality is that Gilligan's insights can be fruitfully integrated into it. *MKH*, pp. 187 ff. See my discussion in the following chapter.
72 *MKH*, p. 127; *REPLY*, p. 259.

4 A minimal ethics and orientation for political theory

1 *WAHR*, p. 251.
2 For critics who imply that Habermas's argument is of this sort, see: Raymond Geuss, *The Idea of A Critical Theory* (Cambridge University Press, 1981), p. 31; Steven Lukes, "Of Gods and Demons: Habermas and Practical Discourse," in Thompson and Held, eds., *Habermas: Critical Debates* (Cambridge, Massachusetts: MIT Press, 1982), pp. 137, 144; Donald Moon, "Political Ethics and Critical Theory," in Daniel Sabia and Jerald Wallulis, eds., *Changing Social Science: Critical Theory and Other Critical Perspectives* (Albany: State University of New York Press, 1983), pp. 181–3; and Russell Keat, *The Politics of Social Theory: Habermas, Freud and Positivism* (University of Chicago Press, 1981), p. 198.
3 See, for example, *LC*, p. 113; and *CES*, p. 93.
4 Cf. William Connnolly, *The Terms of Political Discourse* (Princeton University Press, 1983 edn), ch. 2, esp. pp. 59 ff. Philip Pettit advances a number of arguments against Habermas's notion of justice, but he admits that their validity depends upon his (Pettit's) assumption of the correctness of a strictly biological model of needs, rather than what he characterizes, rather tendentiously, as Habermas's "artistic model." Pettit implies that the latter model is hopelessly utopian. Pettit, "Habermas on Truth and Justice," in G. Parkinson, ed., *Marx and Marxisms* (Cambridge University Press, 1982), p. 227. This charge is an oversimplification. Connolly is particularly good in

pointing out the limitations of a strict biological model. Cf. also Walzer, *Spheres of Justice: A Defense of Pluralism and Equality* (New York: Basic Books, 1983), pp. 8, 66.

5 Cf. Moon, "Political Ethics," pp. 181–2; and Pettit, "Habermas on Truth," p. 219.

6 *CES*, p. 93.

7 *WAHR*, pp. 250–2; *LC*, p. 108.

8 *WAHR*, p. 252.

9 *REPLY*, pp. 227–63.

10 Rawls, *A Theory of Justice* (Cambridge, Massachusetts: Harvard University Press, 1971), pp. 254–6.

11 Adina Schwartz, "Moral Neutrality and Primary Goods," *Ethics* 83 (1973), pp. 302–7; and *CES*, p. 199.

12 Walzer, *Spheres of Justice*, p. 314.

13 John Rawls, "Kantian Constructivism in Moral Theory," *Journal of Philosophy* 77 (1980), pp. 525–7, 554.

14 *MKH*, pp. 76–7.

15 *CES*, p. 90; *REPLY*, p. 257; *MKH*, pp. 175–9.

16 Pettit, "Habermas on Truth," pp. 222–3.

17 "Der Ansatz von Habermas," in Willi Oelmüller, ed., *Transzendentalphilosophische Normenbegründung* (Paderborn: Schöningh, 1978), p. 114; *REPLY*, p. 56, *MKH*, p. 113.

18 Cf. Bernard Williams, "Persons, Character and Morality" in Amelie O. Rorty, ed., *The Identities of Persons* (Berkeley: University of California Press, 1976); Mackie, *Ethics: Inventing Right and Wrong* (Harmondsworth: Penguin, 1977), ch. 4; and Lukes's use of Mackie's argument against Habermas in "Of Gods and Demons: Habermas and Practical Reason," in J.B. Thompson and D. Held, eds., *Habermas: Critical Debates* (Cambridge, Massachusetts: MIT Press, 1982).

19 Williams, "Persons, Character and Morality," pp. 208ff.

20 *REPLY*, p. 257.

21 *CES*, p. 93.

22 *REPLY*, pp. 257–8; *LC*, p. 89.

23 *LC*, p. 108.

24 Keat, *The Politics of Social Theory: Habermas, Freud and Positivism* (University of Chicago Press, 1981), pp. 197–8; Lukes, "Of Gods and Demons," pp. 136–7, 143–4; and John Elster, "Sour Grapes," in Amartya Sen and Bernard Williams, eds., *Utilitarianism and Beyond* (Cambridge University Press, 1982), p. 237.

25 Mackie, *Ethics*, ch. 4, pp. 151–4.

26 Mackie, *Ethics*, p. 93.

27 Mackie, pp. 119, 153. Mackie's position is hardly an isolated one. On this particular point, it coincides with the contractarianism of those who seek to develop normative political theory on the basis of the strategic model. Cf. James Buchanan, *The Limits of Liberty* (University of Chicago Press, 1975), pp. 23–6.

28 *MKH*, pp. 83–4. Hobbes, of course, provides the paradigm case of such con-

fusion: "Covenants Extorted by Fear Are Valid," *Leviathan*, ch. 14.

29 *MKH*, p. 83; *LC*, pp. 111–12. Cf. Martin Golding's discussion of the moral qualities associated with compromise, versus the purely strategic–rational character of a bargain, in "The Nature of Compromise: A Preliminary Inquiry," in J. Roland Pennock and John W. Chapman, eds., *Compromise in Ethics, Law and Politics* (New York University Press, 1979).

30 Paul Ricoeur, *Hermeneutics and the Human Sciences*, edited, translated, and introduced by John B. Thompson (Cambridge University Press, 1981), p. 34.

31 *WAHR*, p. 252.

32 *CES*, p. 84.

33 *CES*, p. 93.

34 *MKH*, p. 114; *TKH*, p. 166.

35 "Zur Einführung," *Die Entwicklung des Ichs*, p. 10.

36 *CES*, p. 85; *RHM*, p. 97; and "Zur Einführung," p. 15.

37 *CES*, pp. 85–6.

38 *CES*, p. 110 (my italics); "Zur Einführung," pp. 9, 15–16.

39 *CES*, p. 91.

40 *RHM*, pp. 93, 96–7; *CES*, p. 108.

41 *RHM*, p. 97. Kohlberg's position is stated in "Education for Justice: A Modern Statement of the Platonic View," in Theordore R. Sizer, ed., *Moral Education* (Cambridge, Massachusetts: Harvard University Press, 1970), p. 59.

42 "On Social Identity," *Telos* 19 (Spring 1975), pp. 95ff. (This is a partial translation of *RHM*, pp. 92–126); *LC*, pp. 48–50, 75–92; and *REPLY*, pp. 278–81.

43 *CES*, p. 110.

44 Seyla Benhabib argues that Habermas's notion of new modes of collective identity still retains traces of a collective Hegelian subject which endangers the value of plurality. Although this concern is a legitimate one, it seems to me that Habermas has, on balance, effectively avoided such implications. See Benhabib, *Critique, Norm and Utopia: A Study of The Foundations of Critical Theory* (New York: Columbia University Press, 1986), pp. 330ff.

45 *RHM*, p. 96. Benhabib argues that the only way to explain how people could be motivated to endorse a communicative ethics is if one assumes a strong "utopian impulse for happiness" which generates the motivation to reflect upon standardized need interpretations. I think Benhabib underplays the argument I have just elaborated regarding Habermas's reading of our concrete historical situation, and this neglect makes her overplay the necessity of Habermas's giving a stronger account of such a utopian impulse. See *Critique, Norm and Utopia*, pp. 324 ff.

46 *CES*, pp. 93–4; *MKH*, pp. 192–4.

47 Given this orientation of communicative ethics, I find it puzzling how anyone could assert that Habermas's position "aspires to take the heat out of the cauldron of contested interpretations and orientations to action. It is in this sense closer to a collectivization of administration than to the democratization of politics." William Connolly, "The Dilemma of Legitimacy," in John S. Nelson, ed., *What Should Political Theory Be Now?* (Albany: State University of New York Press, 1983), p. 326.

48 "On Social Identity," p. 99. Cf. the attempt to draw out some similarities in

the moral–political visions of Rorty and Habermas, in Richard Bernstein, *Beyond Objectivism and Relativism: Science, Hermeneutics and Praxis* (Philadelphia: University of Pennsylvania Press, 1983), pp. 197–206.

49 *MKH*, p. 115; "On Social Identity," pp. 99–100.

50 *CES*, p. 93.

51 "Consciousness-Raising or Redemptive Criticism – The Contemporaneity of Walter Benjamin," *New German Critique* 17 (Spring 1979), p. 59.

52 See especially Carol Gilligan, *In A Different Voice: Psychological Theory and Women's Development* (Cambridge, Massachusetts: Harvard University Press, 1982), and "Do The Social Sciences Have an Adequate Theory of Moral Development?," in Norma Haan *et al.*, eds., *Social Science as Moral Inquiry* (New York: Columbia University Press, 1983).

53 Gilligan, *In A Different Voice*, pp. 19, 30, 73 *et passim*; and "Do the Social Sciences," pp. 34–40.

54 Gilligan, *In A Different Voice*, pp. 164–5.

55 *MKH*, p. 182.

56 Gilligan, "Do The Social Sciences," p. 45.

57 *MKH*, pp. 183, 186–90.

58 *MKH*, pp. 190–1.

59 *MKH*, pp. 191–2. For some thoughtful criticism of Habermas's account of what is involved in moral judgement, see Benhabib, *Critique, Norm and Utopia*, pp. 322–4; 349.

60 *MKH*, pp. 193–4.

61 Gilligan, *In A Different Voice*, p. 156.

62 For an interesting discussion of how communicative ethics must open itself to these sorts of questions, see Benhabib, *Critique, Norm and Utopia*, pp. 340–2. On the importance of the experience of caring for the young, see Sara Ruddick, "Maternal Thinking," in Barrie Thorne and Marilyn Yalom, eds., *Rethinking The Family* (New York: Longman, 1982); and Jean Elshtain, *Public Man, Private Woman* (Princeton University Press, 1980), part II. The importance of appropriating the insights of this "social" variant of feminism should not, however, be allowed to blur the distinctiveness of moral–political problems as conceptualized within communicative ethics. See the discussion in ch. 6, at the end of section 3.

63 Nelson Polsby, *Community Power and Political Theory: A Further Look at Evidence and Inference* (New Haven: Yale University Press, 1980 edn), ch. 12.

64 See Steven Lukes, *Power: A Radical View* (London: Macmillan, 1974); and Connolly, *The Terms of Political Discourse*, chs. 2 and 3. Lukes's and Connolly's positions on power are similar; but for some differences, see Connolly, p. 222 n.

65 See Lukes, *Power*, chs. 7 and 8; and especially John Gaventa, *Power and Powerlessness: Quiescence and Rebellion in an Appalachian Valley* (Urbana: University of Illinois Press, 1980).

66 Lukes, *Power*, pp. 23–5.

67 Connolly, *The Terms of Political Discourse*, p. 64.

68 Cf. Polsby, *Community Power and Political Theory*, p. 229 for just such a reduction.

69 Connolly, *The Terms of Political Discourse,* pp. 69, 192–5, 228, 240–1.

70 Connolly, *The Terms of Political Discourse,* pp. 54 ff, 65–6.

71 I find a similar problem with the model of the agent which Stanley Benn tries to develop in "The Problematic Rationality of Political Participation," in Laslett and Fishkin, eds., *Philosophy, Politics and Society* (New Haven: Yale University Press, 1979). Benn attempts to articulate a model in which intersubjectivity and normativity have an ample place. His key concepts are a non-strategic conception of rationality, which seems close to Weber's "value rationality," and a notion of a "morally responsible person" who "cares about freedom and justice" (pp. 306–8). I have already indicated some shortcomings of this subjective way of thinking about rationality in the first chapter. Further, it does not seem unwarranted to expect a more illuminating way of thinking about normativity than simply asserting that a responsible person "cares about" values like justice.

72 "Toward a Theory of Communicative Competence."

73 *LC,* p. 113.

74 Gaventa, *Power.*

75 *KK,* p. 387; *TP,* pp. 33–4; Cf. Brian Fay, "How People Change Themselves: The Relationship Between Critical Theory and Its Audience," in Terence Ball, ed., *Political Theory and Praxis* (Minneapolis: University of Minnesota Press, 1977).

76 *TCA,* pp. 20–2. Cf. Stephen White, "Reason and Authority in Habermas," *American Political Science Review* 74 (Dec 1980); and "Reply to Comments," *American Political Science Review* 75 (Sept 1981). Gaventa's behavior in pursuing his critical interpretations is exemplary here; see especially his chs. 8–9.

5 Modernity, rationalization and contemporary capitalism

1 *CES,* pp. 97–8

2 *CES,* chs. 3 and 4. Habermas has not attempted the kind of detailed historical and anthropological studies that would be necessary to make his proposed theory of social evolution really plausible. In the absence of these, it seems to me that the effort to make hard and fast judgements about the theory is not very fruitful. Some critics, though, have argued that the entire notion of a developmental logic of "world views, moral representations, and identity formations" is intrinsically flawed; it is theoretically useless, since it has "no explanatory powers whatsoever," compared with a theory of social evolution based on a pure functionalist systems model; see Michael Schmid, "Habermas' Theory of Social Evolution," in Thompson and Held, *Habermas: Critical Debates* (Cambridge, Massachusetts: MIT Press, 1982), p. 174. It is interesting to note here that this is exactly the same sort of complaint that Habermas himself has directed against functionalist systems theories. Again, I think that the controversy over the theory of social evolution yields more heat than light at this most broad and abstract level of analysis.

3 *TCA,* pp. 140, 186, 221.

4 *PDM,* p. 16.

5 *PDM*, pp. 9–11, *TCA*, pp. 145–56.
6 Rogers Brubaker, *The Limits of Rationality: An Essay on the Social and Moral Thought of Max Weber* (London: George Allen and Unwin, 1984), pp. vi, 1–2.
7 Brubaker, *The Limits of Rationality*, pp. vi, 1–2.
8 *TCA*, p. 233.
9 *TCA*, p. 140.
10 For an introduction to these topics, see Hans Gerth and C. Wright Mills, eds., *From Max Weber: Essays inSocioogy* (New York: Oxford University Press, 1946), part III.
11 *TCA*, pp. 143–5, 157–68.
12 Brubaker, *The Limits of Rationality*, pp. 6, 69ff.
13 Brubaker, *The Limits of Rationality*, pp. 69, 82–6.
14 *TCA*, pp. 175ff, 205ff.
15 *TCA*, pp. 61–72, 186ff, 239; *TKH*, pp. 191, 218ff.
16 *TCA*, pp. 163–5, 236–40.
17 *TCA*, pp. 197–8, 219, 242, 254, 260–2, 268.
18 *TCA*, pp. 71–2, 165–6, 340.
19 Habermas sees Weber as maintaining a "cautious universalist position" in relation to the rationalization of worldviews; *TCA*, pp. 155, 178–9.
20 *TCA*, p. 340.
21 *TCA*, p. 198.
22 *TCA*, pp. 222, 231–3, 239–40.
23 *TCA*, p. 43.
24 *TCA*, p. 70.
25 *TCA*, p. 340; *TKH*, pp. 182–3.
26 *TCA*, pp. 70, 340; *TKH*, pp. 218ff.
27 *TCA*, p. 337.
28 *TCA*, p. 337. Also, see McCarthy's explanation of the concept of *Vergesellschaftung* or "sociation", p. xx, n. 10.
29 See the discussion of Alfred Schutz and others in *TKH*, pp. 210–12.
30 *TKH*, pp. 219–20.
31 *TKH*, p. 483.
32 *TKH*, pp. 208–9.
33 *TCA*, 342. Translations slightly altered.
34 *TKH*, p. 179; cf. Nancy Fraser, "What's Critical about Critical Theory? The Case of Habermas and Gender," *New German Critique* 35 (Spring/Summer 1985).
35 Dallmayr, *Polis and Praxis* (Cambridge, Massachusetts: MIT Press, 1984), pp. 243–4.
36 Dallmayr, *Polis and Praxis*, p. 245.
37 Cf. Anthony Giddens, "Commentary on the Debate," *Theory and Society* 11 (July 1982), p. 535.
38 *TKH*, p. 483.
39 *LC*, part I.
40 *TKH*, pp. 222, 293, 490–1.
41 *TKH*, pp. 179, 226.

42 *TKH*, pp. 304, 320–1, 344–6.
43 *LC*, ch. 1.
44 *TKH*, p. 227.
45 See generally, *TKH*, part VI, ch. 1.
46 *TKH*, pp. 347, 447.
47 *TKH*, pp. 269–73.
48 *TKH*, pp. 273–5; *TCA*, p. 341.
49 *TKH*, pp. 348–9.
50 *TCA*, pp. 342–3; *TKH*, pp. 239, 277, 470.
51 *TKH*, p. 504.
52 *TKH*, p. 489.
53 *TKH*, pp. 489, 503.
54 *TKH*, pp. 498–500.
55 *TKH*, pp. 501–3.
56 *TKH*, pp. 293, 417, 483, 488.
57 *TKH*, p. 471.
58 *TCA*, p. 342; *TKH*, p. 400.
59 See the criticism by Fred Dallmayr, *Polis and Praxis*, p. 249.
60 *TKH*, p. 462; *REPLY*, p. 281.
61 *TKH*, p. 462; cf., *LC*, part III, chs. 4 through 6.
62 *LC*, part II.
63 *TKH*, p. 452.
64 *TKH*, p. 514. This has been a theme in Habermas's work since his first book, *Strukturwandel der Offentlichkeit* (Berlin: Leuchterhand 1962).
65 *TKH*, pp. 505–13, 523. For a useful overview of other attempts to understand processes of domination outside of the productive sphere, see Mark Poster, *Foucault, Marxism and History* (Cambridge, Massachusetts: Polity Press, 1984), pp. 16–40. The analysis of Habermas, however, is oversimplistic.
66 *TKH*, p. 524.
67 *TKH*, pp. 531–2.
68 *TKH*, pp. 532–4.
69 Michel Foucault, *Discipline and Punish* (New York: Random House, 1979), part IV, ch. 3. For some parallels between Foucault and earlier critical theorists, see Martin Jay, *Marxism and Totality: The Adventures of a Concept From Lukács to Habermas* (Berkeley: University of California Press, 1984), pp. 526–7.
70 Michel Foucault, *The History of Sexuality* (New York: Random House, 1980), p. 155–9.
71 Nancy Fraser, "Foucault's Body-Language: A Post-Humanist Political Rhetoric?" *Salmagundi* 61 (Fall 1983), pp. 6–7. Cf. Jay, *Marxism and Totality*, p. 528.
72 Cf. the criticism of Foucault in Charles Taylor, "Foucault on Freedom and Truth," *Political Theory* 12 (May 1984), pp. 164–5; also *PDM*, p. 392.
73 *TKH*, p. 537. Cf. John Searle, *Speech Acts* (Cambridge University Press, 1969), pp. 133 ff.
74 *TKH*, p. 536–9.
75 *TKH*, p. 535; cf. *LC*, part III.

76 For some thoughts on the colonization process in the private sphere, see Timothy W. Luke and Stephen K. White, "Critical Theory, The Informational Revolution and An Ecological Modernity," in John Forester, ed., *Critical Theory and Public Life* (Cambridge, Massachusetts: MIT Press, 1985).

77 Foucault, *The History of Sexuality* (New York: Random House, 1980).

78 *TKH*, p. 481; "Modernity and Postmodernity," *New German Critique* 22 (Winter 1981), p. 9.

79 *TKH*, pp. 481, 483.

80 *TKH*, pp. 518–20.

81 *TKH*, p. 521. The notion that science and technology have taken on a role which is functionally equivalent to ideology is an idea Habermas expressed in one of his early essays. See "Science and Technology as 'Ideology'," *TRS*. The new emphasis is on how the phenomena of fragmented consciousness and lifeworld reification help dispose everyday consciousness to an uncritical acceptance of the normative positions cloaked in the mantle of scientific authority and objectivity.

82 *TKH*, p. 522.

83 Cf. White, "The Normative Basis of Critical Theory," *Polity* 16 (1983).

84 "The critique of ideology can no longer set out directly from concrete ideals intrinsic to forms of life, but only from formal properties of rationality structures." *REPLY*, p. 254, *TKH*, p. 522.

85 *LC*, pp. 48–9, 69–84.

86 For a good critique of Habermas's failure, in *LC*, to take into account the problem of fragmented consciousness, see David Held, "Crisis Tendencies, Legitimation and the State," in Thompson and Held, *Habermas*, pp. 189ff.

87 *REPLY*, p. 280.

88 Compare *REPLY*, pp. 280–1 and *TKH*, pp. 565–6. I will assume that the latter text is the controlling one, since the former merely sketched some ideas in response to criticism.

89 *TKH*, pp. 565–6.

90 *TKH*, p. 566.

91 *REPLY*, p. 281. Habermas's recent shift in thinking may make him less susceptible to the charge that he has overestimated the degree to which social stability is always directly dependent on the maintenance of a broadly shared, socially integrative "value consensus." Cf. Held, "Crisis Tendencies," and Nicolas Abercrombie, Stephen Hill and Bryan Turner, *The Dominant Ideology Thesis* (London: George Allen and Unwin, 1980).

92 *REPLY*, p. 281. This would seem to lead in a different direction from *LC*, which predicted the decline of such attitudes as possessive individualism; pp. 80 ff.

93 *TKH*, p. 56 ff.

94 William Connolly, "Discipline, Politics and Ambiguity," *Political Theory* 11 (August 1983), pp. 325–9.

95 *TKH*, pp. 571 ff.

96 See Cohen's excellent article, "Strategy or Identity: New Theoretical Paradigms and Contemporary Social Movements," *Social Research* 52 (Winter 1985). Cohen provides a good overview of recent work on new

social movements. My discussion draws heavily on her insights.

For somewhat more skeptical views of the ability of Habermas's model to account for the origin and characteristics of the women's movement, see Nancy Fraser, "What's Critical about Critical Theory?," and Benhabib, *Critique, Norm and Utopia: A Study of the Foundations of Critical Theory* (New York: Columbia University Press, 1986), pp. 251–2.

97 Cohen, "Strategy or Identity," pp. 664, 690; Cf. *PDM*, p. 423.
98 "New Social Movements," *Telos* 49 (Fall 1981), p. 33. This is a translation of *TKH*, pp. 576–83. Translation slightly altered.
99 See Cohen's survey of rational choice-based or "resource mobilization" theories, pp. 674–90.
100 Cohen, "Strategy or Identity," pp. 693–5.
101 *TKH*, pp. 576 ff.
102 *TKH*, pp. 501–3.
103 See Timothy Luke, "From Fundamentalism to Televangelism," *Telos* 58 (Winter 1983–4).
104 See *Strukturwandel der Offentlichkeit*.
105 Cf. the rather pessimistic prognosis in "Modernity versus Postmodernity," *New German Critique* 22 (Winter 1981), p. 13.
106 *PDM*, pp. 419–21.
107 *PDM*, pp. 418–19, 422–4.
108 *PDM*, p. 423; "The New Obscurity," pp. 13–15.
109 Cohen, "Strategy or Identity," pp. 710–12.

6 The two tasks of critical theory

1 *TKH*, pp. 583–8.
2 *TKH*, p. 588.
3 Cf. Richard Rorty, "Pragmatism, Relativism, and Irrationalism," in *Consequences of Pragmatism* (Minneapolis: University of Minnesota Press, 1982), pp. 173–4; and *Philosophy and The Mirror of Nature* (Princeton: Princeton University Press, 1979), pp. 380–1.
4 "Interpretive Social Science vs. Hermeneuticism," in Norma Haan *et al.*, eds., *Social Science as Moral Inquiry* (New York: Columbia University Press,1983), p. 260.
5 *TKH*, pp. 586–7.
6 "Interpretive Social Science," p. 261; "Philosophy as Stand-In and Interpreter," in K. Baynes, J. Bohman and T. McCarthy, eds., *After Philosophy: End or Transformation?* (Cambridge, Massachusetts: MIT Press, 1987), pp. 310–11; *TKH*, pp. 587–8.
7 See literature cited in n. 12 in the Introduction.
8 "Philosophy as Stand-In and Interpreter," p. 310 (my translation); *TKH*, p. 588.
9 *TKH*, p. 586.
10 Fred Alford, "Is Jürgen Habermas' Reconstructive Science Really Science?," *Theory and Society* 14 (1985), pp. 331–5. Cf. *CES*, pp. 16–25.
11 I also think this way of understanding rational reconstructions of action and rationality makes more sense than trying to understand them as a form of

"pure" knowledge, divorced from cognitive interests altogether, as Habermas originally did in "A Postscript to *Knowledge and Human Interests,*" *Philosophy of the Social Sciences* 3 (Sept. 1973), p. 184. McCarthy rightly points out that the latter strategy radically divorces theory and practice; *The Critical Theory of Jürgen Habermas* (Cambridge, Massachusetts: MIT Press, 1978), p. 101.

12 "Philosophy as Stand-In and Interpreter," pp. 297–8 (my translation).

13 "Philosophy as Stand-In and Interpreter," p. 312 (my translation); *TKH,* p. 584.

14 *TCA,* p. 237.

15 *TCA,* p. 238.

16 Thomas McCarthy, "Reflections on Rationalization in *The Theory of Communicative Action,*" *Praxis International* 4, pp. 177–9; cf. Fred Alford, *Science and the Revenge of Nature: Marcuse and Habermas* (Gainesville: University Presses of Florida, 1985), ch. 9.

17 *TKH,* p. 588.

18 See the critiques Habermas refers to in *REPLY,* pp. 238 ff.

19 *QCQ,* p. 244; and the critique of Foucault in *PDM,* chs. 9–10.

20 *TKH,* p. 588.

21 *REPLY,* p. 262.

22 *TCA,* p. 240.

23 *REPLY,* p. 262.

24 *TCA,* pp. 73–4; *REPLY,* p. 262; *QCQ,* p. 242.

25 *QCQ,* p. 242; "Philosophy as Stand-In and Interpreter," pp. 312–14 (my translation).

26 *REPLY,* p. 250; "Philosophy as Stand-In and Interpreter," p. 313 (my translation).

27 *QCQ,* p. 244.

28 *REPLY,* p. 245.

29 McCarthy, "Reflections on Rationalization," pp. 188–9. It should be noted that the kind of philosophy of nature McCarthy suggests retains an anthropocentric core, something which might be quite unacceptable to some proponents of such a philosophy.

30 In regard to moralizing relations with animals, it is important to emphasize some of the drawbacks that would follow from failing to recognize clearly that normative legitimacy questions apply with full force only to reflective and accountable (speech competent) beings. Failure to maintain this distinction can lead quickly to positions such as the one recently defended publicly by some animal liberationists: dangerous, medical experimentation, when necessary, should be done not on "innocent" animals but on guilty humans, i.e., those in prison.

For Habermas's attempt to suggest a way of thinking about some of these problems, see *REPLY,* pp. 244–7.

31 Cf. *REPLY,* pp. 247–8.

32 See Luke and White, "Critical Theory, The Informational Revolution and an Ecological Modernity," in J. Forester, ed., *Critical Theory and Public Life* (Cambridge, Massachusetts: MIT Press, 1985) for an overview of some of these kinds of alternative practices.

33 *TKH,* p. 580.
34 *TKH,* p. 507.
35 "The New Obscurity," esp. pp. 12–17.
36 "New Social Movements," p. 35.
37 Luke and White, "Critical Theory, The Informational Revolution and an Ecological Modernity," section IV.
38 "On Social Identity," pp. 99–103.
39 Habermas is, of course, aware that such new technology can just as easily be turned to uses which expand the colonization of the lifeworld; *TKH,* pp. 571–5. Cf. Luke and White, "Critical Theory, The Informational Revolution and an Ecological Modernity."
40 "Civil Disobedience: Litmus Test for the Democratic Constitutional State," *Berkeley Journal of Sociology* 30 (1985), pp. 110–11.
41 "Civil Disobedience," p. 99.
42 For the criticism that Habermas takes us no further than Weber, see Anthony Giddens, "Reason Without Revolution? Habermas's *Theorie des kommunikativen Handelns,*" in Richard J. Bernstein, ed., *Habermas and Modernity* (Cambridge, Massachusetts: MIT Press, 1985), pp. 120–1.
43 Nancy Fraser, "What's Critical About Critical Theory?," p. 111.
44 Fraser is fairly sensitive to the resources Habermas has for meeting her criticisms.
45 Cf. Martin Jay, *Marxism and Totality: The Adventures of a Concept from Lukács to Habermas* (Berkeley: University of California Press, 1984), pp. 509, 518 ff; and Mark Poster, *Foucault, Marxism and History* (Cambridge, Massachusetts: Polity, 1984).
46 Foucault, "What is Enlightenment?," in Paul Rabinow, ed., *The Foucault Reader* (New York: Pantheon, 1984), p. 45.
47 "Consciousness-Raising or Redemptive Criticism," p. 56.
48 Cf. Poster, *Foucault, Marxism and History.*
49 Foucault, *The History of Sexuality* (New York: Random House, 1980).
50 Cf. Nancy Fraser, "Is Michel Foucault a Young Conservative?," *Ethics* 96 (Spring/Summer 1985). Habermas himself considers this possibility in "Consciousness-Raising or Redemptive Criticism," pp. 57–9.
51 Cf. Fraser, "Is Michel Foucault a Young Conservative?"
52 Foucault, "The Subject and Power," in Herbert Dreyfus and Paul Rabinow, eds., *Michel Foucault: Beyond Structuralism and Hermeneutics* (University of Chicago Press, 1983 edn), p. 216.
53 Foucault, *The History of Sexuality,* pp. 155–9.
54 Fred Dallmayr, *The Twilight of Subjectivity: Contributions to a Post-Individualist Theory of Politics* (Amherst: University of Massachusetts Press, 1981), pp. 205 ff; and Joel Whitebook, "Reason and Happiness: Some Psychoanalytic Themes in Critical Theory," *Praxis International* 4 (April 1984). Reprinted in Bernstein, *Habermas and Modernity.*
55 Foucault, "Body/Power," in *Power/Knowledge: Selected Interviews and Other Writings 1972–1977,* edited by Colin Gordon (New York: Pantheon, 1980), pp. 58–9; and *History of Sexuality,* pp. 140 ff.

56 Here "otherness" is an *intra*subjective category as opposed to the *inter*subjective one discussed in ch. 4. Foucault's challenge here is one which Habermas finds to be common among post-modernist attacks on modernity and the Enlightenment. What is at issue is the attempt to raise "Reason's Other to the position of a court before which modernity can be called to order," *PDM,* p. 128.

57 Foucault, "On the Genealogy of Ethics: An Overview of Work in Progress," in Dreyfus and Rabinow, *Michel Foucault,* pp. 230-1, 235.

58 Foucault, "What is Enlightenment?," pp. 41-2.

59 *TCA,* p. 20.

60 *QCQ,* p. 240; *TKH,* pp. 584-5.

61 *QCQ,* pp. 235-6.

62 *QCQ,* pp. 235-6; "Modernity versus Postmodernity," pp. 4-5; "The Entwinement of Myth and Enlightenment," *New German Critique* 26 (Spring-Summer, 1982), p. 25; *PDM,* ch. 4.

63 *QCQ,* p. 240.

64 Cf. Charles Taylor's remarks about the difference between our symbolic activity and that of primitive societies, in "Rationality," in Martin Hollis and Steven Lukes, eds., *Rationality and Relativism* (Cambridge, Massachusetts: MIT Press, 1982), pp. 98-100.

65 Habermas suggests that Nietzsche's critique of modernity is also guilty of forgetting this point, "The Entwinement of Myth and Enlightenment," pp. 23ff.

66 "Modernity versus Postmodernity," pp. 4-5.

67 *QCQ,* p. 236.

68 On the irony of the achievements of the modern, rational self, cf. William Connolly, "Discipline, Politics and Ambiguity," *Political Theory* 11 (1983), pp. 334-6.

69 Another source of provocative ideas about an aesthetic of everyday life is to be found in feminist writings. See, for example, Nancy Hartsock, *Money, Sex and Power* (New York: Longman, 1984), chs. 7-11.

70 Foucault, "On the Genealogy of Ethics," p. 231.

71 Foucault, "On the Genealogy of Ethics," p. 230.

72 Foucault, "On the Genealogy of Ethics," p. 239; and "The Confession of the Flesh," in *Power/Knowledge,* p. 208.

73 In the final analysis, Foucault was humane enough to see the limits of his own line of thinking. In an interview the year before he died, he admitted that "the idea of a consensual politics" was important as "a critical principle with respect to other political forms;" and, moreover, that there might be such things as "consensual disciplines." "Politics and Ethics: An Interview," *The Foucault Reader,* pp. 378-80. But it is precisely with remarks such as these that all of the "juridical" problems Habermas has been wrestling with come flooding back in. Clearly Foucault did not want to close off all access to intersubjective otherness, but his comments about "consensual politics" have a blatantly *ad hoc* quality to them. Within the framework of his model of subjectivity, these problems must appear alien; from within the communicative

model, on the other hand, they are inherent

74 Cf. Dreyfus and Rabinow, *Michel Foucault,* p. 258.
75 Horkheimer and Adorno, *Dialectic of Enlightenment* (New York: Seabury Press, 1972); Adorno, *Negative Dialectics* (New York: Seabury Press, 1966); and Adorno, *Aesthetic Theory* (London: Routledge and Kegan Paul, 1984).
76 See Albrecht Wellmer, "Truth, Semblance, Reconciliation: Adorno's Aesthetic Redemption of Modernity," *Telos* 62 (Winter 1984–5); and Dallmayr, *The Twilight of Subjectivity: Contributions to a Post-Individualist Theory of Politics* (Amherst: University of Massachusetts Press,1981), pp. 133–43.
77 Albrecht Wellmer, "Reason, Utopia and The Dialectic of Enlightenment," *Praxis International* 4 (April 1983), p. 94, reprinted in Bernstein, *Habermas and Modernity.* Cf. Seyla Benhabib's critique of Adorno in *Critique, Norm and Utopia: A Study of the Foundations of Critical Theory* (New York: Columbia University Press, 1986), pp. 219–21.
78 *QCQ,* p. 237.
79 See, for example, Sara Ruddick, "Maternal Thinking," in B. Thorne and M. Yalom, eds., *Rethinking The Family* (New York: Longman, 1982); and Jean Elshtain, "Antigone's Daughters," *Democracy* 2 (April 1982).
80 Mary Dietz, "Citizenship with a Feminist Face: The Problem with Maternal Thinking," *Political Theory* 13 (Feb. 1985). Cf. the interesting exchange between Seyla Benhabib and Nancy Fraser in the special issue on "Feminism as Critique" of *Praxis International* 6 (Jan. 1986).
81 This objection was made to me by Fred Dallmayr.
82 *TKH,* pp. 555, 560–2.
83 *TKH,* pp. 555–60, 562 ff. For how this research program throws light on systems of "bureaucratic socialism," see especially pp. 563–7.
84 Geertz, *Local Knowledge: Further Essays in Interpretive Anthropology* (New York: Basic Books, 1983), p. 234.
85 Geertz, *Local Knowledge,* p. 234. See the various essays in this book for how such commentaries are developed. Walzer's *Spheres of Justice: A Defense of Pluralism and Equality* (New York: Basic Books, 1983) is also instructive in this regard.

Bibliography

WORKS BY HABERMAS CITED IN THE TEXT

Stukturwandel der Offentlichkeit. Berlin: Leuchterhand 1962.
Zur Logik der Sozialwissenschaften. Frankfurt: Suhkamp 1970.
Toward a Rational Society, translated by J. Shapiro. Boston: Beacon Press 1970.
Toward a Theory of Communicative Competence, in H. Dreitzel (ed.), *Patterns of Communicative Behavior,* pp. 115–48. New York: Macmillan 1970.
Knowledge and Human Interests, translated by J. Shapiro. Boston: Beacon Press 1971.
Theorie der Gesellschaft oder Sozialtechnologie: Was leistet die Systemforschung?, with Niklaus Luhmann. Frankfurt: Suhrkamp 1971.
Kultur und Kritik. Frankfurt: Suhrkamp 1973.
Theory and Practice, translated by J. Viertel. Boston: Beacon Press 1973.
Wahrheitstheorien, in H. Fahrenbach (ed.), *Wirklichkeit und Reflexion: Walter Schulz zum 60 Gebürtstag,* pp. 211–63. Pfüllingen: Neske 1973.
A Postscript to *Knowledge and Human Interests. Philosophy of the Social Sciences* 3 (1973), 157–89.
Legitimation Crisis, translated by T. McCarthy. Boston: Beacon Press 1975.
On Social Identity. *Telos* 19 (1975), 91–103.
Zur Rekonstruktion des Historischen Materialismus. Frankfurt: Suhrkamp 1976.
The Analytical Theory of Science and Dialectics, in T. Adorno *et al.* (eds.), *The Positivist Dispute in German Sociology,* pp. 131–62. New York: Harper and Row 1976.
A Positivistically Bisected Rationalism, in T. Adorno *et al.* (eds.), *The Positivist Dispute in German Sociology,* pp. 198–225. New York: Harper and Row 1976.
Zur Einführung, with R. Döbert and G. Nunner-Winkler, in R. Döbert, J. Habermas and G. Nunner-Winkler (eds.), *Die Entwicklung des Ichs,* pp. 9–30. Köln: Keizenheimer 1977.
Der Ansatz von Habermas, in W. Oelmüller (ed.), *Transzendentalphilosophische Normenbegründung,* pp. 123–30. Paderborn: Schöningh 1978.
Philosophy as Stand-In and Interpreter, in K. Baynes, J. Bohman and T. McCarthy (eds.), *After Philosophy: End or Transformation?,* pp. 296–315. Cambridge, Massachusetts: MIT Press 1987.
Communication and the Evolution of Society, translated by T. McCarthy. Boston: Beacon Press 1979.
Consciousness-Raising or Redemptive Criticism. *New German Critique* 17 (1979), 30–59.

Bibliography

Interview with Habermas. Interviewed by D. Horster and W. van Reijen. *New German Critique* 18 (1979), 29–43.

Theorie des kommunikativen Handelns, vol. II, *Zur kritik der functionalistischen Vernunft.* Frankfurt: Suhrkamp 1981.

New Social Movements. *Telos* 49 (1981), 33–7.

Modernity versus Postmodernity. *New German Critique* 22 (1981), 3–22.

Reply to My Citics, in J. Thompson and D. Held (eds.), *Habermas: Critical Debates*, pp. 219–83. Cambridge, Massachusetts: MIT Press 1982.

The Entwinement of Myth and Enlightenment. *New German Critique* 26 (1982), 13–30.

Moralbeweusstsein und kommunikatives Handeln. Frankfurt: Suhrkamp 1983.

Neo-Conservative Cultural Critique in the United States and West Germany. *Telos* 56 (1983), 75–89.

Interpretive Social Science vs. Hermeneuticism, in N. Haan *et al.* (eds.), *Social Science as Moral Inquiry*, pp. 251–67. New York: Columbia University Press 1983.

The Theory of Communicative Action, vol. 1, *Reason and the Rationalization of Society*, translated by T. McCarthy. Boston: Beacon Press 1984.

Vorstudien und Ergänzungen zur Theorie des kommunikativen Handelns. Frankfurt: Suhrkamp 1984.

Questions and Counterquestions. *Praxis International* 4 (1984), 229–49.

Uber Moralität und Sittlichkeit: Was Macht eine Lebensform 'Rational'?, in H. Schnädelbach (ed.), *Rationalität*, pp. 218–35. Frankfurt: Suhrkamp 1984.

Der Philosophische Diskurs der Moderne: Zwölf Vorlesungen. Frankfurt: Suhrkamp 1985.

Civil Disobedience: Litmus Test for the Democratic Constitutional State. *Berkeley Journal of Sociology* 30 (1985), 96–116.

The New Obscurity: The Crisis of the Welfare State and The Exhaustion of Utopian Energies. *Philosophy and Social Criticism* 11 (1986), 1–17.

OTHER WORKS CITED

Abercrombie, N., Hill, S. and Turner, B. *The Dominant Ideology Thesis.* London: George Allen and Unwin 1980.

Adorno, T. *Aesthetic Theory.* London: Routledge and Kegan Paul 1984.

Negative Dialectics. New York: Seabury Press 1966.

Alexy, R. Eine Theorie des praktischen Diskurses, in W. Oelmüller (ed.), *Normenbegründung und Normendurchsetzung.* Paderborn: Schöningh 1978.

Alford, F. Is Jürgen Habermas' Reconstructive Science Really Science? *Theory and Society* 14 (1985), 421–40.

Science and the Revenge of Nature: Marcuse and Habermas. Gainesville: University Presses of Florida 1985.

Apel, K-O. *Analytic Philosophy of Language and the Geisteswissenschaften.* New York: Humanities 1967.

Towards a Transformation of Philosophy, translated by G. Adey and D. Frisby. London: Routledge and Kegan Paul 1980.

Austin, J. L. *How to Do Things with Words.* Cambridge, Massachusetts: Harvard University Press 1975.

Axelrod, R. *The Emergence of Cooperation.* New York: Basic Books 1984.

Ball, T. From Paradigms to Research Programs: Towards a Post-Kuhnian Political Science. *American Journal of Political Science* 20 (1976), 151–77.

Barry, B. *Sociologists, Economists and Democracy.* University of Chicago Press 1978.

Barry, B. and Hardin, R. (eds.), *Rational Man and Irrational Society.* Berkeley: Sage 1982.

Benhabib, S. *Critique, Norm and Utopia: A Study of the Foundations of Critical Theory.* New York: Columbia University Press 1986.

Benn, S. Rationality and Political Behavior, in Benn and G. W. Mortimore (eds.), *Rationality in the Social Sciences,* pp. 246–67. London: Routledge and Kegan Paul 1976.

The Problematic Rationality of Political Participation, in P. Laslett and J. Fishkin (eds.), *Philosophy, Politics and Society,* Fifth Series, pp. 291–312. New Haven: Yale University Press 1979.

Berlin, I. Rationality of Value Judgements, in C. J. Friedrich (ed.), *Rational Decision* NOMOS VII, pp. 221–3. New York: Atherton 1964.

Bernstein, R. *Beyond Objectivism and Relativism: Science, Hermeneutics and Praxis.* Philadelphia: University of Pennsylvania Press 1983.

Introduction, in Bernstein (ed.), *Habermas and Modernity,* pp. 1–32. Cambridge, Massachusetts: MIT Press 1985.

Brigham, J. *Constitutional Language.* Westport: Greenwood Press 1978.

Brubaker, R. *The Limits of Rationality: An Essay on the Social and Moral Thought of Max Weber.* London: George Allen and Unwin 1984.

Buchanan, J. *The Limits of Liberty.* University of Chicago Press 1975.

Cohen, J. Strategy or Identity: New Theoretical Paradigms and Contemporary Social Movements. *Social Research* 52 (1985), 663–716.

Connolly, W. The Dilemma of Legitimacy, in J. Nelson (ed.), *What Should Political Theory Be Now?,* pp. 307–37. Albany: State University of New York Press 1983.

The Terms of Political Discourse. Princeton University Press 1983.

Discipline, Politics and Ambiguity. *Political Theory* 11 (1983), 325–41.

Dallmayr, F. *The Twilight of Subjectivity: Contributions to a Post-Individualist Theory of Politics.* Amherst: University of Massachusetts Press 1981.

Polis and Praxis: Exercises in contemporary political theory. Cambridge, Massachusetts: MIT Press 1984.

Dietz, M. Citizenship with a Feminist Face: The Problem with Maternal Thinking. *Political Theory* 13 (1985), 19–37.

Dirksen, A. I. On an Unnoticed Key to Reality. *Philosophy of the Social Sciences* 8 (1978), 209–25.

Downs, A. *An Economic Theory of Democracy.* New York: Harper and Row 1957.

Dryzek, J. The Progress of Political Science. *Journal of Politics* 48 (1986), 301–20.

Dworkin, R. Review of Michael Walzer's *Spheres of Justice. New York Review of Books* April 14 (1983), 4–6.

Bibliography

Elshtain, J. *Public Man, Private Woman*. Princeton University Press 1980.
  Antigone's Daughters. *Democracy* 2 (1982), 46–59.
Elster, J. *Ulysses and the Sirens*. Cambridge University Press 1979.
Fay, B. How People Change Themselves: The Relationship Between Critical
  Theory and Its Audience, in T. Ball (ed.), *Political Theory and Praxis*, pp.
  200–69. Minneapolis: University of Minnesota Press 1977.
Ferejohn, J. and Fiorina, M. The Paradox of Non-voting. *American Political
  Science Review* 68 (1974), 525–46.
Foucault, M. *Discipline and Punish*. New York: Random House 1979.
  The History of Sexuality vol. 1. New York: Random House 1980.
  Power/Knowledge: Selected Interviews and Other Writings 1972–1977, edited by C.
  Gordon. New York: Pantheon 1980.
  The Subject and Power, in H. Dreyfus and P. Rabinow (eds.), *Michel Foucault:
  Beyond Structuralism and Hermeneutics*, pp. 208–26. University of Chicago
  Press 1983.
  On the Genealogy of Ethics: An Overview of Work in Progress, in H. Dreyfus
  and P. Rabinow (eds.), *Michel Foucault: Beyond Structuralism and Hermeneutics*,
  pp. 229–52. University of Chicago Press 1983.
  The Foucault Reader, edited by P. Rabinow. New York: Pantheon 1984.
Fraser, N. Foucault's Body Language: A Post-Humanist Political Rhetoric?
  Salmagundi 61 (1983), 55–70.
  What's Critical about Critical Theory? The Case of Habermas and Gender.
  New German Critique 35 (1985), 97–131.
  Is Michel Foucault a Young Conservative? *Ethics* 96 (1985), 165–84.
Gaventa, J. *Power and Powerlessness: Quiescence and Rebellion in an Appalachian
  Valley*. Urbana: University of Illinois Press 1980.
Geertz, C. Thick Description: Toward an Interpretive Theory of Culture, in
  Geertz, *The Interpretation of Cultures*, pp. 3–30. New York: Basic Books 1973.
  Local Knowledge: Further Essays in Interpretive Anthropology. New York: Basic
  Books 1983.
Geuss, R. *The Idea of a Critical Theory*. Cambridge University Press 1981.
Gewirth, A. *Reason and Morality*. University of Chicago Press 1978.
Giddens, A. Commentary on the Debate. *Theory and Society* 11 (1982), 527–39.
  Labor and Interaction, in J. Thompson and D. Held (eds.), *Habermas: Critical
  Debates*, pp. 149–61. Cambridge, Massachusetts: MIT Press 1982.
  Reason without Revolution? Habermas's *Theorie des kommunikativen Handelns*,
  in R. Bernstein (ed.), *Habermas and Modernity*, pp. 95–121. Cambridge,
  Massachusetts: MIT Press 1985.
Gilligan, C. *In a Different Voice: Psychological Theory and Women's Development*.
  Cambridge, Massachusetts: Harvard University Press 1982.
  Do the Social Sciences Have an Adequate Theory of Moral Development?, in
  N. Haan *et al.* (eds.), *Social Science as Moral Inquiry*, pp. 33–51. New York:
  Columbia University Press 1983.
Goffman, E. *The Presentation of Self in Everyday Life*. New York: Doubleday
  1959.
Golding, M. The Nature of Compromise: A Preliminary Inquiry, in J. R.

Pennock and J. Chapman (eds.), *Compromise in Ethics, Law and Politics*, pp. 3–25. New York University Press 1979.

Hampshire, S. Morality and Convention, in A. Sen and B. Williams (eds.), *Utilitarianism and Beyond*, pp. 145–57. Cambridge University Press 1982.

Hampton, J. Contracts and Choices: Does Rawls have a Social Contract Theory? *Journal of Philosophy* 77 (1980), 315–38.

Hardin, R. *Collective Action*. Baltimore: Johns Hopkins University Press 1982.

Hart, H. L. A. Positivism and the Separation of Law and Morals. *Harvard Law Review* 71 (1958), 593–529.

The Concept of Law. Oxford University Press 1961.

Hartsock, N. *Money, Sex and Power*. New York: Longman 1984.

Hekman, S. *Hermeneutics and the Sociology of Knowledge*. Notre Dame University Press 1986.

Hesse, M. Science and Objectivity, in J. Thompson and D. Held (eds.), *Habermas: Critical Debates*, pp. 98–115. Cambridge, Massachusetts: MIT Press 1982.

Hobbes, T. *Leviathan*. New York: Macmillan 1962.

Horkheimer, M. *The Eclipse of Reason*. New York: Seabury Press 1947.

Traditional and Critical Theory, in Horkheimer (ed.), *Critical Theory: Selected*

Horkheimer, M. and Adorno, T. *Dialectic of Enlightenment*. New York: Seabury Press 1972.

Horkheimer, M. and Adorno, T. *Dialectic of Enlightenment*. New York: Seabury Press 1972.

Jay, M. *Marxism and Totality: The Adventures of a Concept from Lukács to Habermas*. Berkeley: University of California Press 1984.

Kambartel, F. Wie ist praktische Philosophie konstruktiv möglich? in Kambartel (ed.), *Praktische Philosophie und konstruktiv Wissenschaftstheorie*, pp. 9–33. Frankfurt: Suhrkamp 1974.

Keat, R. *The Politics of Social Theory: Habermas, Freud and Positivism*. University of Chicago Press 1981.

Kohlberg, L. Education for Justice: A Modern Statement of the Platonic View, in T. Sizer (ed.), *Moral Education*, pp. 57–83. Cambridge, Massachusetts: Harvard University Press 1970.

From Is to Ought: How to commit the Naturalistic Fallacy and Get Away with It in the Study of Moral Development, in T. Mischel (ed.), *Cognitive Development and Epistemology*, pp. 151–235. New York: Academic Press 1971.

The Claim to Moral Adequacy of a Highest Stage of Moral Judgement. *The Journal of Philosophy* 70 (1973), 630–46.

Justice as Reversibility, in P. Laslett and J. Fishkin (eds.), *Philosophy, Politics and Society*. Fifth Series pp. 257–72. New Haven: Yale University Press 1979.

A Reply to Owen Flanagan and Some Comments on the Puka–Goodpaster Exchange. *Ethics* 92 (1982), 513–28.

Lakatos, I. Falsification and the Methodology of Scientific Research Programs, in Lakatos and A. Musgrave (eds.), *Criticism and the Growth of Knowledge*, pp. 91–196. Cambridge University Press 1970.

Luke, T. From Fundamentalism to Televangelism. *Telos* 58 (1983–4), 204–10.

Luke, T. and White, S. Critical Theory, The Informational Revolution and an Ecological Modernity, in J. Forester (ed.), *Critical Theory and Public Life*, pp. 22–53. Cambridge, Massachusetts: MIT Press 1985.

Lukes, S. Some Problems about Rationality, in B. Wilson (ed.), *Rationality*, pp. 194–213. New York: Harper and Row 1970.

Power: A Radical View. London: Macmillan 1974.

Relativism: Cognitive and Moral, in Lukes, *Essays in Social Theory*, pp. 156–76. London: Macmillan 1977.

Lyotard, J.-F. and Thebaud, J.-L. *Just Gaming*, translated by W. Godzich. Minneapolis: University of Minnesota Press 1985.

MacIntyre, A. The Idea of a Social Science, in B. Wilson (ed.), *Rationality*, pp. 112–30. New York: Harper and Row 1970.

After Virtue. University of Notre Dame Press 1980.

Mackie, J. *Ethics: Inventing Right and Wrong*. Harmondsworth: Penguin 1977.

Margolis, H. *Selfishness, Altruism and Rationality*. Cambridge University Press 1982

McCarthy, T. *The Critical Theory of Jürgen Habermas*. Cambridge, Massachusetts: MIT Press 1978.

Reflections on Rationalization in the *Theory of Communicative Action*, in R. Bernstein (ed.), *Habermas and Modernity*, pp. 176–91. Cambridge, Massachusetts: MIT Press 1985.

Megill, A. *Prophets of Extremity: Nietzsche, Heidegger, Foucault, Derrida*. Berkeley: University of California Press 1985.

Meuller, D. *Public Choice*. New York: Cambridge University Press 1979.

Moon, J. D. The Logic of Political Inquiry, in F. Greenstein and N. Polsby (eds.), *Handbook of Political Inquiry*, vol. 1, pp. 131–228. Reading: Addison Wesley 1975.

Values and Political Theory: A Modest Defense of a Qualified Cognitivism. *Journal of Politics* 39 (1977), 877–903.

Political Ethics and Critical Theory, in D. Sabia and J. Wallulis (eds.), *Changing Social Science: Critical Theory and other Critical Perspectives*, pp. 171–88. Albany: State University of New York Press 1983.

Moon, J. D. and Fay, B. What Would an Adequate Philosophy of Social Science Look Like? *Philosophy of the Social Sciences* 7 (1977), 209–27.

O'Neill, J. Critique and Remembrance, in O'Neill (ed.), *On Critical Theory*, pp. 1–11. New York: Seabury Press 1976.

Offe, C. The Two Logics of Collective Action, in Offe, *Disorganized Capitalism: Contemporary Transformations of Work and Politics*, pp. 170–220. Cambridge, Massachusetts: MIT Press 1985.

Olson, M. *The Logic of Collective Action*. Cambridge, Massachusetts: Harvard University Press 1971.

Pettit, P. Habermas on Truth and Justice, in G. Parkinson (ed.), *Marx and Marxisms*. Royal Institute of Philosophy Lecture Series 14, Supplement to *Philosophy* (1982), pp. 207–29. Cambridge University Press 1982.

Polsby, N. *Commmunity Power and Political Theory: A Further Look at Evidence and Inference*. New Haven: Yale University Press 1980.

Popkin, S. *The Rational Peasant: The Political Economy of Rural Society in Vietnam.*

Berkeley: University of California Press 1979.

Poster, M. *Foucault, Marxism and History*. Cambridge, Massachusetts: Polity 1984.

Rasmussen, D. Communicative Action and Philosophy: Reflections on Habermas's *Theorie des kommunikativen Handelns. Philosophy and Social Criticism* 9 (1982), 3–28.

Rawls, J. *A Theory of Justice*. Cambridge, Massachusetts: Harvard University Press 1971.

Kantian Constructivism in Moral Theory. *Journal of Philosophy* 77 (1980), 515–72.

Ricoeur, P. *Hermeneutics and the Human Sciences*, edited and translated by J. Thompson. Cambridge University Press 1981.

Riker, W. and Ordeshook, P. *An Introduction to Positive Political Theory*. Englewood Cliffs: Prentice-Hall 1973.

Rorty, R. *Philosophy and the Mirror of Nature*. Princeton University Press 1979. *Consequences of Pragmatism*. Minneapolis: University of Minnesota Press 1982.

Rose, G. *The Dialectic of Nihilism: Post-Structuralism and Law*. Oxford: Blackwell 1984.

Ruddick, S. Maternal Thinking, in B. Thorne and M. Yalom (eds.), *Rethinking The Family*, pp. 76–94. New York: Longman 1982.

Schwartz, A. Moral Neutrality and Primary Goods. *Ethics* 83 (1973), 294–307.

Searle, J. *Speech Acts*. Cambridge University Press 1969.

Selman, R. *The Growth of Interpersonal Understanding*. New York: Academic Press 1980.

Taylor, C. *Hegel*. Cambridge University Press 1975.

Rationality, in M. Hollis and S. Lukes (eds.), *Rationality and Relativism*, pp. 87–105. Cambridge, Massachusetts: MIT Press 1982.

Foucault on Freedom and Truth. *Political Theory* 12 (1984), 152–83.

Thompson, J. *Critical Hermeneutics: Paul Ricoeur and Jürgen Habermas*. Cambridge University Press 1981.

Thompson, J. and Held, D. (eds.), *Habermas: Critical Debates*. Cambridge, Massachusetts: MIT Press 1982.

Turnbull, C. *The Mountain People*. New York: Simon and Schuster 1972.

Walzer, M. *Spheres of Justice: A Defense of Pluralism and Equality*. New York: Basic Books 1983.

Weber, M. *From Max Weber: Essays in Sociology*, edited by H. Gerth and C. W. Mills. New York: Oxford University Press 1946.

Economy and Society: An Outline of Interpretive Sociology. Berkeley: University of California Press 1978.

Wellmer, A. Truth, Semblance, Reconciliation: Adorno's Aesthetic Redemption of Modernity. *Telos* 62 (1984–5), 89–115.

White, S. Reason and Authority in Habermas. *American Political Science Review* 74 (1980), 1006–17.

Reply to Comments. *American Political Science Review* 75 (1981), 463.

On the Normative Structure of Action: Gewirth and Habermas. *The Review of Politics* 44 (1982), 282–301.

The Normative Basis of Critical Theory. *Polity* 16 (1983), 150–64.

Review of Susan Hekman, *Hermeneutics and the Sociology of Knowledge. The Journal of Politics* (forthcoming, 1987).

Post-Structuralism and Political Reflection. *Political Theory* (forthcoming, 1988).

Williams, B. Persons, Character and Morality, in A. Rorty (ed.), *The Identities of Persons*, pp. 137–216. Berkeley: University of California Press 1976.

Wilson, J. Q. *Political Organization*. New York: Basic Books 1973.

Winch, P. *The Idea of a Social Science*. New York: Humanities Press 1958.

Understanding a Primitive Society, in Winch (ed.), *Ethics and Action*, pp. 8–49. New York: Routledge and Kegan Paul 1972.

Index

action, *see also* communicative action
  dramaturgical, 38–9
  norm-guided, 13–18, 37–8
  strategic, 10–13, 37
  teleological structure of, 46
  understanding-oriented vs success-
    oriented, 45–7
Adorno, T., 3, 5, 25–6, 32, 90, 104, 151,
    153–4
advanced capitalism
  identity formation in, 78–81
  legitimation and motivation problems in,
    118–23
  new forms of opposition in, 118–27,
    137–43
  and the "new obscurity," 2–6, 9
  resilience of, 118–23
  and subsystems of economy and
    administration, 107–15
aesthetics
  autonomy of, in modernity, 147–50
  enhanced role in balanced society,
    134–53
  expressive capacity, 46–7
  and language, 31–6
  and practical discourse, 82–3
  and subjectivity, 144–53
argumentation
  and accumulation of knowledge, 131–6
  and "performative contradiction," 50–65
  presuppositions of modern, 55–8
  specialized forms and corresponding
    cultural value spheres, 131–4
Austin, J. L., 28, 34, 45

Baudelaire, C., 146, 148–9
Berlin, I., 16, 52

Chomsky, N., 29, 58
class conflict, 108, 112
class interest, 111–12
class relation to expert cultures, 118
cognitive development psychology, 48,
    57–67

Cohen, J., 123, 126
communication, systematically distorted,
    32, 45, 88, 117–18
communicative action, 25–47
  and cooperation, 37
  and ideal speech situation, 56–7
  importance in social theory, 98–100
  as medium of lifeworld reproduction,
    97–100
  normative force in, 50–8
communicative competence
  in modernity, 43–4, 55, 90
  relation to other competences, 28–9, 58
communicative ethics
  cognitivist claims of, 44–65
  context sensitivity in, 82–5
  and fallibility, 88–9
  and indeterminateness, 73–4, 77–83
  minimal character of, 23–4, 69–83
  and motivation, 77–83
  and nature, 136–53
  and needs, 69–83
  and otherness, 81–3, 136–53
  place of compromise in, 75–7
  procedural character of, 48, 69–83
communicative rationality, *see also* rationality
  and action, 25–47
  and consensus, 42–3, 55–8
  and ethical universalism, 1–2, 22–3,
    69–85, 154
  and modernity, 90, 96
  as the most comprehensive conception,
    26–7
  and motivation, 14, 40–4, 52, 110, 154
communicative sociation vs systems
    integration, 100–27
Connolly, W., 87
consciousness
  magical–mythical vs decentered, 94
  modern structures of, 23, 57–8, 90–127,
    131–6
  philosophy of, 4
consensus, 42–3, 55–7
contextual rationality, 10, 11–23